ALSO INNOVATORS

How one computer salesman
contributed to the digital revolution

ALSO INNOVATORS

How one computer salesman
contributed to the digital revolution

Christopher B. Yardley, PhD

PRESS

Published by ANU Press
The Australian National University
Acton ACT 2601, Australia
Email: anupress@anu.edu.au

Available to download for free at press.anu.edu.au

ISBN (print): 9781760462987
ISBN (online): 9781760462994

WorldCat (print): 1099184186
WorldCat (online): 1099184654

DOI: 10.22459/AI.2019

This title is published under a Creative Commons Attribution-NonCommercial-NoDerivatives 4.0 International (CC BY-NC-ND 4.0).

The full licence terms are available at
creativecommons.org/licenses/by-nc-nd/4.0/legalcode

Cover design and layout by ANU Press. Cover photographs: Marcin Wichary via flic.kr/p/bXqtAs and flic.kr/p/4AftJ1.

First edition © 2016 ANU Press
Second edition © 2019 ANU Press

Contents

Preface vii
1. 'A proper job' 1
2. Once were cowboys 23
3. A working 'home away from home' 41
4. A taste of Northern bitter 53
5. Eddie French's rainbow 73
6. The brewer's assistant 95
7. Pursuing my own rainbow's end 105
8. The tallyman and other endeavours 115
9. Adventures in Southeast Asia 125
10. As far south as we could go 203
11. Working with the airlines in the Australasia-Pacific region 223
12. The ups and downs of a contractor 257
13. Not a multinational this time 267
Afterword 281

Preface

I have relished my working life in the computer industry. I enjoyed every day. I was lucky enough to be at the front-end of the developing business of data processing, working in small, focused units selling systems. For half of my working life, I was with the Sperry Corporation (through many name changes), before it merged with the Burroughs Organisation in the late 1980s to form Unisys. I do not know if it was deliberate policy, but every two years or so my sales role within Sperry changed, from salesman, to technician, to manager. I was never confused, but as I was to learn this was not common practice at Unisys, which had problems putting me into a neat box.

I have always thought of myself as a salesman, although job titles may have obscured that simple definition and I did not always conform to my own definition of a salesman. I was certainly never any good at telling jokes, although for a short while I did make notes of some punchlines for what I thought were good things to remember. For me, this was a mistake. My strength was in sharing my experiences in the industry, which became particularly relevant as computers evolved through designated generations and the same mistakes were repeated with each cycle. I was a mainframe salesman, and remain a novice in understanding the full potential of my PC.

Every work opportunity that came up was more than likely accepted by my wife and me. We moved home 14 times, and lived and worked in five different countries with our two boys.

I managed to resist the challenge of working for myself until 2001. Opportunities arose, but I was happy to keep working in a multinational organisation, where experts were available if you had the courage to ask for help. When running my own small software shop, with limited resources, I was caught out by my lack of training and preparedness for protracted legal disputes, although in the early days as a salesman I was confident enough to draft customer contracts.

ALSO INNOVATORS

I decided to retire in 2005. In preparation for retirement, while I reduced the number of days in my working week, I wrote the following story. I was testing myself to remember events and names. Most of the events have survived the process of editing, but many names have been cut, and I need to apologise to a few hundred or so work colleagues. The question I had to ask myself in preparing the book for publication was: does the name make a significant contribution to the story? If it did not, it was cast aside. But all those names still live in my memory.

I was not quite sure what my book was trying to describe until I read Walter Isaacson's book, *The Innovators: How a Group of Inventors, Hackers, Geniuses and Geeks Created the Digital Revolution*. Isaacson's story follows the ups and downs of the innovators of computing and programming through to the challenges presented by the internet. I was interested to read about a few persons I knew, one or two I had the privilege of meeting, as well as others who were just famous names. I got to thinking about the purpose-built computing machines of the World War II and their development into the general purpose entities initially described by Alan Turing in the 1930s. My first experience of a computer was as a university undergraduate writing a simple formula for determining the amount of reinforcing steel needed in a beam to carry a specific load. We had been taught how to use a translation set of rules called Fortran — short for 'formula translation'. Our scribbles were encoded in paper-tape, as were the results from the computer, which required another human–machine intervention to view. Today we expect to see such a result within seconds on the PC or tablet on our desk. Such has been the development of technology.

Walter Isaacson's book features a number of key designers and visionaries who were seen as driving this technological change. My perspective is that the laboratory designer who strove to get a circuit to run at its fastest was certainly an enabler, but that the everyday user — in my case, the computer salesman — is also an innovator. Under pressure to sell products, I had to derive and sell the solutions to problems. In this, the development of my career has run in parallel to the development of computing.

I hope you enjoy the narrative.

Christopher B. Yardley
September 2016
cannava@iinet.net.au

1
'A proper job'

A career in computing was not planned. I had worked towards joining the (UK) Royal Navy, as a lad attending the Skinners' School in Tunbridge Wells, Kent, in the 1950s. I was a member of the school cadet corps, and as a 16-year-old I had signed up to the school and university branch of the Royal Navy Volunteer Reserve. I was called for service in 1956 while still at school, and only escaped going to war when the captain of HMS *Ocean*, on his way to the Suez engagement, realised he had schoolchildren on board. We were unloaded onto HMS *Vanguard*, the only battleship in the British fleet, and kept in a secure environment for two weeks, as Prime Minister Anthony Eden had not publicly declared that he was sending gunboats to Egypt. At the time, Australian Prime Minister Robert Menzies was negotiating for a peaceful resolution to the crisis. The experience of being aboard the *Vanguard* further whetted my ambition to be a sailor.

My ambition was partly satisfied when in 1958 I was offered a place, and officer training, in the navy. My dad had served in the Royal Air Force during World War II, qualifying as a codes and cyphers specialist; he had to sign my application. He was, however, loathe to sign the mandatory 29-year service agreement, asking what would I do when I demobilised as a 47-year-old lieutenant commander. He suggested I undertake a university course and then decide if I felt the same way. With the study I had taken to get into the navy, I was able to procure a place at the University of Leeds, studying civil engineering. I thoroughly enjoyed my time at Leeds, but was unsure about spending the rest of my life in Wellington boots in and around building sites.

Figure 1.1: Schoolboy and sailor, Royal Naval Reserve service on HMS *Zest*, 1957.
Source: Author's collection.

1. 'A PROPER JOB'

'Grow up, son. Get a proper job, the same as everyone else.' That was mum and dad's resolution to my uncertainty when I arrived home at Tunbridge Wells in 1961, after three years at the University of Leeds, with a shiny new civil engineering BSc and an understanding of the design of hyperparabolic shells. I also had a girlfriend, Audrey, who I hoped would be my wife. I had fulfilled the two principal ambitions I took to the North of England as an undergraduate. At Leeds I had also taken the coursework of a new curriculum BSc (Econ.) in business management and I had passed these final examinations in addition to the degree course — not well, but passed.

What to do next? I had spoken to the faculties of medicine and law at Leeds and made enquiries of Kent County Council for an extension of my education grants. I was keen but unrealistic in thinking that events would let me drift into continuing my student lifestyle. It was not to be.

That one sensible conversation with mum and dad had me back in the real world. What was a proper job? I targeted Friday's *Daily Telegraph* employment pages and responded to four generic advertisements that were seeking 'an ambitious graduate'. I was invited to two interviews.

IBM was looking for trainee salesmen. At the time, IBM was the world's largest information technology company, with 80 per cent of the market of what was then called 'electronic data processing'. IBM had placed three of the advertisements I had answered, with slight variances in the text and reply addresses, and was not offended that I had picked it out more than once. Nothing was said about my multiple applications when I attended IBM's office in London's Wigmore Street for an interview. I was shown into a dingy little cubicle where an IBM aptitude test and answer paper awaited me. This was unexpected, but I was naively confident. It was a bright, sunny day outside and beams of sunlight cut through grimy windows, showing the dust in the Soho air. This diffusion of sunlight highlighted that the original aptitude test booklet had been previously completed by another candidate — the pencil indentations were obvious. I tried to ignore that I had answers in front of me and started off with my own responses on the answer paper. 'This is stupid,' I thought. I was getting the same answers as my predecessor. So I copied out those answers, completed the sections that were unanswered, and spent some time checking my answers. I rang the bell for attention as the clerk had asked me to do when I was invited to take the test.

The clerk arrived and was quite concerned.

'Can't you do it?'
'Well I have finished and checked the answers.'

She countered:

'You should not have finished this quickly. The HR manager is still interviewing another candidate. You'll have to wait. I'll process the test, but you will not be able to see him for another 23 minutes. Please wait here.'

She brought me a newspaper to read.

After precisely 23 minutes she collected me, and I went for my interview with the HR manager, who was big, sweating, and smarmy. He got up from behind his desk.

'My name is Godsland; whenever you think of me, you will think of heaven.'
A silent 'Yuk — this guy is a real creep.'

The interview was short. IBM's assessment of me was that I was 'probably unemployable in a commercial sense'. Mr Godsland counselled that the aptitude test analysis showed that I was probably more suited to academia as a career.

Undeterred, I attended an interview at the National Trade Press (NTP) in Drury Lane and was interviewed by Dai Watkins, a young Welshman with a lived-in face. He was a very keen Welshman. Many are, it's a national trait. Dai explained that he had joined NTP — the trade and technical publications arm of the Daily Mirror Group — straight from the London School of Economics as an economist and statistician. He had outgrown the job, and I was being interviewed as a potential chief statistician and economist to replace him. He was leaving to set up his own marketing consultancy.

There was something familiar about Dai Watkins. I let him continue to enthusiastically explain the market research aspects of the job, particularly regarding new journals in the emerging technical industries of the early 1960s. Then I remembered: I had played rugby the previous Saturday for the Blackheath Rugby Club Second XV in a trial game at the Rectory Fields. Dai had played on the right wing; I had played on the left wing. He remembered me when I made him aware of the connection. In no time at all I was in front of the NTP managing director, S. Chas Burt, and Dai was recommending me as a suitable candidate for the job. Mr Burt agreed with him, and I negotiated an annual salary of £850 — £50 more than I had heard any of my pals getting as civil engineers. That was OK.

The next day I had a telephone call at home from Mr Burt. 'How do you feel about attending an introduction to data processing course at IBM, starting Monday of next week?' Of course, I had to agree to that.

I was back at the IBM Wigmore Street office, but did not see Mr Godsland during the four weeks of attendance at the course. It was a good course, with about 20 participants, all male, mostly accountants. We were taught to use the IBM Series 3000 system hardware and how to program the plugboard system. We learned to program the system using wires plugged into a control panel to carry electrical signals around and through the equipment, rather like the old-fashioned telephone operator control panel. A full board required a cover to stop wires being accidentally knocked out. Changing a program could be a nightmare, feeling your way through to the backplane and several inches of cables.

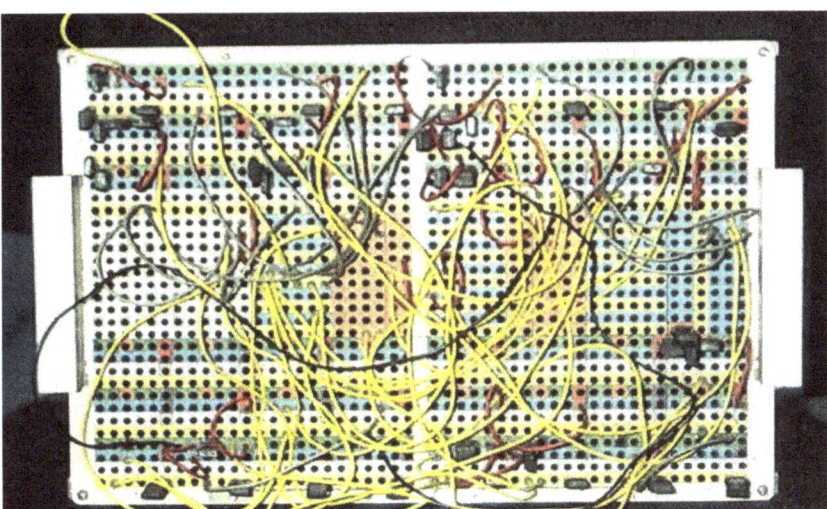

Figure 1.2: A small plugboard with not too many connections made.
Source: Wikipedia Commons.

The Series 3000 was a punch-card oriented system, with the choice of an 80- or 90-column card. We learned on a 90-column card system. The system was, at that time, an unannounced IBM product from IBM Germany. The course material was all very new to me. We had done some theoretical programming at the University of Leeds, writing basic routines on coding pads, verifying instructions as well as we were able after they had been punched into paper tape, and reading our output as produced on the computing department's Ferranti Pegasus system, which had been installed in 1957. As civil engineers, our university computer experience consisted of three lectures and the chance to write and run a simple test program using the Fortran programming language.

Figure 1.3: The University of Leeds Ferranti Pegasus as installed in 1957.
Source: Author's collection.

The Series 3000 course was certainly a hands-on experience. The lady teacher was excellent and very patient in explaining business processes to me, as I was the only person attending the class without business experience. It was all going well until, at the end of the third week, it was announced to the class that IBM Armonk (the IBM headquarters in the US) had cancelled the IBM 3000 system and would instead extend the life of the IBM 420 Alphabetical Accounting Machine in the UK. This was a bit of a blow, but we kept going on the now redundant equipment and completed the class.

1. 'A PROPER JOB'

It was another blow to realise, when I got to NTP four weeks later, that Dai Watkins had left, and was not able to perform a logical handover of responsibilities. I had seen Dai at rugby training and played a couple of games with him, but we had not really talked about work. I had inherited Dai's secretary, but she was very pregnant and was waiting to quit working.

My first morning at work, I experienced S. Chas Burt's notoriously autocratic approach to handling people first hand. I had found Dai's old office and was sitting there talking to my secretary, asking her what to do in order to start work, when the telephone rang.

'Come up here!'

was the concise and clear instruction. It could only be the boss, and I asked for directions to his office. On this occasion Mr Burt was more than charming.

'How did the course go?'

I replied that it had been fine, although I had some problems with business processes, and had found the final test paper and test routine exercise somewhat tricky because of this.

'I am still mixing up credits and debits.'

Mr Burt told me not to worry.

> 'I think you have done really well. IBM has given you a score of 78 per cent for the course, which was higher than the class average. I want you to take on the role of data processing manager as well as being the market research manager. You can use a computer for your statistical work.'

'Thank you, Mr Burt. But … what does a data processing manager do?'

> 'Well, Chris, I cannot really tell you. We have never had one before. We had an IBM 3000 on order, which is why you attended the course, but, as you know, IBM has withdrawn that product. We want you to buy us a system to automate the readers' enquiry department. The manual systems cannot cope with the volumes we now have, and we are introducing additional magazines every few months.'

His further advice was for me to talk to his secretary, who would tell me the name of the IBM salesman who looked after the Daily Mirror Group account. She also introduced me to George Martin, who ran the classified advertising department, and who seemed to be Mr Burt's deputy.

ALSO INNOVATORS

George Martin was an ex-army officer, the holder of a Military Cross. A large man with a receding red hairline, he controlled a large, open plan office from a corner vantage point. Radiating outwards from this point, everyone else, mostly young men, sat in small cubicles. Today they would be called telemarketers, but instead of sitting at a computer screen they had newspapers and a telephone in front of them. Their job was to scrutinise the classified advertisement columns of rival publications for prospective buyers of our more directed service, and ring advertisers and convince them that their money would be equally well, or better, spent putting their advertisements in the relevant specialist technical journal published by NTP.

George introduced me to Jean Smith, the supervisor of the readers' enquiry department, the responsibility for which I had just acquired. In addition to classified advertisements, the NTP technical journals also carried display (mostly full-page) advertisements, which were given a code number. Each journal carried three pre-paid postcards listing the advertisement code numbers from that issue. Our readers were encouraged to circle the code numbers on the postcards as a request for more information. Jean and several ladies sat at typewriters and typed out readers' names and the relevant code numbers, which were then sorted and sent to the advertiser. If the reader was interested in more than one item, their name would be carbon copied onto a second piece of paper. Some readers would seek information on several products, so names and details were typed onto flimsy paper in order to get as many legible copies as possible. Company librarians from the Indian subcontinent and the Middle East were prone to ask for additional information on every product and service mentioned in every issue of the journal. Jean had not been told that her department was going to be upgraded to a data processing environment.

My status allowed me a secretary. Dai's ex-secretary only stayed with me a few days, so I placed an advertisement in the *Daily Mirror* and quickly selected a super girl, Hilary Cutna, to help me. Hilary was 21 years old, like me, and had secretarial and accounting experience. She and I set out to learn our new jobs together. Another source of help was the NTP marketing director, who took us under his wing and looked out for us in every way. A short session we found invaluable was when he sat us down to explain how to write a business letter.

1. 'A PROPER JOB'

'Always start with "I am writing to …" and explain simply the reason for the letter. Always keep your initial letter to a single page. Sign the letter off in the way you would expect the recipient to address you when he calls back as a result of the letter.'

This was simple stuff, but was valuable to us both.

Hilary and I agreed on some objectives: to learn the reader enquiry business in order to be able to select the best data processing system; to select a suitable system while handling the day-to-day market research responsibilities left by Dai Watkins; and to learn the journals and the idiosyncrasies of each.

We had something like 40 specialist technical journals, with titles such as *Electronic News* (NTP's first newspaper format publication); *The Watchmaker, Jeweller and Silversmith*; *Engineering Materials and Design*; *Interior Design*; and *Laundry and Dry Cleaning News*.

Dai Watkins had recommended that I try and regularly read one of our publications for an insight into the trade and in order to learn its language to use in surveying the readership. I had an office on our floor of Drury House. Also here were the display advertising manager of each publication, editors and clerical staff, and George Martin's empire of classified advertisement salespeople, who were young, keen, and ambitious to become display advertising representatives. The older magazines were subscription based, but NTP increasingly added controlled circulation publications, choosing to whom it (initially) sent the publication free of charge. Lists of professional people in each of the specialist markets covered by a journal were our potential readers; especially valued were that group of readers who had previously used the readers' enquiry system. We sold access to these readers to advertisers as potential buyers. Lists of names were our lifeblood.

What was becoming increasingly important for the advertiser to know was the profile of the readers of a particular magazine. It was an easy job to work it out for *The Watchmaker, Jeweller and Silversmith*, as the largest part of the mailing addresses included the word 'jeweller' or were in London's jewellery quarter of Hatton Garden. The magazine's circulation was small — perhaps 3,000. Dai Watkins had been conducting readership surveys by sending out questionnaires to a sample group from our circulation lists to be able to define readership profiles. We submitted the results of the survey to the Audit Bureau of Circulation, and the figures were published by the bureau for the benefit of potential advertisers. *Electronic News* had an unknown readership, although the original mailing list had been compiled from the membership lists of engineering associations. However, when a reader made an enquiry we also asked, on the submitted postcard, for his or her job title, as well as giving a multiple choice list of industries to which he or she might belong, and codes for articles and products of interest.

Mr Burt had been sold on the idea of data processing enabling him to capture readership profiles of readers who made enquiries. He also expected to be able to replicate the list of enquiring readers for the display advertising manager to use as an inducement for follow-on advertising. NTP had ordered the IBM 3000 system following an intensive IBM sales campaign prior to my appointment.

The IBM salesman was Robin Brown. I asked him to come in and see me. He was quite unflappable about the cancellation of the IBM 3000 series and followed the party line, suggesting that the IBM 420 would do us just as well, or maybe the IBM 424 WTC Computing Accounting Machine (with solid state computing device). I learned very early that IBM never made a specific recommendation. The sales argument was that the buyer would only need to consider an 'IBM A' or 'IBM B' solution. IBM salespeople were taught not to discuss or even countenance the thought of a competitive supplier.

Robin Brown was an excellent companion. He had been a Guards officer during his national service and was not much older than me, around 27 to 29 years old. He had a lovely story about standing guard along the route of Queen Elizabeth's Coronation eight years earlier, in the rain, dressed in his red tunic and bearskin cap. The guards had been provided with Horlicks tablets for sustenance during the expected six hours of duty. He had taken his from their wrappings and put them in the breast pocket of his tunic, where they melted into a sticky mess and obvious stain, for which he was subsequently charged and disciplined.

Robin did his best to walk me through the requirements study that led to his proposal for the IBM 420 plus a card sorter and 12 IBM 031 card punch verifiers. I also asked International Computers and Tabulators (ICT) and De La Rue of Paris to bid. All three suppliers recommended similar plugboard systems. I was secretly favouring the De La Rue bid, as product training was to be in Paris. Perhaps Robin sensed this: IBM came in with an offer too good to turn down. As we were a disappointed IBM

1. 'A PROPER JOB'

Series 3000 customer, IBM would provide the IBM 420 equipment free of charge for one year, with delivery in two weeks. No further consideration was required. I knew that much about business.

The quick delivery of the hardware put me under immediate pressure to find a suitable office, as the existing readers' enquiry office housed just eight desks, and we were installing a large processor with in-built printer — the size of a pair of sideboards — the card sorter, and the dozen card punch verifiers. I needed to find four additional staff to work the card punches, someone to conduct initial training in the use of the card punches, and to learn the purchase of consumables (cards and printing paper), as well as a printer for continuous paper to feed the printer, with different stationery for each journal. And somehow I had to program the IBM 420 with the help of manuals. Luckily, I had only recently done the IBM course, albeit focusing on another hardware system. Although I did not have the equipment, I was able to plan and chart the route of signals from the card reader on the 420 through the arithmetic and comparative processes to the printer. Market research would have to be put on hold.

The equipment was installed over a weekend. We had to partly close Drury Lane for the heavy-duty mobile crane to lift the 420 processor and printer into the building through the second-storey window space. The card punches and card verifiers were installed at the same time. IBM 031 card punches did not come with the drawer space or modesty panels that the copy-typists were used to. A rush order overcame that difficulty. I had not budgeted for the hire of the crane and the removal and replacement of second-floor windows when estimating costs.

But we got things going. At first we accumulated a backlog of work as we learnt the new equipment and the tricks of the trade. An early shortcut we used was not verifying the punched data. Verification involved a duplication of the input process and cards were notched to show if they had been checked or corrected if necessary. This was obviously of huge advantage in an accounting application, but it was not working for us with a free-form input of names and addresses — with cards formatted with names, first line of address, second line of address, and so on. As copy-typists, each lady had adopted her own style of input and, to an extent, her own set of abbreviations. Our reader enquirers did not help the process either, as many left out a lot of information and would use their own forms of shorthand. We looked at standardising the input, and therefore the verification process, but it did not work. So the decision was made not to verify. This upset IBM through Robin Brown, and resulted in the first of the letters in which IBM suggested to Mr Burt that its recommendations were not being followed and this would prejudice NTP operations.

If the reader enquirer was requesting a follow-up on more than one item in the journal, he or she entered more than one product code. Some people asked for additional data on up to 100 items. We therefore duplicated the name and address punch cards the appropriate number of times, marking each name and address card set with the code number requested. The names and addresses were then sorted, in the card sorter, and printed on the 420 processor. The initial program was relatively simple and involved a new page list for each change of code number.

The covering letter to the advertiser was also printed through the system using continuous stationery, pre-printed with the journal name, upon which we listed the advertised item's code number, a short product description, and the relevant reader names and addresses. We originally intended sending conventional-sized letters to advertisers, but I soon changed them to a smaller size, which would not require folding, with the advertiser's address showing through a window envelope. To improve the look of the output form, I had the journal stationery printed without sprocket holes, to save the stripping task, using the platen-feed feature — this brought another letter from IBM to Mr Burt.

Other quick equipment changes included upgrading the punches from the IBM 031 to the IBM 026 model. The travel of the card through the IBM 031 was directed via a formica strip into which notches, at the position of the column that was the start of a new field, were cut with a sharp knife or a purpose-built notch guillotine. With continuous use, the notch in the formica became larger through impact and the field positioning became erratic. The IBM 026 punch allowed us to punch a master format card which controlled the fields. We also upgraded the IBM 420 processor to the IBM 424 model and acquired a faster card sorter. It has to be said that IBM accommodated these changes at similar advantageous rates as the original offer, and we only paid the nominal difference between the list prices — keeping a credit for the equipment that was initially delivered for the first year. We used a huge number of cards. They were expensive. Subsequent study has shown that a large part of IBM's profits were from the sale of punch cards. Dai Watkins, with whom I kept in regular contact, had a Canadian pal called Dan Smith who had brought his company, Precision Data Card, to the UK. I used them. Another IBM letter to Mr Burt suggested that the Precision Data Card stock was of inferior quality. That was three letters, and I had hardly started.

The system was working quite well. The advertisers certainly appreciated getting printed names and addresses of readers with an interest in their products. Some asked for multiple copies of lists in order to cut them up to use as stick-on addresses for their sales force. We were also, at times, very quick. This was especially the case when new magazines introduced the reader enquiry service or a new magazine was introduced. At times this caused delays for the established journals, but I tried to gloss over this deficiency. Eventually we would have as many as 26 data preparation clerks. Our floor of Drury House had originally been used as a paper store, so we had no reservations about putting the tabulator on the floor, but when we were using the printer — and we often printed for 10 hours a day — the reverberation of each line, with the printer operating at approximately 60 lines a minute, was obvious, and at a noise level that would not be permitted today.

We were able to identify 20,000 readers in the general engineering business who had made enquiries through *Electronic News* and *Engineering Materials and Design* and use these names as a subscription base for a new weekly newspaper, *Engineering Weekly*. At this time, NTP was extending its relationship with QB Printers in Colchester, which was implementing web-offset newspaper technology, which gave us the promise of colour.

Electronics was a fertile market in the early 1960s. We introduced a glossy journal called *Design Electronics* and were able to define a narrow readership profile for early copies of this magazine, which was circulated only to persons who had told us they were electronics design engineers. I compiled the lists, but the technology did not extend to us being able to print regular labels, so we continued to use steel plates with impressions of the reader's address to print journal wrappers.

I extended the use of the data processing equipment when we had to implement a full subscription fulfilment system for a small, paid circulation monthly magazine. IBM was most interested in this application and issued the set of NTP guide notes, which I had written, within its supported applications library — application descriptions were something that was missing in this hardware-oriented data processing industry. The work we were doing was also of interest to our Daily Mirror Group parent, International Publishing Corporation (IPC), and I joined the group data processing committee, led by Bernard King from the Daily Mirror Group head office in New Fetter Lane. IPC acquired an early IBM 1401 system and, when it was available, the first IBM 1440 in Europe, as well as an early IBM 1460. I did some assembler programming on the 1400s and got a feel for storage media other than punch cards.

Figure 1.4: The IBM 1401 of the early 1960s incorporated tape drives as storage media for sequential processing.
Source: Wikipedia Commons.

I did some advisory work with Ken Cohen, the data processing manager of Tothill Press (another IPC trade and technical publishing house which later merged with NTP) during the implementation of its reader enquiry system, using ICT equipment. It was again a punch card and sorter system, but incorporated a typed reader enquirer name and address that was photocopied for the advertiser. The card was used in much the same way as we used it, the difference being that we incorporated the name and address details within the punch card rather than on it.

I may have given the impression that IBM was a difficult supplier. This was not really the case. I learned to appreciate that IBM was being careful in covering themselves in a developing industry. I always enjoyed Robin Brown's input as our salesman, and we became good friends. Robin was promoted within IBM and was replaced by Tony de Glanville. Tony was equally personable, but was more interested in the main IPC account, which I also understood. We had regular faults with the card punches and sorter, and the IBM 424 processor demanded regular preventive maintenance. Rod Smith was the IBM engineer we saw the most of. He was excellent. If he and I ever had too many beers at lunchtime, we would retire to a position hidden from view behind the card sorter, endeavouring to replace the electronic brushes and switches that comprised the basic sorting mechanism. This was a preventive maintenance job that had to be done some time, after all.

I did not find it easy to manage the punch room, especially when it got larger. The girls were more worldly-wise than I, and would try and manipulate me in any way they could. I tried to hide behind Hilary Cutna, and later Audrey Davies who became my personal assistant, but eventually I employed a punch room supervisor. The early days were not always easy. Mr Burt sent for me one day to ask why I was favouring one particular punch operator (let's call her Gabriella), and giving her one half-day a week leave of absence. The union had raised it as an issue. Gabriella had been told to explain her domestic situation to me by her doctor, who had also called me to discuss her situation. Gabriella, an Italian, had married an Englishman and come to London. They had never properly consummated their marriage (I did not want to know this): 'Tom is so big. I get so very nervous. My body goes rigid.'

My schoolboy counselling did no good. Hilary was unmarried and Gabriella would not discuss it with Jean. Her doctor had suggested remedies that might relax the woman, including the three-hour psychiatric sessions for which I gave her leave. The other girls in the office had complained to their shop steward about the favouritism I was exhibiting — if only they had known. Mr Burt listened, but quite correctly told me it was my problem. He suggested I talk to the shop steward.

Within the printing business, the shop steward is known as the 'Father of the Chapel'. Wally Sollioux was NTP's Father of the Chapel. He and I discussed in masculine isolation what we might do to overcome Gabriella's problem and drew cards to see who would take responsibility for coming up with a solution. I lost. I was so relieved. To this day, I do not know how Wally addressed the issue, but Gabriella certainly became less erratic, and I would quite often see Tom when he collected her from work at the end of the day. They eventually appeared content in one another's company.

I had other responsibilities in NTP apart from the new data processing adventure. Dai Watkins had left a readership survey to be completed. He had also pointed out that it would make sense for me to join the Market Research Society and take a postgraduate statistics course at his alma mater, the London School of Economics, which was in easy walking distance of the office. I took his advice and enjoyed both activities. Our readership survey contained the obvious questions, with tick-a-box options to prompt answers. Dai had been working on the basis of 10 surveys per year. With some 40 journals on the presses, this meant we would survey the readership every three to four years. I have to say I found Dai's approach a bit amateur, although this attitude might have been due to the enthusiasm generated by my attendance of the London School of Economics class. The school's pub was also a convenient watering hole and meeting place for guests.

NTP contained a wealth of characters. Tony Gottelier and Roy Shorter, who were the same age as me, were working as classified advertisement telephone salespersons when we became pals. They could not have been more different. Tony Gottelier was polished and refined, public-school educated, and very much a man of the world. Tony was destined to be a star in our mundane workplace. Roy Shorter, his competitor and colleague, was just the opposite: a proud East Ender with Cockney emphasis and aspirations. As a team they were outstandingly successful as telephone salesmen and were soon promoted to be display advertisement representatives — with business cards and, eventually, business cars. Perhaps to keep Tony's feet on the ground, he was appointed as advertising manager of *Laundry and Dry Cleaning News*. Roy furthered his apprenticeship with one of the technical magazines before getting the job of advertising manager for a new publication, *Building Industry News*, which was a huge success from day one. George Martin, who had been the manager of the classified advertising department, was appointed to one of the flagship publications, *Engineering Materials and Design*. His journal, which was perhaps 300 pages thick every month, generated a huge number of enquiries and George kept the pressure on us for rapid turnaround and inventive presentation of facts and figures. He was also close to Mr Burt and was therefore a useful ally.

Perhaps my best pal at NTP was Dick Gibson, an older Dubliner with one of the less fashionable household textiles journals, which was without the reader enquiry service and which may have helped us stay friends. Dick always seemed a bit of a loner. I enjoyed his company, and after a couple of years we began to socialise. Dick would accompany Hilary Cutna to the London theatre with me and Audrey, who became my wife after I had been at NTP for about a year. Audrey moved from Middlesbrough and we settled in an 1890s terrace house in Orpington, 30 minutes by train from central London. Audrey was a school teacher.

I took advantage of *The Watchmaker, Jeweller and Silversmith* magazine. The advertising manager, having done his best to dissuade me from marriage, introduced me to a manufacturing jeweller in Hatton Garden. I met with Mr Chalfen of H. Chalfen and Company at his office. We chatted with one of his jewellers for a while before walking into a huge safe, a room lined with velvet-lined pull-out drawers, upon which sat cut diamonds. My purchase was destined to be modest, but Mr Chalfen and his colleague played the game to the full, and I was left with a choice of two diamonds that were only marginally more expensive than my upper spending limit. One diamond did look bigger than the other. I was invited to inspect the colour through an eyeglass to make my final selection. I went through the motions and emotions while in the background an assistant questioned Mr Chalfen offering me the smaller of the two, which was of 'exceptional colour and should have been in a higher price bracket'. It had to be a con, but it was so nicely done. I bought the smaller stone and Mr Chalfen had it mounted as a solitaire in a platinum setting. I was happy with my purchase — I still am. Less happy, initially, was my future mother-in-law, as I sent the token of our engagement to Audrey in Middlesbrough, in the North of England, via Royal Mail and the small (uninsured) parcel had been left on the doorstep. But it had got there. Audrey was happy, which is what mattered.

ALSO INNOVATORS

Figure 1.5: This is the only work photograph I have from the National Trade Press days. Note the bowler hats on the hatstand. I owned a bowler for just one day.
Source: Author's collection.

The chairman of NTP was Vere Sherrin — tall, silver-haired, dignified, and every inch my image of the successful businessman. Mr Sherrin was a director of the Daily Mirror Group and held several other directorships. Mr Burt introduced me to the chairman's son, Graham Sherrin, who I helped with some exploratory market research. Our work resulted in the publication of a new weekly newspaper, *Medical News*, which was jointly published by NTP and *The Financial Times*. My little team took considerable care with the development of the circulation list, having conducted a small postal survey to determine if doctors would read a newspaper — even one written specifically for them — such was the volume of material these people could expect every day. We were surprised at the level of pre-publication interest and absolutely overwhelmed by the response to a readership survey conducted after 12 months of the publication. The response rate was over 60 per cent, and the two open-ended questions elicited pages of difficult to read script. The response was reflected in the advertising revenue the publication generated. It was a huge success. *Medical News* was a prestige publication, and its offices near Harley Street reflected that success. Mr Burt was pleased to have been able to offer NTP expertise to *The Financial Times*.

I also did some work with the Daily Mirror Group with readership surveys. I put together some basic questionnaires and conducted personal interviews in the street, mostly at the exits to the London Underground, with readers we could see carrying the better known of the group's publications — the *Daily Mirror*, *Woman's Own*, and *Woman's Weekly* amongst others. The high-profile editorial teams of these consumer publications were much less amenable to any suggestions arising from market research than their trade and technical editorial colleagues, especially when I suggested we reprint a two-year-old edition and see if any readers noticed.

Commuting was a way of life for London office workers. During my first year of work I travelled the 40 miles to London from Tunbridge Wells with my younger brother, Butch, who was then working in the estate office of St Bartholomew's Hospital. He was a commuter for the 40 years of his working life. Butch and I took the bus to Tunbridge Wells Central Station, or to Tonbridge, to pick up the Hastings–Charing Cross train. He had been doing this for a year already and had a group of pals who met every day in the same carriage of the train. It was a cheerful group of young people who — initially — unintentionally made life a bit noisy on the hour-long journey. Older travellers were as equally set in their ways as the youngsters and an uneasy truce was eventually achieved.

I quickly conformed to the train platform etiquette. The regulars would congregate on the platform in anticipation of the train, talking together. When the train approached the platform, we formed a single line in order of the time we had arrived. The single line was positioned directly opposite the place where the train door was expected to stop. Once through the door, the rush was on to your own preferred seat or alcove. We even knew the drivers, including those who were consistent in where they stopped. If the driver did not play the game correctly, the single file queue would break like the drivers at the start of the 24-hour Le Mans race, chaos ruled, and it was push and shove with energetic elbows to tussle to be first to the door. The South-East Railway system was known for its problems.

Ice and fog were always good for long delays. The platforms would be filled to overflowing and a new strategy prevailed. We nearly all carried a square key that gave access to the guards' van and we would travel in that space. The railway police were not happy with this situation, so we would leave the train at a run, alighting prior to the train stopping, mostly avoiding any confrontation with the waiting railway policemen. Butch told me that the situation has improved 40 years on: the trains stop at less stations, and with maturity has come the opportunity to arrive in the office later. His same group is still travelling. Commuting becomes a way of life. The commuter knows no better. Thank goodness I escaped that fate before becoming too set in my ways.

London had its advantages. I learned to make the most of theatre. The cinema did not appeal nearly as much. Audrey and I enjoyed a monthly evening out with Hilary Cutna and Dick Gibson, and there were very few shows we did not enjoy. Our office in Drury House overlooked the Drury Lane Theatre stage door and some of the dressing rooms, and we regularly met the current crop of performers in and around the Covent Garden facilities we shared. Laurence Harvey was a real favourite when he was appearing in *Camelot*. There were always young women waiting for him to use the stage door. One evening after seeing a show, Audrey and I were walking my father- and mother-in-law down Maiden Lane, a back lane of The Strand, when we collided with an elegant man coming out of a stage door. The gentleman doffed his trilby and made a great fuss of my mother-in-law to facilitate her passage. She never forgot the experience — she had been feted by Rex Harrison. *My Fair Lady* played for several months in Drury Lane, and Rex Harrison, Stanley Holloway, and Julie Andrews became familiar to us.

Just prior to Christmas 1964, Tony Gottelier at NTP sold me four 5-shilling tickets to a show to be held at the Hammersmith Palais. Tony recommended we enjoy a new singing group and predicted that they would become very successful. Audrey and I took my brother Butch and sister Libby to a concert by the Beatles. We knew we were to experience something special when we were offered £5 each for our tickets as we fought the crowds to get into the theatre. We had tickets to the full set of future pop stars, at that time unknown, managed by Brian Epstein. The Liverpool-based set of artists included not only the Beatles, but Gerry and the Pacemakers, Freddie and the Dreamers, Billy J. Kramer and the Dakotas, and Cilla Black. My 16-year-old sister screamed herself hoarse. We did not hear very much, but it had been a memorable evening.

Everything was going quite well at NTP, until Christmas 1964. I had damaged my right knee playing a game of soccer in Corsica while on summer holiday. This required the removal of a torn cartilage and had me on crutches and absent from the office for six weeks — which is why I had chosen to have the surgery done at Christmas. Despite it being the holiday season, six weeks was too long away.

Two things had happened. One was a move by another manager to take over the readers' enquiry department. His authoritative, more disciplined approach had met with success while I was away. He had also discovered that, in my absence, one or two of the punch room girls were secreting reader enquiry forms in their desks and prejudicing the integrity and timing of the system. The other was a move from Drury House to new offices in Bowling Green Lane in Clerkenwell, quite close to Smithfield Market. A merger of NTP and the Tothill Press was on the cards. I managed to keep Hilary and Audrey, and we looked to make more use of technology in the research-related activities I had joined the company to pursue. The Daily Mirror Group had the IBM 1460 system by this time, and I looked at converting the magazine subscription fulfilment system to run using magnetic tapes or disks as the storage medium. There was also quite a bit of work through the Daily Mirror Group data processing committee, and I became more involved in computers.

I had learned through experience but was conscious that the only training I had had was in punch card tabulator technology, and I thought to make a career change to computers. Bernard King, the Daily Mirror Group data processing manager, had been impressed with what he was being told by Honeywell, and arranged for me to meet with them. I also spoke to the UNIVAC division of Remington Rand, and it was UNIVAC I joined in mid-1965.

2

Once were cowboys

I wanted a move that would have me working with computers. Bernard King, the Daily Mirror Group data processing manager, said that if I was seeking a job in the computer industry, I should apply for a job with Honeywell, which was challenging IBM for the commercial market in the UK. He believed that the Honeywell 200 was a real competitor to and a possible replacement for the IBM 1401 that we had bought on behalf of the Daily Mirror Group. But I did not enjoy the Honeywell interview. It was without direction. The emphasis of the available literature and wall posters was hardware control systems rather than computers, which was my burgeoning interest.

My interview with the UNIVAC division of Remington Rand, on the other hand, was quite different.[1] John Woods, the UK sales and marketing manager, came across as an enthusiastic kid playing with new toys, and he showed great interest in the extent to which I had been able to pick up the new technology at the National Trade Press (NTP), including my ability to program plugboard systems and the fact I knew some (IBM 1400) NEAT programming language. Remington Rand supplied general office equipment and systems, including Remington typewriters, and Kardex

---

1   UNIVAC is an abbreviation of UNIVersal Automatic Computer, referring to a line of electronic digital stored program computers. The UNIVAC 1 (delivered in 1951) was the first commercial computer produced in the US and the BINAC built by the company was the first general-purpose computer for commercial use. After I joined the company, it went through a number of name changes, while still wanting to retain the name UNIVAC and its association with the first commercial computer ever sold. In 1965, the computer was in its second generation, having moved from valve technology to solid state electronics.

filing systems and filing cabinets. Remington Shavers was somehow included in the portfolio. It made some sense that computers fitted into the division, although we had nothing to do with the established product lines. I joined UNIVAC as John's personal assistant in the High Holborn office opposite the Old Bailey. This was a good central place to be located in 1960s London, with The Strand, Fleet Street and Covent Garden on our doorstep.

We were keen amateurs in a developing profession, but we were eager to learn. On my first morning I was sent to the West London Air Terminal, as a part of the BEACON project team installing UNIVAC 490s for British European Airways. I was to learn that UNIVAC was good at real-time computing. At the time, we convinced ourselves that we were the only computer company that could readily link terminal equipment to our mainframe computers — the terminals were teletypewriters working at 50 bits per second, very slow. I was sent to West London Air Terminal to wire as much of a UNIVAC 1004 plugboard as I could. Working on something that looked like the old-fashioned telephone exchange panels with removable connectors, we wired the computer instructions by physical wire connections rather than using software stored in the computer's memory. I was good at this from my experience with the Daily Mirror Group. A UNIVAC 1004 was the input/output device, card reader, card punch, and 600 line per minute printer for the airline reservation system. I was very pleased that I was able to contribute.

I had seen computer rooms before, but I was not prepared for the reservation hall at British European Airways, where 256 purpose-designed and -built desks awaited the reservation clerks who would use the system. I was later to learn of the work that John Woods and Bill Dunlop had contributed to and supervised during the pre-sales work to win the British European Airways order. This had included the engineering design and construction of these purpose-built workstations. I later maintained the library of material that comprised the history of the sale as a part of my duties. The desks were quite close to one another and I was told of the design and tests that went into determining the correct strength of the spring on the seat which ensured it settled back under the terminal desk when the agent left his/her position for whatever reason. The terminal on the desk was a modified teletype with coded acetate overlays printed with the details of particular flights to give each terminal and flight its unique identity. Notches in the bottom of the overlay tripped switches to achieve flight identity, such as the London–Paris schedules. The operator read the available schedules to the telephone caller from the acetate sheet. If the flight was appropriate, the operator was able to see if there were seats available and reserve them seats while confirming passenger details. The desks were grouped by destination and area under a team leader. Today we would recognise the hall, with its public viewing gallery along one wall, as a call centre. I had never seen anything so large and dedicated to a single function.

My boss, John Woods, liked to keep on the move. Indeed, his three sales managers complained about the fact that he was always on the move — a lot of the time he was on foot somewhere in London, as he did not like using taxis. John looked like a bespectacled academic and often behaved like an impulsive schoolboy. He would roll his yellow woollen gloves into a ball and drop kick them down the office corridor to aid his progress. I did not see much of John during the first month I worked with him. I had to guess what it was he wanted me to do for him as his personal assistant. I took a lead from Bob O'Brien, who was personal assistant to the managing director, Charles W. Elliott. But it was not working.

I requested a showdown. We sat down to review a set of notes that I had prepared and John had notated: 'y' represented yes, and 'n' represented no. That was easy enough. It was 'ω' that was causing problems. I was treating 'ω' as a symbol for Woods signifying agreement for the proposed action. Our problem in communicating soon became apparent as John went through his instructions verbally: 'yes, yes, no, bollocks, yes, no …'.

Having sorted that little difficulty out, we managed fine. I shared John's office.

One of my jobs was the preparation of sales prices we could offer to potential customers — not the published price list, but the lowest price mandated by company policy. I worked with individual salesmen to determine the appropriate system components that would comprise the hardware we were expecting to sell. I then worked out the inter-company transfer price for hardware and software, added the cost of extras such as freight, insurance, technical support, and a cost of sales figure, to which I added the mandated 28 per cent gross profit. That was the minimum figure acceptable to the company. This price passed through management to gain approval before submission to the customer as part of a proposal. Quite often we built in an additional discount, one that might be offered during a positive negotiation. These were the days, of course, when we sold hardware, and software and support were bundled into the hardware cost. The reason we could do this was because we had no software. The salesman had a list of the engineering specifications for the components of a computer system and the availability of specific programming languages, but in the mid-1960s there was nothing as specific as application software. From the list of hardware components, the salesman had to develop a solution to a specific task or problem the potential client wanted to address. But first the salesman had to isolate what that task or problem might be. This process was called systems analysis: the job of the initial computer salesman.

Our hardware transfer costs varied by the type of system component — a new central processing unit (CPU) might have a transfer cost greater than 100 per cent, and an older model magnetic tape unit a transfer cost of 20 per cent of the sale price. I needed a 28 per cent gross margin to get to an approved selling price. It was often possible to optimise the system components, perhaps using slightly different components with advantageous transfer prices. The selling price was authorised by Roger Hunziger, the financial controller, and Charles Elliott, the managing director. I cannot remember many fights over prices. Charles Elliott was ex-army, a colonel from World War II, tall and dignified. It was rumoured that he turned off his hearing aid when meetings became long and boring.

Other front-line parts of the computer company included technical support and field engineering, which in my early days at UNIVAC were managed by John Kason, who was often at loggerheads with John Woods. I relished the day that one of the sales managers came into the office I shared with John to report that a computer language specialist was leaving the company and that his car was sitting in the garage under the building. If we did not grab the car it would be retained by the technical group. John looked at me and asked if I drove. I did, and took the car home that evening. I continued to use public transport travelling from Orpington, because the train was so convenient. It was about 18 months later when the two-year lease of the car ran out, prompting concern in the office about where it was. It was in my garage. I had made good use of the car, thank you. Possession being a determining precedent meant that my company car was replaced — and very convenient too, as it was about this time that I transferred into one of the three direct selling teams and needed a car.

The selling teams were the commercial sales team, selling to commercial customers; the government sales team selling to government, including defence; and the real-time sales team, selling systems into the commercial arena that required a terminal input and response rather than using batch input. Only UNIVAC was confident in this computing mode — or so we thought. Real-time was by definition the response needed by the user to make optimum use of the equipment we were selling. Seeing something happen almost immediately was what real-time implied.

The computer product mix was interesting. We had computer processing units with word sizes of 6, 18, 30, and 36 bits. The greater the number of bits in the word, the greater the power of the built-in machine instruction. The UNIVAC 418, as used by Intinco, for example, had an 18-bit word, and was ideal for the level of communications it was expected to achieve. The airline system at British European Airways was based upon the UNIVAC 490 family of 30-bit word machines, which required more power. The UNIVAC 1100 used 36 bits and was initially designed for scientific compute-intensive applications but was with time also used with advantage for commercial applications.

In 1965, UNIVAC and IBM were vying for dominance in the computer market. IBM had announced the 360 computer series in mid-1964 and was almost ready to start delivering on its promises. Theoretically, IBM 360 architecture meant that any program written and operated on any machine within the IBM 360 series of processing units would run on (almost) any other. IBM almost went broke with the launch of this most ambitious project, but it won the battle through superb marketing. The UNIVAC 9000 series response looked like a lame copy, using the same 8-bit byte architecture. It took a long time to mature into a saleable product.

As John Wood's personal assistant, I had a charmed introduction into the selling environment. I was appointed account manager to International Computers and Tabulators (ICT), which became International Computers Limited (ICL) when it merged with the computer division of English Electric in 1968. When I came across them, ICT was the principal UK computer manufacturer, formed in 1959 by a merger of the British Tabulating Machine Company and Powers-Samas. In 1963, it added the business computer divisions of Ferranti, whose earliest designers included Alan Turing. It had success reselling the UNIVAC 1004 as the ICT 1004 computer system. We sold some 250 1004s to ICL in the UK, some of which ended up across the globe as ICT pursued its international ambitions. I became good friends with Bill Downing, the ICT 1004 purchasing and project manager in its Putney headquarters — it was good to get out of town occasionally. UNIVAC was the original equipment manufacturer supplying ICT, who re-badged the 1004 to complement its own product portfolio. It was good business as we also sold spare parts to ICL, but did not have to provide other technical support.

I was also assigned account responsibility for International Investment Company, Intinco, later acquired by the Daily Mirror Group and renamed International Data Highways two decades before the term 'information superhighway' was coined to describe the future of information communication technology. Intinco offered a service to stockbrokers through which — via teletypes in their office, connected by slow telephone lines — they could get information on the latest stock-trading prices, using the stock exchange code listing. Intinco would update the last selling price at the end of every trading day so that the price was available at the open of the next day. The service was extended to include individual and company portfolio listings and online valuations for the client. With the Daily Mirror Group acquisition of Intinco, I had the challenge of selling to my first boss, S. Chas Burt, who had appointed me data processing manager of National Trade Press, a Daily Mirror Group subsidiary, a month after I left university in 1961.

I was still very green when I went to Intinco on Clerkenwell Road for the first time and asked to speak to Bill Dunlop, the technical director. Bill took me under his wing. Indeed, I was somewhat taken aback during our initial discussion when he recommended I address, via telex, specific questions to named managers at UNIVAC headquarters in Blue Bell, Pennsylvania. I asked how he knew so much about the company. He replied that he had been the acting general manager of UNIVAC just a few months earlier. I certainly learned from Bill Dunlop that the salesman does not have to be a know-all. Bill taught me to listen, and (initially) do what he advised. As I grew in the job, and Bill's knowledge rapidly became outdated, I was able to contribute more to the relationship, and I well remember the delight of us both when I was first able to make a sensible recommendation in my own right.

Bill Cox was the senior UNIVAC project support engineer on site. He was very tall and very intense, with a hatchet beard, and the elbows of his voluminous jumpers worn through. He programmed the operating system and rectified possible system problems via the engineer's panel, where he could change individual bits in the instruction buffers as he went along. This was great in the short term, but it was all done too fast to be documented and caused repeated headaches when we updated the software operating system and re-introduced the previously corrected errors.

We had a team of engineers on site for two shifts to cover evening data entry and the continual system tinkering that went on. Etele Hustie, a small, modest engineer who was a refugee from the Hungarian uprising of 1953, was the chief engineer. Etele and I became friends and shared many weekends at Intinco installing additional equipment, closing the main road on many Sundays as we had to lift the heavy equipment into the building by overhead crane. At Intinco we always had the very latest in mass storage devices — in today's terms the storage was minuscule, measured in thousands of words; we were not into mega-anything at this stage. The UNIVAC technologies were drum oriented and it was to be 10 years before we started to see disks as we know them today.

We had a few panics sustaining the online system, one of which certainly sticks in the mind. I got into the Holborn Viaduct office at the normal time of 9.00 am to be told that Intinco was down, had been down all night, and that Bill Dunlop was apoplectic. I got to Clerkenwell Road within minutes to find all of Intinco management in the operations manager's office looking through the observation window at Etele. He was skipping rope.

I went into the computer room through the engineer's office where Etele's staff were cowering, poised to take spare parts to Etele when called upon. I ventured into the computer room and spoke softly to Etele as I approached him from behind.

'Hi Etele, it's Chris. What can I do to help?'

He stopped his exercise and, turning, said:

'Thank goodness you are here. Keep that lot off my back. I cannot think when they keep interrupting, every two minutes, to ask when the fault will be fixed.'

'OK. I can do that. But what's with the skipping?'

'A moving wire is the only way I can keep Bill Dunlop and Cliff Griffith away from me, and I have told them it helps me concentrate.'

Needless to say, Etele fixed the fault within a reasonable time and no major harm was done. Etele was my kind of engineer. When the NASA space program used a dual UNIVAC 418 system as a part of its world-wide network from an office in Holborn, Etele and his lads were on standby during critical space missions.

I stayed with the BEACON project as John's representative until completion. The BEACON project team was an interesting mix of experts. The senior members were Phil Fellows, an American with airline experience; deputy project manager John ('um-yeah') Harrison, a fast-talking chain-smoker who was recorded at one presentation uttering 'um-yeah' 30 times in one minute; Ed Mack, an American albino who was the programming genius who made it all happen and worked closely with Brian O'Heron (the two later joined forces in the US to develop computer medical systems); and Dave Phillips, a voluble Welshman who worked on planning and scheduling aspects of the project.

Phil Fellows's number one rule on the project was the integrity of program interfaces. He kept repeating that the only reason for instant dismissal from the project would be the failure to gain agreement for, and documentation of, an interface change. Once he even added: 'Not even sex on the computer console will constitute a reason for dismissal, provided the project is not inconvenienced.'

Of course, the challenge was accepted. We waited anxiously for the outcome of that very act enjoyed by Ian Douglas and Pam Sainsbury, who were discovered by British European Airways security staff overnight, when they were 'working over'. No disciplinary action was taken — only notoriety for the perpetrators.

Another overnight activity remains a mystery to this day: the 1004 printer would burst into life and print reams of gibberish for no known reason. This happened a few times. The attendant computer operator was not able to cancel the print file and fed boxes of continuous stationery until the system had disgorged itself. These files became affectionately known as the 'Dead Sea Scrolls' and were recorded as such.

The BEACON project team became the founding members of the UNIVAC London Real-Time Research and Development Centre later established in Paddington. There they continued to develop airlines systems as a part of the UNIVAC Standard Airline System, which helped the company to share that particular market segment with IBM for many years.

David Streeton, an engineer who understood the technology we were selling, managed the real-time sales group. I always felt that his team had the most fun and were the most technically-competent selling group the company had. I was later fortunate enough to join this group.

As a group we had considerable success, and tended to play too hard. A crestfallen John Oswald came into work one morning dressed in the same clothes he had worn to work — and the pub — the day before. He was late home. His wife took exception to his lateness, and believed she could smell perfume on John's suit, so she threw him out of home. As he tried to sleep in his car, in the driveway, he was kept awake as his possessions were thrown on the front lawn. Thankfully, there was no lasting drama — he got into his home the next evening and we understand nothing else was said.

Brian Lawrence, an old-school engineer, and I took Ed Mack to meet the Trustee Savings Bank in Altrincham, Cheshire, for its presentation to explain a request for proposal it was going to issue. We decided to drive up. Ed started telling rude jokes from the moment he got into the car, continuing until we found the hotel in Altrincham, and then on the way back. The bank's plans were innovative and Ed gave another virtuoso performance in assuring them that Sperry had the hardware, software, and the plans to meet its every wish. Bob Brotherton, head of data processing at Trustee Savings Bank, explained to us the bank's relationship with the Bank of England, which would be influential in any final decision. We submitted a proposal, which Mr Brotherton recommended, but was overruled, and the bank acquired an ICL System 4 configuration. It would take Mr Brotherton 14 years to win approval for a Sperry 1100 system.

One of the reference accounts that David had sold was to Rediffusion Television, where a six-bit word commercial system was used for real-time advertisement booking and scheduling. The UNIVAC 1050 was not really built for real-time operation, but David's design and Bill Chatham's technical management worked wonders.

David Streeton did not need to use his team very much when he sold the Corporation for Economic and Industrial Research (CEIR) a large mainframe for scientific processing. Initially, Mike Seaton was the assigned

CEIR salesman. But Mike was too precious and thin-skinned, flouncing into David's office and refusing to deal with CEIR because they were not nice to him. So David was obliged to run with the account.

Eventually UNIVAC moved the real-time group within Remington House, and David was relegated to a windowless office that he did not like and which left his team in an open-plan environment. Not to be defeated, our David spent a weekend wallpapering his cubbyhole with wood-grain pattern wallpaper and installing a fridge, which ensured he still got visitors. For the open-plan office, he installed an early model coffee percolator and we learnt, over time, not to need six coffees each morning and afternoon.

We all worked on the sale of the Sperry 1100 system to Shell International Petroleum Company. Shell had been using the Computer Services Bureau in Birmingham for linear programming (the logical solution of multiple simultaneous equations), and our solution introduced remote job entry to its UK operation. Our remote job entry equipment was a UNIVAC 1004, the same hardware we had been selling directly through ICL, as a small commercial system, at sites geographically separate to the main computer centre and connected by telephone line to the main computer. We were still working with punch cards, although the remote job entry system could include magnetic tape storage. Ian Meeker, who was rather pompous, carrying a tightly rolled umbrella that matched his bowler hat, nominally headed the sales effort. He used the Shell Pecten symbol as inspiration for the project name: 'poly-entrant computing through (the) entire network'.

As always seemed to be the case, Ian and I worked at the photocopier all night before the proposal was due. We were still sorting pages and hole punching them for insertion into three-ring binders on the back seat of the taxi as we drove to Shell Centre to meet the tender submission deadline.

We won the bid. Ian moved out of our open-plan office at Remington House and into an office at Shell Centre, despite the fact that the lead-time for delivery of the 1100 was 24 months away. Ian also employed his own secretary at Shell. He established a solid relationship with Norman Rosenthal, the Shell manager for the project. Everything worked, and eventually David Streeton demanded that Ian return to Remington House.

2. ONCE WERE COWBOYS

Ian arrived on a Monday morning at home office and we could hear an almighty row coming from David's wallpapered enclave. Ian Meeker's belief and David's denial that the 'sale to Shell was enough to guarantee his position for life' caused Ian to storm out. An equally angry but determined David Streeton stalked into the open-plan office and announced to his expectant audience:

> 'You are all promoted to senior sales executives. Ian Meeker's excuse for not wanting to come back from Shell Centre is that he refuses to have to share any office with "junior" sales executives! I have told him he will not have to.'

The team accepted that. Funny how that decision has permeated the whole industry. You would only ever meet senior sales executives in the computer sector from that day on.

It was inevitable that Ian would move on. He joined the international division of the company and worked in Eastern Europe — we presumed that he would still have his bowler hat on, even in Russia. He was attending to Aeroflot business when he died suddenly in Moscow.

With Shell and British Petroleum (BP) as customers, it was natural that the team would focus its attention on the tender request put out by Shell-Mex and BP Ltd, the marketing company for Shell, BP, National Benzole and Power Petrol. Norman Blatch was the lead salesman. Large and almost larger than life, Norman would brighten even a dull day with his enthusiasm and barrow boy, finger-flicking mannerisms when making a point. Norman was ecstatic when we won the job, but we lost regular contact with him as he devoted himself to setting up the project. The Shell-Mex and BP Ltd representatives were a charming crowd. They killed a bottle and a half of scotch with Norman and David in David's office one afternoon. The session ended with the unanimous acceptance of the fact that Shell-Mex and BP Ltd people compared very well with the more ruthless staff we dealt with at Shell and BP.

I think the team was jealous of Norman. We were all formally invited to dine with Norman at a restaurant in the Aldwych one Saturday evening to celebrate the installation of the first Shell-Mex and BP computer system at their Hemel Hempsted computer centre, north of London. Norman had the reputation for being a bit stingy, so the lads met for a pint or two before going to the restaurant where we dined in a private room. Norman had also invited along Shell-Mex representatives and the team mood became blacker as we were suddenly obliged to have to work for our supper and be nice to our new customers. But at the conclusion of the meal, each member of the team was presented with gold engraved cufflinks as a thank you for helping during the sales process. That humbled us. I still wear those cufflinks.

Our specialisation in real-time computing led to a request from UNIVAC Scandinavia, hoping to sell a UNIVAC 418 system to a prospect in Lapland. Tjaereborg Rejser A/S was a travel agent and airline owner, and a user of an early Control Data Corporation (CDC) 3300 system. Per Krogiger, the Tjaereborg pastor, had initially started a small business taking his parishioners on bus and coach trips. The business had grown very large, and had offices in the Scandinavian capitals and a booking and reservation system for Stirling Airlines, also owned by the pastor. He also operated a conventional travel agency business. It was a fascinating trip, and I got to travel in a sled pulled by reindeer within the Arctic Circle. But more significant was a lesson in pragmatism and a new definition of 'real time' from the pastor. He told us that the response times from the CDC system were:

> Tjaereborg Town Office: 30 seconds
> Copenhagen: 10 minutes
> Helsinki: 20 minutes
> Oslo: 30 to 40 minutes

Foolishly, we decried these as meaningless response times and argued that people would not wait this long. Per Krogiger knew better than we did. The Copenhagen office was in a coffee shop, where the waiting public sampled the coffee; the Helsinki office was associated with a newsagents and book shop; and the Oslo office was based in a department store. Per Krogiger certainly provided a complete service and made money at every turn. He did not need response times under three seconds to be satisfied with his installed system.

The government sales group found it difficult to penetrate and win government business, which was given to ICL, the only UK computer maker, as government policy. One day we received a request for tender from the Royal Navy for a system to handle the logistics of the Polaris submarine system. The request called for two computer centres, one in Bath and one in Darlington. Was it worth UNIVAC bothering to tender? We discussed this at length. We decided to bid. We knew we would not win the business, and so gambled upon making the expected sale as unprofitable for ICL as possible. We put in a bid, using the latest technology to further test ICL, at 50 per cent of the published price list. We were also very generous in our support offer. The bid was forgotten.

After several months interval and no prior indication, we received notification from the navy that we had won the business. A quick run through of the figures showed that there was no way we would be able to show the necessary 28 per cent gross margin. Worse, we had lodged no paperwork with the company to state that we had bid, and certainly had no approvals, at the winning price. We brainstormed long and hard about what to do.

Eventually we decided that we would have to cheat the system. We fabricated the paperwork that should have been produced months earlier. Once this course of action was determined it should have been simple, but it was not. The company name had changed and for a while we could not find any of the old stationery. The pre-dated document looked awfully pristine. It was aged under the mat just inside John's office for half a day and surreptitiously lodged in Charles Elliott's office, at the bottom of secretary Rona Cook's in-tray.

That afternoon we marched into Charles's office with the good news and the order letter from the navy. It was never publicly disclosed how hard he and Roger Hunziger had to fight to get approval for the navy business from UNIVAC headquarters, but they managed it.

But the navy saga did not stop there. Out of the blue, Dennis Bizeray, who managed the government sales team, sent John Woods a note, the intent of which was to deprive Mike Norman of his rightful commission. Dennis argued that Mike did not deserve the full commission and that he was too young to be able to handle the responsibility of so much money. Fortunately, common sense prevailed and Mike got his money. But he did not stay much longer with the company.

Yes, there were times when we were cowboys.

We could not have enjoyed the success we had without the help and constant attention of our secretaries. Jane Newsome and Sue Dixon were great and, if anything, put in even longer hours than we did. They were in the team and were included wherever possible in social as well as business functions.

Jane and Sue came into their own at proposal time. As salespeople, we were looking for the opportunity to bid systems to prospective customers. We would do our very best to make sure we wrote the requirements contained in the request for tender on our prospect's behalf if at all possible. This did not happen that often. The date of submission for a proposal has a life of its own. Initially, we would have plenty of time and when compiling the proposal schedule we would allow for slippage, anticipating that it would not be needed. But it always was, and last-minute panic was the norm. These were the days when reproduction of a number of copies was achieved by using a Roneo-Vickers reproducing machine. Pages were typed onto 'skins' that took the impression from the electric typewriter through which the ink would permeate on to plain paper. If the impression was too hard ('o's were notorious), the centre of the letter would fall out and the resultant print image would be a filled-in letter. The skins could be corrected using a product called Snopake. We were able to change the skins a few times in an attempt to reuse previous work, but always got into trouble with the pricing section. This would be changed so often, as the proposal developed, that the layers of the red-coloured corrections were multiplied until the offending numbers were positioned on blisters on the skin. As the proposal neared completion, every part of the organisation wanted to add its thoughts. Quite often, the print reproduction was severely prejudiced by the thickness of the skin and the actual prices were almost indecipherable on the finished product. We used three-ring binders and I can remember us submitting three copies of a set of more than 20 volumes. Manuals were photocopied more often than not, and there were many overnight efforts to meet submission dates.

The chain-smoking Ann Whiting was our advertising and public relations manager. Ann was a champion. She did the UK subsidiary great service in that we were able to invite Grace Murray Hopper to London as a guest. Grace was one of the acknowledged pioneers of computing from the Eckert and Mauchly Electrical Research Laboratories and the University of Pennsylvania from which originated, under the Remington Rand banner, the UNIVAC 1 (UNIVersal Automatic Computer 1), arguably the world's first computer. When I first heard Lieutenant Commander US Navy (Reserve) Murray Hopper speak, she was already over 60 years old, severely dressed in her navy uniform. She carried an enormous handbag out of which she would produce the tools of her trade, as well as her knitting. To illustrate her talk she showed the speed of the computer through a 30 cm long piece of wire. This was the length of wire that, at the speed of light, represented one nanosecond: one millionth of a second. Even then, we were working in nanoseconds. Grace was eventually promoted, in her 70s, to be a Rear Admiral in the US Navy and was made a Fellow of the British Computer Society.

Our customers were always keen to receive such famous visitors and I was fortunate enough to accompany her on several visits and have time for one-on-one discussions over lunch. She loved the Connaught Rooms off the Aldwych for afternoon tea.

Figure 2.1: Grace Murray Hopper as I remember her.
Source: Wikipedia Commons.

Training did not seem to be an issue, but I do remember Mike Lewis from the Shell project team teaching us the 1100 assembler language on Monday evenings. I was also extremely lucky to be able to attend the first European project management course, which was run from the company's European headquarters in Zurich. I was the only UK student in attendance. The first two weeks involved daily visiting lecturers from the British European Airways BEACON airline project. I suspect we were taught 'ideal' project management, as it included sessions on pricing and public relations, items that were not generally the UNIVAC project manager's business. We were also told that UNIVAC expected its programmers to be able to produce six lines of computer code per day. This included the writing, testing, and documentation of the code as it stood, as well as its place in the system. Six lines of code per day did not seem very much, especially when we knew that an airline reservation with all the checking that takes place could be around 30,000 lines of code long. In simple terms, it would require two-and-a-half man years of effort to produce one reservation, and this was using the most effective software code, the code designed for the computer upon which it was to run. This fact was the rationale for UNIVAC to write a generalised software system, for airline applications, that might be sold to many different customers. Also, if the airline itself decided to write a generalised system that was capable of adaption, it would eventually become a software competitor to UNIVAC. Both UNIVAC and IBM set themselves the airline business as a target and each would achieve approximately a 50 per cent share of the market.

It did not matter how good a system UNIVAC had implemented at British European Airways: when it was absorbed into the British Overseas Airways Corporation there was going to be a competition between BEACON and BOADICEA (the British Overseas Airways Digital Information Computer for Electronic Automation system that was running on large IBM platforms). The data processing director of BOADICEA was Peter Hermon. We knew Peter Hermon at UNIVAC, as he had been a prospect when he worked at Dunlop Engineering in Birmingham. He had never been an easy person to approach, and we feared the inevitable face-off. Peter always preferred IBM, but for the British Airways system we could also expect that the UK Government would bring pressure to bear for them to consider ICL, the indigenous supplier. ICL by this time had absorbed English Electric Computers whose genesis had been LEO Computers, developed for Lyons Tea Houses.

As occurred 30 years later when Qantas took over Australian Airlines, the technical, independent view was that the Sperry+UNIVAC system was the most comprehensive and advanced of available facilities. In both these cases, the decision was made to consolidate on the IBM platform, as operated by the major airline partner.

The UNIVAC division of Sperry Rand increasingly became the dominant division of the company and we enjoyed almost annual name changes to reflect the changes in the conglomerate. Other divisions included the original Remington division, with its Kardex filing systems, and Remington typewriters and shavers. We were given Remington shavers at Christmas for distribution to our best customers as gifts, which were always welcome. The New Holland division made and distributed a range of heavy farm machinery. The New Holland name was better known in rural communities than UNIVAC or Sperry. Frank Moore sold a computer system to the Sperry Gyroscope Company in Bracknell, Berkshire, which became another reference site for us, as most technical people were aware of the Sperry Gyroscope connection.

We anticipated and learned to live with annual organisational changes, and in the sexy industry in which we were working, jobs were not hard to come by. At the start of the 1969 fiscal year, the company decided to change the structure of the sales organisation to a purely geographic structure. Sales teams were reassigned, and Midlands (Birmingham), and Northern Region (Altrincham) offices were established. There were many changes at the top, we had an influx of recruits across the company, and UNIVAC House was acquired above Euston Station to house the growing community.

One project that the new London region sales group undertook was fascinating. EMI Records worked with us to evaluate the potential of a real-time manufacturing system that would control the day's production of records to reflect the wholesale orders it had received that day, rather than it making guesses as to what might be ordered for storage prior to distribution. With the system we proposed, we were looking to coordinate the actual manufacture of vinyl records through the merging of many conveyor belts from the multiple vinyl presses available, so that a particular wholesaler's order would arrive at dispatch at the appropriate time. The mathematics were horrendous. As UNIVAC salespeople, we knew the rudiments of queuing theory to be able to explain to our prospective customers how the interrupt processing of our equipment worked to handle communications, but we were all stretched coordinating the travel of records down numerous conveyor belts. The system was never built, but I was able to use skills acquired from this exercise when I got to Control Data Corporation and became involved in process and production control.

They were busy, interesting times, and a lot of fun.

3
A working 'home away from home'

I had kept in contact with David Streeton when he moved from UNIVAC to Control Data Corporation (CDC), and when our families holidayed together during the summer of 1968 David asked me to join him at CDC. At the time, UNIVAC was not the fun it had once been, partly because of the organisational changes that were realigning the company. I also believed that the specialisation we had acquired in the real-time group would be dissipated and lost.

Before I could represent CDC, it was necessary for me to attend an induction course at CDC headquarters in Minneapolis–Saint Paul, Minnesota. I was excused the first week of the four-week course, as I already had a background in computer sales, and joined the class of 25 presentable young men at the start of the second week. We were housed in serviced apartments along Interstate Highway 494, and I called into CDC on Saturday evening to pick up a key and was in bed asleep before my roommate came in from his night out. He woke me. Jerry, who was from South Carolina, and I stayed up half the night talking. As David had recommended that I hire a car, Jerry and I had a Ford Mustang to play in.

The general format of the remaining days of the induction course was for a senior CDC manager to tell us about his role and for us to get to know him and new aspects of the company. CDC was small enough that the company would encourage dialogue from the field to head office, and it helped that we would have already met. It worked. I had been told that CDC was an extension of UNIVAC, but it was a surprise to learn how much of an extension it was.

The first 36-bit word machine designed by UNIVAC was its 13th project. Rather than designate it with that number, the binary form for 13 was used: 1101. General manager of the UNIVAC division of Remington Rand, William D. (Chuck) Norris, and designer Seymour Cray had the principal say in the design of UNIVAC processors until that time. Seymour Cray's interest was in extending the word size of the processor to expand the instruction set repertoire and build more powerful processors. We learned that Messrs Norris and Cray had approached UNIVAC management with the plans and design for a 60-bit word machine — this would have been the 1103. But their proposal was rejected by UNIVAC, so they left and set up CDC.

Was it a coincidence that by taking the designator of the new system from the old company (1103) and adding it to the street number of its Park Avenue address (501) you came up with a total of 1604? The CDC 1604 was the first processor sold by the new company.

A number of the senior CDC managers we met also had UNIVAC backgrounds.

To this day, I am surprised that the most interesting of the specialist presentations was on pricing policy, followed by the talk by the corporate lawyer. We were addressed by and met Chuck Norris, Seymour Cray and Jim Thornton, Mr Cray's second-in-command on the CDC (flagship and largest mainframe) 6600 and the major research project the String Array Processor (STAR).

We had great fun socially and met for many beers most evenings in the Holiday Inn on 494. It was a good group of people and we worked to make it successful — especially the older Swiss man who was the general manager designate for his country, who was initially concerned that the class would be too technical for him. He just about coped, but he did not enjoy the course.

Figure 3.1: The formal class photograph — CDC induction class of September–October 1968.
Source: Author's collection.

We enjoyed an Indian summer until the third week of the class, when the first winter blast of the US Midwest lowered the temperature from a pleasant 70°F to freezing. My roommate, a few classmates and I were back in our apartment quite early with a pizza and an American football game on the television. One of the class had played college football and he was explaining the niceties of the game. We had a few beers and finished the bottle of duty free whisky I had brought in for whoever put his hand up. I was in bed when the telephone rang. It was another classmate. He had spent the evening with a United Airlines hostess who had thrown him out of her apartment, and asked if I would pick him up, as he had no money for a taxi and the young lady was not prepared to call one on his behalf. I dressed and set off on the highway to meet him. It was bitterly cold. I was driving determinedly when a car, perhaps 100 yards in front of me, put on its brakes. My reflex was to do the same. Big mistake. The roads were covered in black ice and the Mustang pirouetted along the highway until it fell off the embankment into a field. The highway patrolmen who found me were, fortunately, intrigued to find an Englishman in a field and not too concerned that I was full of Scotch. They had chains on their wheels and a tow rope, and I was soon back on my mission. Dan McHarg was suitably pleased when I eventually picked him up and drove him, very carefully, back to the apartments.

On the last Friday, the class had an election for class president and vice president, and I learned one of the most important lessons of working with a US multinational. I knew David Streeton had been elected class vice president of his induction group, and it had immediately stood him in good stead with CDC. I was nominated for class president, but lost by one vote to an ex-IBM salesman, who was very smooth and deserved the accolade. However, I was publicly castigated by the class leader for not voting for myself, which would have meant my winning.

Back home, I had to buy my own car and it was fortunate that I bought a Mini — if the car had been any larger I should not have been able to park it in an unused corner of the underground car park of the St James's Square office. It was nice office, close to St James's Park and Whitehall, with good restaurants around us.

Frank Boyle was the managing director. I found Frank to be a bit reclusive at CDC, although I had met him previously at the Corporation for Economic and Industrial Research, a consultancy with a good reputation for understanding data processing. David Streeton had a very good relationship with Frank and his yellow accountant's lined pad. The pad came out whenever prices were being discussed, and the jottings were treasured as a reminder to Frank of the prices we might get away with. David Streeton was the commercial sales manager, and would eventually entice nine of his former UNIVAC colleagues to CDC. Dr Keith Corless was the government sales manager. He had tasted success with large installations at London University and at the Meteorological Office.

The existing salesmen were initially a bit put out when I was given the sales responsibility for the Société Information Automatique computer bureau, located by the side of Victoria Railway Station. Société Information Automatique was the UK subsidiary of a French parent which operated a CDC 6600, at the time the most powerful computer commercially available. The two UK joint managing directors were John Wootton and Peter Hutton. I knew John Wootton. He had been a lecturer in the second and third years of my civil engineering course at the University of Leeds and had taught me highway engineering. He was small, fair and very precise. John had a certain immediate notoriety at the university, having taken his wife on honeymoon to a practical two week university surveying exercise held in Whitby on the Yorkshire Coast. John and his wife were teased unmercifully. Perhaps I would have been less of a leader in that activity had I known John might one day be a customer. In the event, he was fine about our previous history. Peter Hooper was tall, dark, and wore heavy spectacles, and was the more obvious salesman of Société Information Automatique management. The Société Information Automatique customers were the petroleum companies David Streeton and I already knew. Shell and BP ran their really big linear programs on the CDC 6600 rather than the Sperry 1100s, which were being used for commercial projects. Obviously, the pricing algorithm also made sense.

The CDC 6600 was not a particularly sensitive hardware system but we did have a few interesting hardware experiences.

The petroleum companies used the CDC 6600 for linear programming — the resolution of multiple simultaneous equations — the results of which would influence the flow of raw material through the exploration, acquisition, and processing process to its ultimate destination: the petrol pump. The programs ran for several hours. Occasionally, we would have a problem. An electrical fault or spike was often diagnosed as a possible cause to bring the hardware down. But Société Information Automatique had incorporated the latest smoothing equipment into the motor alternator set-up, and we were at a loss to discover the cause of a problem that had stalled the operation. This happened more than once. The computer was attended by full operations staff when these programs were running and they were not able to shed any light on the cause. We even had building consultants investigate. We knew we were above the London Underground, the tube, because of an occasional mild tremor, hearing the train, and knowing our proximity to Victoria Station. Then, somehow, the reason and solution became clear: if individual tube trains did not cause any problems for us, what was the effect of two trains passing directly under us travelling in different directions? The consultants did the calculations and confirmed this as a probable cause. A constant electrical charge was put across the basement and the fault disappeared.

More obvious, and embarrassing, was an engineering field change order from CDC head office which instructed the on-site engineers to change the lubricating oil associated with the main drum storage as a matter of urgency. It was done, but with the wrong oil, which brought the system to a crashing halt. The Société Information Automatique Paris CDC 6600 was out of action for the same reason, as well as other systems that had been recognised as potential back-up systems in the event that the London machine failed. The London University installed CDC 6600 also failed.

A back-up computer was found and jobs were taken overseas to run, but it was an expensive mistake. The correct oil was provided probably no more than three days later, but it was a salutary experience.

British Petroleum (BP) was a prospective customer for CDC. BP made extensive use of the SIA 6600, in addition to the Sperry 1108 we had sold them while representing UNIVAC. Seymour Cray, the hardware genius of CDC, had encouraged Jim Thornton to design and build a new system called the String Array Processor, the STAR system. It carried a starting price tag of US$10 million and was represented in the sales and marketing brochures as a mahogany and glass structure with a high central core, surrounded by cabinetry, and eventually what looked like a continuous leather seat around the structure. It was an ultra-modern design concept for its day. The compute power was enormous. Each sub-system was controlled by an IBM Series 360/40 processor to provide enough data to keep the STAR busy. CDC did not have time to design its own input/output processors for the STAR; the IBM 360/40 was a machine in common use and was available.

The CDC STAR support team from the Minneapolis–Saint Paul headquarters came to London and we spent two full days discussing the STAR potential with BP, who agreed to visit Minneapolis–Saint Paul. On my way to the US, a couple of days before the BP team arrived, I called in for an overnight stop in Chicago to catch up with Dan McHarg from the induction class. I was supposed to stay with Dan and his wife, but we never made it home and I arrived in Saint Paul very much the worse for wear. The senior BP representative was head of the operations research department, Colin Williamson, a large impressive businessman who exuded confidence and could have been taken for a politician or lawyer. We stayed for a few days at the Holiday Inn opposite the CDC office and enjoyed the best hospitality.

Our sales strategy was to demonstrate the raw power of the hardware, discuss the potential of STAR for a multi-thread operating system, and invite BP to determine if and how it could use such a system. Eventually, on the last morning of the trip, CDC laid its cards on the table. CDC would give BP a STAR system if, in return, BP would provide the linear programming expertise and software know-how that would optimise the hardware and operating system. I do not think that Colin Williamson had any warning that we were about to make such an offer. He was superb. He got up from the conference table and went to the blackboard. There he drew a normal curve.

> 'You will recognise a normal curve.
>
> 'This curve represents the intellect of the 230 systems engineers in the BP operations research department.
>
> 'We are proud of our recruitment techniques. So if the right tail of the curve represents the "genius" end of the curve, the normal axis of our curve will be biased towards the left. We have more clever people than not.
>
> 'We can recognise that five or six people in my department are absolutely outstanding. Five or six people upon whom the core of the real software development would depend.
>
> 'Now, this is a normal curve. Let's say that three people have the genius we believe they have. What about the three people at the other end of the curve? These engineers, through no fault of their own, will thwart any successful software build.
>
> 'We are flattered to be asked, but we are not software writers, we are an operational research house. I shall make representations to my management but I do not think this is a commitment we can take on.'

It was a telling argument, simply and effectively presented. It left CDC management, and me, without an immediate logical response.

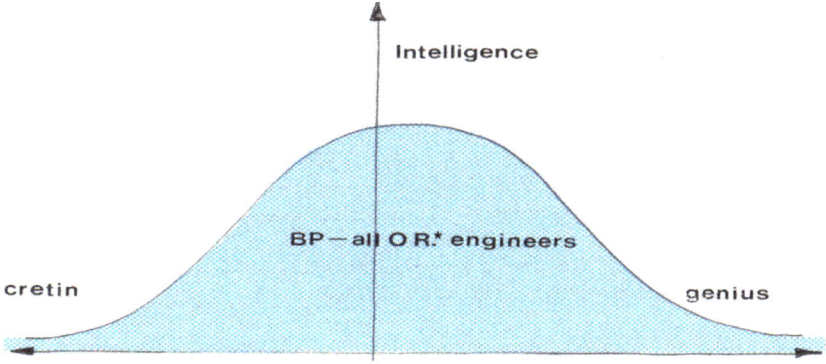

Figure 3.2: Colin Williamson's argument.
Source: Author's recollection.
* operations research.

Colin was as good as his word, and we were aware that he made a strong case to his management that BP should be involved in some capacity to produce software for the STAR, but approval was not forthcoming.

At the other end of the computing scale, CDC also sold process control computer systems. My lay definition of process control, at the time, was that a system was monitoring a continuous flow situation, and measurements were made within that flow that prompted changes to the course and/or speed of the flow. Our immediate prospect was Shell Petroleum and the flow was petroleum refinery distillation. I visited the Shell refinery at Stanlow, in Cheshire, to see early CDC analogue instruments used in a semi-automatic solution in operation. It was fascinating. I climbed up and over a distillation plant and ended the day filthy, but with an appreciation of what Shell wanted to control with as much automation as we could introduce. Shell was the expert in this field, and its request for proposal was extremely detailed and had been written with an understanding of CDC specifications and capabilities.

I travelled to Shell headquarters in Holland to meet with Shell engineers and was accompanied by and teamed with a most personable young Dutch CDC engineer, Henk Isselt, who held my hand through the learning curve and guided me through Shell politics. For six weeks we were based on the Dutch coast at the offices of Bataafse Internationale Petroleum Maatschappij NV Company, the Dutch Shell refinery arm. I commuted from Kent every week and enjoyed temporarily living in Holland. We played hard, but also worked long hours to get the job done.

An interesting facet of the proposal was the requirement for the electrical contacts on the printed circuit boards (that would constitute the SC-1700 central processing unit and peripherals) to be gold, as any other metal would corrode in the refinery environment. The CDC system controller was an 18-bit word machine acquired whilst CDC was in that mode.

The system we designed to meet the Carrington (Cheshire) refinery needs was a two processor configuration with the larger (32K memory) processor monitoring the 1440 digital input control points and the 560 digital outputs. The smaller (28K memory) system was to take over the monitoring function during times when the larger was unavailable (broken), or being tested during a period of preventative maintenance. In normal operation, the small system would run the Shell-authored linear program that examined the state of the refining process every five minutes and advised when changes to flows, temperatures, etc. were required for optimum performance of the plant and the crude oil input. Henk and I worked through almost every word of the proposal with the Dutch Shell engineers. We also fully argued and agreed an acceptance test criteria for the unit components and the complete system at their request. The acceptance test procedures became a standard for both companies.

At the end of the day, the final document was not as professional as I would have liked when we started, but logistics became difficult, with me in The Hague all week and typing support in St James's Square back in London. But we were successful, and our tender was accepted. Better still, it was accepted as the basis for 13 process systems through Shell's European refining operation. This was the most technical proposal for which I had responsibility, and it needed a steep learning curve. That experience, and that of the negotiation of the acceptance test criteria, have proved invaluable over the years.

After winning the Shell business, I started having problems with walking and was diagnosed with gout back in the UK. 'Overly good living' was the traditional cause of this complaint, and I did have to admit to the doctor that I had been eating very rich food three meals a day for the past few weeks. We were also in the habit of slipping out of the office mid-morning and -afternoon to enjoy soused herrings, the local delicacy, which were sold on the seafront, whatever the weather. And at home were pottery bottles of Dutch gin and port, courtesy of the duty-free entitlements at Schiphol Airport. Never again! As you can imagine, I took some ribbing from my colleagues as I hobbled round the office once I got back.

One interesting anomaly within CDC was the fact that employees — even salesmen — were issued with 35 pence 'luncheon vouchers' to help with the cost of lunch in this expensive part of town. We were not that often in St James's Square, and should not have been if we were doing our jobs. It became tradition that we saved our luncheon vouchers and periodically went out as a group to an expensive restaurant. We would splurge on an expensive boozy meal, payment for which would be a whole stack of the unopened books of vouchers. We took it in turns to have to negotiate with the restaurant management, who were somewhat taken aback by our effrontery.

Buoyed by the impending success with Shell, I sought permission from David Streeton to bid for a traffic-flow control system for the City of Liverpool. The idyllic situation that the city wished to implement would have all the traffic lights on arterial roads through the centre of the city at green for an ideal driver maintaining the legal speed limits. I believed I understood the mathematics from what I had learned in answering the Shell refinery request and the work we had done for EMI systems at UNIVAC. That was not enough. As with most advanced projects, the city did not want to be a first-time user of a CDC kit in an unproven application, and our solution would have been in that category. We lost that order to Nixdorf of Germany, who had automated several German towns and was very professional in its approach to Liverpool. It was the first time I had met Nixdorf as a competitor.

Working with CDC as an ex-UNIVAC employee was almost like being at a home away from home. Many of the CDC managers were ex-UNIVAC, and while I was working with David Streeton, John Ware and Brian Lawrence had also come to CDC. The company had almost the same real-time team as UNIVAC during 1966–1967. It almost felt the same, but something was different. In my case, I think it was a growing awareness that there had to be a different style of living that did not involve a difficult two-hour drive to get to and from work. Of course, that two-hour drive was a more manageable 40 minute trip leaving Farnborough at 6.30 am rather than 7.10 am, and a similar time saving could be made in the evening by working late or spending time in the pub at the close of work. My two boys were aged two and four, and were an engaging handful, but I was not seeing much of them, as I was also training two evenings a week at Blackheath Football Club and playing rugby every Saturday. It did not seem fair.

I knew that Ted Jones (by this time established as northern region director of the UNIVAC division of Sperry Rand) had offered John Ware the job of northern region sales manager. John turned Ted down. When Ted asked me, I took the opportunity to go to Altrincham in Cheshire, during one of my trips to see Shell, and talk to Ted and Roger Notman-Watt, both of whom had been good friends at Remington House. I liked what I saw. Ted was very relaxed. Roger was off to Brazil to work and had a house for sale, which would suit my family very well, being only a seven-minute drive from the office.

Telling David Streeton that I was going to leave CDC was probably the most difficult thing I have ever had to do in business. We are still friends, and I was saddened that David commented that the UNIVAC days were his happiest and most successful days in business: 'everything we touched turned to gold'. I had to admit to him that I have enjoyed all of my career; UNIVAC and CDC were only highlights.

A short while after I left CDC, I was advised by Brian Lawrence that Shell had ordered 11 refinery control systems based upon the proposal I had submitted to the Carrington Refinery — a total order worth some US$6 million. Brian was pleased, as Shell had been allocated to him and he collected a fat commission cheque.

4
A taste of Northern bitter

Ted Jones had been an ally during my Remington House days. A Kiwi, from Wellington, and an accountant by training, he was a few years older than the rest of us, and wore his greying hair long and affected his own style with a quiet authority. He took the role of the first northern region director for Sperry+UNIVAC, although we were still using the UNIVAC acronym to sell products. His first recruit was Roger Notman-Watt. Audrey and I had been quite close to Roger and his wife Rita in London when we socialised outside of the business environment. Ted had an obligation to Roger from a few years back in Remington House. Ted had developed a relationship with a young lady from work, Joanne, who already had a boyfriend; a jealous boyfriend. The boyfriend came into Remington House one evening after office hours, and was met and challenged by Roger Notman-Watt. An altercation ensued that left Roger bruised and bleeding. It was never stated whether Roger claimed to be Ted, or was simply aggressive in denying the boyfriend access to the office. Ted subsequently married Joanne and they moved to Prestbury, Cheshire, when he took up the role of director. Roger moved with Ted as his administration manager, living just a few moments from the office in Hale Barns, Cheshire.

I knew that Ted had offered John Ware the job as Sperry+UNIVAC northern region sales manager, and that John had preferred to stay in the South with CDC. John and Margaret's children were about 10–12 years old, and he enjoyed living in Croydon. I had been surprised when Ted called to offer me the role of sales manager, but was flattered to be asked. I was about to visit Carrington, also in Cheshire, on CDC business, so agreed to meet Ted and Roger after I had finished at the Shell refinery. It was not a job interview in any sense of the word. Ted and Roger enthused about how happy they were to have made the move from London, and were aggressive about the sales potential they were exploring. Roger took me to his home, a large family home with a fantastic open view across the Cheshire Plains, and told me that he was actually leaving Sperry to move to Brazil. The house was for sale and, because he was going overseas, he wanted to sell all of the furniture at what he claimed were very keen prices. I was certainly of a mind to consider a move back to Sperry. The closeness of Rivershill Gardens to the office, the availability of a home without the aggravation of an extended search, and the chance to take a sales management role combined to make it an attractive proposition. Audrey endorsed the move. I started six weeks later.

Whoever chose the office location in Station Street, Altrincham, chose well. The office was next door to the Lawnswood Arms, an upmarket hostelry, and was opposite the Ploughman, a spit-and-sawdust setting that became our home away from the office, particularly for lunch. The Cresta Court Hotel was the other side, towards Altrincham. Also on the town side, on the other side of the road, was a really nice smaller establishment, the Orange Tree, for Friday evening and quieter functions.

The first surprise was a sales director to contend with. Ted had not mentioned Peter Lea, who he had recruited from the customer engineering ranks. Unsurprisingly for an engineer, Peter saw things in black or white, and was at a complete loss in dealing with the greys of the selling process. Nor did he really have a sense of humour. But he did have a sense of honour, and gave up the big ground-floor office that was designated for the sales manager. He joined forces with Ted Jones when I immediately rebelled over the allotment of car parking spaces. I lost that fight. My ethic is always 'first-come, first served', although if the car park nearest to the door was left empty as a courtesy for Ted Jones, as the regional director, so be it. Peter was dark and mostly smartly dressed. He had the tendency to hunch his shoulders and with his thick dark eyebrows could look a bit intimidating.

4. A TASTE OF NORTHERN BITTER

Figure 4.1: Ted Jones and myself at the Wig and Pen in Fleet Street, the pub used for Sperry functions.
Source: Author's collection.

My first assignment was to attend a regional sales conference. It was a good opportunity to see each of the salesmen in my team presenting his sales plan for his geographic area, and to compare them with the salesmen from the Midlands Region who were based in Birmingham and in attendance. The Midlands team had outstanding salespeople who I knew.

Laurence O'Neill, a dark, well-groomed Welshman, gave a wonderful presentation that took every advantage of his natural lilt on 'how to present' by making every mistake in the book with a superb timing and just the right degree of embarrassment to have me asking 'Was this for real?' Alan Stevens, a tall, ascetic, bald, slightly stooped technician turned salesman, was our expert on the products of International Computers Limited, for whom he had previously worked.

My own sales team looked solid. I was pleased. The conference also gave me the opportunity to stand up and explain my motives for rejoining Sperry. My team included salesmen who worked from home around Liverpool, Leeds, Newcastle, and Sheffield. The Scottish representative was luckier, as he had the advantage of a Sperry manufacturing plant in Scotland, a base from which he could reference sell. Sperry was assembling card punches at the Livingston factory, obtaining government grants and the justification for claiming a 'Made in Britain' cachet. It became my habit to spend a week, sequentially, with each salesman on his territory while trying to maintain the flexibility of being available when required to attend to Manchester business and respond to Sperry's needs. Each salesman was different, with their local accents, backgrounds, and ways of selling. Hands-on training had not been a feature of the northern region. There was also a sales team selling into local government. Central government sales were still conducted from London.

I knew two of the technical support folk from Remington House. Bernard Place and Dave Range were now based in Altrincham, living in Knutsford in new houses and enjoying new lives. Bernard was a conscientious software man, without having a particular flair. He had an IBM background and knowledge, and enjoyed arguing the toss with Barry Graham, who was to join us as regional software manager from the Birmingham office. Bernard had an interest in project management and the planning aptitude for that element of the task. He enjoyed a flutter on the horses and would spend time, over a coffee, in the mornings with the form guide. He claimed to beat the bookies, occasionally. David Range was large, fair, and impressed everyone with his gentleness. He was teamed with Bernard on a number of projects and they enjoyed joint success. When I met them again, Bernard was project manager for the Sperry 1100 site at Wythenshawe, and Dave was his assistant. (This was one of the computer systems credited to Ian Meeker from the real-time sales team led by Dave Streeton, as discussed in Chapter 2.)

At about the time that I left Sperry for CDC, Sperry had entered the card punch verifier business with its 1701/1710 products in direct competition with, and with a price advantage over, the IBM 026/029 alternatives. The thought of having to sell card punches was perhaps an additional reason for my looking at CDC. I had been proven wrong. With the right salesman, the card punch business could be good, and it certainly opened doors that Sperry would not have opened without this entry-level equipment. I had a good door opener on my sales team, an irrepressible character who would not and could not take 'no' for an answer, a team-player who alerted us when he made contact with a computer prospect. He wowed and feted the formidable ladies who seemed to fill the position of punch room supervisor in the Northwest. David was a hard worker and put in a lot of time to earn our respect.

We had a number of interesting customers to look after, including:

- The Shell International Petroleum large Sperry 1100 installation. Ian Meeker's PECTEN submission had recommended a two computer centre approach, with one in London and one in the Manchester area.
- William Timpson and Son, a shoe manufacturer, with one of the UNIVAC second generation systems (featuring vacuum tube technology), a UNIVAC Solid-State 80. We wanted to sell them a third generation system.
- Robinsons Brewery, the local Stockport brewery. This was an order previously won by Pat Cullen. This was a good customer to have at Christmas time as, every year, it allowed us to buy from the complete stock list at wholesale prices. The house port was particularly good.

My initial task was for Ted Jones and me to sell our first Sperry 1100 in the region. That determined an approach to the larger organisations.

Bob Brotherton, the head of data processing at Trustee Savings Bank, was still in the same position in Altrincham as when I had talked to him a few years before. The International Computers Limited (ICL) System 4 equipment (from the former English Electric Company) was doing all that was required of it in a very limited communications environment. Bob Brotherton knew that when Trustee Savings Bank moved to online banking, Sperry would be a contender for that business again. On my recommendation, Bob had been amenable to undertaking a regular presenter role for us at the Nice Sperry Management Training Centre, and we paid for his trip. The program seminar, held every six months, was sold to other prospective clients in the finance and insurance sector. Mr Brotherton undertook his presenter and consultant role, which he enjoyed, and for which he was paid a handsome fee. He justified it on the basis that it enabled him to keep in touch with new Sperry technologies and the other players in the sector. Eventually he was allowed, by the legislative changes to the Bank of England control of the financial services sector, to go to tender. Trustee Savings Bank ordered from Sperry 14 years after Ed Mack, Brian Lawrence, and I made the first contact from London — but that is another story.

We were able to mount a combined approach to British Insulated Callender's Cables (BICC), who was headquartered in Prescot, Lancashire, as it was in the market for card equipment, and David Swanston rapidly developed a good relationship with its punch room supervisor. I made a friend and ally of Frank Cunliffe, who was applications and programming manager at the main data centre. BICC was using ICL equipment in two centres and was a satisfied ICL customer. It is often easier to sell to the happy customer than the disgruntled user who is already looking for what might go wrong. Frank arranged for Sperry to make a formal presentation of Sperry competencies to a senior level management team. As BICC was steeped in ICL, we co-opted Alan Stevens from the Birmingham office to assist with the presentation. In these circumstances we worked with 35 mm slides, and the usual format would be to discuss hardware, then (our lack of) software, before a services segment during which we would show our (growing) understanding of the data processing aspirations of BICC. Perhaps Frank had agreed to the presentation a bit too early in the relationship. Ted Jones and I were not making any progress during our introductions; our audience truly was not interested. Alan Stevens was having an equally unrewarding response during his dissertation extolling the virtues of the hardware, with lots of facts and figures, speeds and capacities, until:

> '… and this slide, gentlemen, shows the new Sperry Uniservo 12C tape unit. It is very fast, with the industry's smallest inter-block gap and f-f-f-f …'

Alan did stutter at times, but this was worse than I had seen him. He stopped, took several deep breaths and started out again.

> 'Very fast and f-f-f-f …' — another pause — 'Very fast and f-f … fucking expensive.'

The room exploded with laughter and delight that he had mastered his problem. Alan now had his audience eating from his hand, and those who followed him were also given a good hearing. BICC acquired punch equipment and we continued to push the mainframe case with them.

BICC asked to visit Sperry customers. We were pleased to comply, and decided to visit London and put together a visit schedule for six senior managers. We travelled down one afternoon on the Manchester Pullman (a luxury rail service), having been driven to Wilmslow Station from Prescot in the BICC Rolls-Royces. That first evening, we visited the West London Air Terminal to view the still operational reservation system and talk future software concepts with the London Development Centre staff who had built the reservation system. We attended Rules of Maiden Lane, one of my favourite restaurants in central London, for dinner. The oldest restaurant in London, Rules is all polished wood and red velvet, and is very posh. We ordered three courses and, quite properly, the wine-list was brought to me as host. I ordered a bottle of every drink I knew I could pronounce, and was seemingly — given the interest shown by my neighbour, the chief accountant of BICC — doing quite well. I asked if he had an interest in wine. Quick as a flash, he had his diary out, opened at the wine vintage page. He complimented me on my order so far, and added two more bottles. I looked across at Ted Jones. His face was thunderous. Through head movements he indicated that he wanted to speak to me privately. We met in the toilet. There he told me: 'Never, ever, do that again. You are the host. You order the wine — all of the wine.' I thought that reaction was a bit over the top, but I had other concerns in making the trip a success. Our subsequent trip to the theatre, where we saw *Annie*, set us up in good humour for the next day's visits to Shell and Abbey National Building Society, during which we heard only good news. The Pullman back to Cheshire was another gourmet close to the trip.

Figure 4.2: Rules of Maiden Lane, London.
Source: Author's collection.

BICC did not buy from us. Frank Cunliffe and his boss and I had developed a strict timetable against which they would recommend to their board that Sperry be considered to provide an additional technology specific system for the Prescot site. But, as it happened, another agenda intervened. Des Pitcher, the Sperry UK managing director, called the CEO of BICC, who he knew through the Directors' Association, to ask for an early order offering a substantial discount. This occurred without any discussion with

Ted Jones or me. It showed us up for what we were — desperate for the order. It disappointed the BICC team, who were already going out on a limb for us. We never recovered. BICC fleetingly considered us during upgrades to the installed ICL systems in order to keep us interested, but we had certainly blotted our copybook. Frank Cunliffe and I remained good friends, and he was adamant that we would have success, eventually, but he was seconded to BICC Australia, in a managerial rather than an IT managerial role, and I had moved on. It was Des Pitcher's intervention that cemented, in my future business dealings, the realisation that the only real virtue of management was to give discounts.

I generally asked my team to meet with me on a monthly basis in Altrincham. Following Ted Jones's comments to me at Rules, I arranged a 10-unit course in wine tasting which would conclude the business aspect of our meetings. Ted joined us for the final class and was in no position not to approve the substantial course fee, which he did with great humour.

James Neill and Sons was a steel company in Sheffield whose products included specialised and cutting tools such as hacksaw blades. We sold to David Baker, the company's recently recruited data processing manager, who was keen to implement a manufacturing system. We had to decide what to sell. Sperry had introduced a cut-down model in the 1100 family, the 1106, and the price was approximately £500,000 for a bare bones configuration and a limited number of terminals. For that money, we could bid a large model of the 9,000 byte family and a fair number of terminals. We decided upon the 1106 as the candidate most likely to replace ICL, and Pat Cullen and I were targeted to sell an 1100. We had an excellent pre-sales engineer, Phil Williamson, whose background was large systems, assigned to the account. Phil was an essential member in the sales team and built a formidable reputation with the prospective engineer users at James Neill. Hugh Neill, the son of the founder of the company, was a high-profile toolmaker in Sheffield; in the mid-1980s, he became the Lord Lieutenant of South Yorkshire. Selling a big system made sense in terms of growing the company's prestige in the market. David Baker was malleable and was there to be sold. It was a matter of putting the time in with him. David was resolute that he would not accept lunches or any other benefits from us during the sales process, but did agree to a dinner after a contract was signed. ICL did not put the necessary time in and were finessed out of the business.

4. A TASTE OF NORTHERN BITTER

We were confident of a sale to James Neill when we were invited to meet its board prior to its formal decision. Des Pitcher, the Sperry UK managing director, was keen to join Pat Cullen and me when we presented to the board. We did not make a good job of briefing Des about James Neill's business interests, and he was correctly annoyed to be exposed to James Neill's aggressive expansion plans and the possibility that the Sperry 1106 we had proposed might need to be expanded to accommodate them. I accepted this as a justifiable criticism — after the event. Des was put in the unfortunate position of having to think on his feet, and he responded by increasing the amount of time we would buy back from James Neill as a part of the overall pricing package. We had proposed to buy back four hours of time per day for Sperry's own use. Des increased that to a full shift at the same rate. We were assured of the order by Hugh Neill at the conclusion of the meeting. We left a contract for their signature.

We were, of course, part of the bigger Sperry+UNIVAC. I gained a certain notoriety from participation in the UNIVAC Users Association Europe Conference in Copenhagen. We were close to signing William Timpson up for a third generation system, and the suggestion was made that Bert Brownhill, the company's data processing manager, might like to attend. Sperry used the conference for product updates and networking, and we were able to extend invitations as a recognised aspect of a full sales campaign. Bert was an older man. I had met him just a couple of times, and had enjoyed talking data processing management with him. He used training and customer visits as perks for his own staff and was delighted to accept our invitation. The conference was always very well organised, with full days and good food expeditions arranged for each evening. Bert and I got on well together. On Thursday he told me that he had never had a sauna and asked if I would take him to the sauna in the hotel. I had no problem with that. I had no problems at all and was enjoying the sauna until Bert commented, 'I am not sweating at all'. I was perspiring copiously, but attempted to raise the temperature and humidity in the sauna. Still Bert was not satisfied. So, more water on the coals. Then Bert remarked: 'Isn't it strange, I have never been able to sweat?'

I looked at him for the first time, sitting with a towel across his thighs, and the start of huge water blisters on his shoulders. After all the years I had played rugby and shared baths and showers with other men, I had avoided looking at a naked Bert. I had him out of that sauna fast and into the dipping pool, but it was too late, he had burnt and had to spend a couple of nights in hospital. He was not on the plane with me when I got back to Manchester. I called Mrs Brownhill to explain what had happened and she was fine with the explanation. Not so Ted Jones, who suggested I might not be allowed to take customers on trips any more if I did not learn how to take care of them.

Ted Jones was keen on expanding his knowledge of selling and, after attending a training course conducted by the Kepner-Tregoe consultancy, came back into the office with an enthusiasm to put into practice what he had learned. The 'scoring' assessment of a probability to sell a system shown below is the result of some modification of the analysis system he had derived.

We attempted to determine whether selling was a science or an art, and asked if we could apply a scientific approach to help our selling. We put together a form that looked at 10 indicators that our prospective client was interested in what we were saying to him.

Checklist for appraising prospect probability Score 1 to 10 (Don't know = 1)		
1	Your instinctive feeling we'll get the order	
2	The strength of our contact's desire for UNIVAC	
3	His status in the contract signature hierarchy (score 10 if he signs, 8 if once removed, 6 if twice, etc.)	
4	The degree of our contact's personal antipathy towards IBM or ICL (insert the higher of these)	
5	His opinion of our technical competitive position	
6	Level of inside information	
7	UNIVAC strength in the organisation or hardware area or aspect of the industry	
8	Our competitive price position	
9	Our degree of access to the man or body which makes the final decision	
10	The firmness of the prospect's implementation plan	
	Score:	

In a sales meeting, I asked my guys to complete an assessment of their best chance to sell a system in the current fiscal year and come up with a score. I then asked them to consider whether we should concentrate all of our selling competences to secure the order rated as our best opportunity. Salesmen are sensitive creatures. There was not much chance that anyone would want to move from his allocated geographical territory to help a colleague. Nor did they want to be reminded too often of these 10 rules of selling. I used the prompt on a quarterly basis with my sales team, with the chart on a transparency projected onto a screen and completed with the responses of the salesman responsible for an account. The argument then would be: If the calculated probability of Alan Walton's sale to Roneo Vickers has not gone up in the past three months, why are we bothering to continue to sell to them? What have we done wrong in the past quarter? Let us examine if our score has gone up or down for any factor. This type of analysis always created worthwhile discussion.

Ted and I considered it worthwhile to pursue these ideas. Within Sperry+UNIVAC, we were confronted with the requirement to complete monthly, quarterly, and annual assessments of whether a prospective customer was going to buy from us. The assessment was recorded as a percentage chance to sell. This could be a purely subjective single assessment, but the implications were huge.

For example, if we reported according to the below figures, the factory would decide from our forecast that it needs to produce 1100/60 product to the value of US$4 million (the extended figure in the last column) in quarter 6–9/72, and 1100/70 equipment to the value of US$1.5 million in the quarter 10–12/72.

Prospect	UNIVAC system	Value	Month of order	Probability	Extension
A Company	1100/60	US$2 million	6/72	20%	US$400K
B Company	1100/60	US$3 million	6/72	40%	US$1.2m
C Company	1100/60	US$4 million	8/72	60%	US$2.4m
D Company	1100/70	US$1.2 million	10/72	30%	US$300K
E Company	1100/70	US$1.6 million	11/72	50%	US$800K
F Company	1100/70	US$1 million	12/72	40%	US$400K

Product forecasting must be a horrendous task for a company working across the world. Does the factory only consider probabilities above 60 per cent? I do not want to examine that too much. What interested Ted and I was an examination of the validity of the probability figures we used.

Looking back to the 10 factors that we considered as influencers of probability, we recognised that if any of the 10 factors was not understood by the salesman and were acted upon, he would not reach a probability factor that would result in an order.

Is selling art or science? My belief is the salesman has to understand and empathise with the needs of the potential customer. He can then contribute his knowledge and experience in meeting those needs. The only obstacle to meeting that ideal is that, as a Sperry+UNIVAC salesman, I only had the UNIVAC portfolio of products to offer. The customer knows this. The brave salesman will walk away, saying, 'I cannot provide a solution. Please ask me back should your needs change.' He will save himself time, the company money, and will have left a good impression. Next time, at least he starts with having left the impression of integrity. (It does not work that way, of course. But the principle is legitimate.)

It was about this time, 1971, when we were confronting the new IBM 370 computer family (which evolved from the 1964–65 360 range) that Sperry went through one of its habitual reorganisations. It came at a bad time. We had just implemented, for the first time in my experience, a formal company-wide performance appraisal scheme. We had no formal instruction on the scheme and only cursory notes about its completion. I had met with each of my guys, and we were agreed it was a step in the right direction. Performance was rated A–E in eight subjective areas. The job was done and seemingly forgotten, until a swap of marketing vice presidents between Europe and the US. The US won John 'um-yeah' Harrison and we got Ted Springstead, who was initially based in Lausanne. Um-yeah fired 200 salespeople in the US, so Springstead fired 201 salespeople in Europe. The criteria used for this was the performance appraisal scheme. Ted Jones's secretary found me on a Friday morning in Leicester, mid-presentation at the East Midlands Gas Board, and demanded of its staff that I come immediately to the telephone. So I took the call, to be told:

> 'A message from Ted Jones. You are required by midday to contact [three names] and tell them that they are given one month's money in lieu of notice, but that they must leave Sperry employ at the end of today. And we want their cars back next week.'

I asked to speak to Ted and told him that I would be unable to carry out these instructions, as I was committed with customers for the day, and that if these instructions were real, he would have to do the dirty work.

I was able to reflect during the weekend that maybe I could agree with one of the three names, but would argue strongly for the retention, if possible, of at least one person. I called Ted on the Sunday and he told me that the selection had been made from the performance review, and that anyone who scored a C was on the list for dismissal. This was Des Pitcher's decision, as he was required to lose something like 30 staff. Ted admitted the anomaly of the criteria, as I had nominally lost three people, but any manager who had evaluated his people more sympathetically might not have lost anyone. More power to Ted in that he had not spoken to the two people about whom we shared a similar enthusiasm. After a fraught week in the office, I lost only the Liverpool-based salesman.

Ted Jones was promoted to marketing director of Sperry back at UNIVAC House in London. The new regional director was Alan Campbell, a feisty Scot who strode with broad-chested aggression. He had played top-level soccer with Glasgow Celtic and was all action, with a very defined set of rules and methodology. He was built like the soccer inside-forwards of his era, short and defiant — you could almost call it pugnacious. He had a softer side that took some searching for and a tradition of attending Ladies' (Final) Day at Wimbledon, which in the 1970s was on a Friday. Alan had held the same position of regional director at Honeywell, and his declared intention in joining Sperry was to replace the Honeywell systems he had sold previously. He brought a number of managers with him. I remember a count reaching 19 ex-Honeywell people working in the region. That number rather unfairly included a couple of people who were indeed ex-Honeywell but were not a part of the exodus instituted by Alan.

Alan took me to one side and explained that he was going to move me sideways in the company, with Liverpool being my sales patch until he was able to convince Sperry to adopt a vertical, industry-specific selling strategy. He wanted me to be his industry sales manager in the new structure.

Alan took time to explain the influx of former Honeywell employees as being necessary — he had accepted such a tough sales target that he needed to work with an established team of people who knew how he worked and whose capabilities he knew. There was nothing new here. David Streeton had taken a group of us from UNIVAC to CDC for the same reason, and I would see it again, for sure.

Alan had strict rules. He had an open-door approach for any salesman in the region, provided that the salesman's activity was meeting his criteria of three sales calls per day, submission of one proposal per month, and three outstanding proposals at any time. His theory, which he claimed had been proven at Honeywell, was that any salesman who did not meet this profile of activity would fail. Any salesman who met these targets would be successful, and if all salesmen were successful, so was he.

Alan had not been able to crack the J. Bibby & Sons account while at Honeywell. He asked me to take him in to meet Geoff Codd, who had replaced Bernard King as data processing director in Liverpool. Alan insisted on a very detailed profile of the people he was going to meet. He wanted to know about their age, marriage status, spouses' names, age and names of any children and where they lived, personal preferences (such as food), smoking habits, favourite restaurants, business history, companies worked for, and the computer manufacturers they were familiar with. Alan's briefing and notes were something I could cope with.

After I effected Alan's introduction to Geoff Codd, I was promptly dismissed from the meeting to move Alan's car, even though it was adequately parked in a public car park. I had a look around the bookshop downstairs before rejoining them, and we went to lunch. I later learned from Geoff that Alan had explained his priorities and need for fast business in straightforward terms, and that his door was also to be open to our prospects if they were going to be able to order quickly. Obviously Alan believed he was the person to close any quick business deals in the region. The two of them obviously had spoken heart-to-heart and Tom Williams, Bibby's top technical man, joined Sperry soon after.

I quite enjoyed my stint looking after Liverpool. The insurance and shipping companies were based there, so there was an obvious market for larger systems. The Merseyside branch of the British Computer Society was active, with regular monthly meetings. I got myself elected as secretary, and then deputy chairman, in order to get access to the British Computer Society membership lists and make the best use of that information. Eric Williams, of the consulting house Fraser Williams, was the branch chairman. He and I became quite good friends. A particular interest in talking to Fraser Williams was to reach an agreement whereby Sperry might base proposals on the Fraser Williams software set. Alan Campbell and I sung from the same song-sheet in knowing that software would drive future sales — not hardware.

Another adventure occurred when David Baker of James Neill called in the invitation — made as an inducement to recommend Sperry — to dine in Paris. The offer was put on the table during the selling of the 1100.

4. A TASTE OF NORTHERN BITTER

Ted Jones had been aware that the offer had been made and had turned a blind eye to it. We now had Alan Campbell as regional director and Pat Cullen was not prepared to raise the issue with Alan, who had just been promoted. So it was left to me to argue the case for the travel and expenses for David Baker and someone to accompany him. I had not expected to, or wanted to, win that distinction. It was not going to be a straightforward trip. David was a private pilot and his plan was to hire an aeroplane and fly us to Paris. The economics of £8 per flying hour made sense as Pat outlined the plan. I was not a participant in the planning exercise. Pat just prompted me to be ready to travel from an airport in Sheffield early next Monday morning.

I paid for a two-day hire of the plane, a two-seater Piper Cherokee, and David and I were soon strapped in and he was talking to the air traffic controller, seeking permission to take off. He was perspiring quite heavily, but we had soon taken off, and I was beginning to enjoy the trip. David advised me that he had been taking time off from work to be able to swot for his pilot's licence extension that allowed him to navigate by radio. He had passed that test the previous day. I still had no concern, and learned the art of locking into a radio frequency, which we would follow until the next tower, to progress into Dartford. We landed to refuel and were advised not to take off as fog was expected across the channel, so we stayed in Dartford.

We were again delayed the next morning, but eventually got away about lunchtime and headed for Beauvais in Northern France, again to refuel. Our next target was Versailles, but somehow we got lost. The trip then started to take on surreal dimensions. David found a railway line and flew at a very low level over a couple of railway stations in the hope I might be able to read the station signs. I am left with the impression that French station designers do not position the signs to be read from the air — more likely that they should be legible from train level. We flew around for perhaps an hour, with David making continuous radio requests seeking help from anyone who might be listening. Eventually we got a response from Versailles, who had been tracking our machinations across the countryside on radar — and what a good job it was someone who had excellent English. We were talked down into Versailles just before dark — what a relief, and it was still only Tuesday.

We booked into a hotel, cleaned ourselves up and went into Paris. We found the perfect place for the evening in Montmartre. Not quite the Moulin Rouge, but next door. I have never seen prettier girls than those who entertained us in the cabaret. I am sure the food was fine. Girls approached us, not unexpectedly. David took a shine to one of them, who asked for some money. I definitely thought I was going to see (or not see) another side of my companion. He engaged her in conversation: 'What is a nice girl like you …'. Unabashed, he must have negotiated a deal and asked me for cash, which he passed over to her whilst we were still in the restaurant. David left the table with her, the money firmly in her possession. They were gone for no more than three minutes. David had had second thoughts. His bluff had been called. My reaction was to pursue the girl for restitution of the money, but David was satisfied. He had tested himself and not been found wanting. Oh well. We spent two days at Versailles Airport waiting for permission to take off for the return trip, again delayed by fog in the South of England. Suddenly it was Friday. But we did get away early on the Friday and with two refuelling stops were back in Sheffield late Friday afternoon.

My conversation and justification for a five-day trip and unreceipted expenses with Alan Campbell was not easy, and did nothing to endear me to my new boss. However, with the stewardship of Phil Williamson as project manager, the James Neill installation was a success and became a reference site for us.

Within my Liverpool sales area, Hygena, the manufacturer of excellent kitchen furniture, was an ex–Alan Campbell customer with a Honeywell 200 system installed. Alan aggressively targeted his old customers as potential Sperry customers and used past contacts to get us talking to the decision makers. Hygena signed for a Sperry 9400 system and the Sperry Universal Manufacturing Information System (UNIS) software toolset for implementation of new applications after conversion of the existing software to the new equipment. We had some software tools but it also required a dedicated programming effort. Despite this sale, I was obviously still not Alan Campbell's favourite salesman. He instructed me that I should pay half of my commission to Mike Hall (another Honeywell recruit who had taken over as pre-sales support manager), as it was Mike who had actually won the business. It was not something I was prepared to make a stand about. I was upset though when Alan told me that he wanted to invite some of the new Honeywell recruits to the Sperry

100 Per Cent Salesman's Club in Marbella, Spain, and would be sharing my credit from the James Neill and Hygena sales with selected engineers. I was still entitled to attend the club, but not in the high percentile of achievers.

The guest motivational speaker at the club that year was Walter Schirra, the only NASA astronaut who had flown Mercury, Gemini, and Apollo missions. I had a five-year-old son who at that time had a real fascination with the space program, and he gave me a space textbook and two postage stamps that featured Walter Schirra, asking that I get them autographed. After the formal dinner at the club, we were invited to meet the great man. Many asked for his autograph, but it seemed that my lad had been the only one who had prepared suitable material for signature, as Mr Schirra was pleased to notice. After the dinner we talked a bit and he suggested we might go into Marbella for (even more) drink. This we did, getting back to the hotel in the small hours.

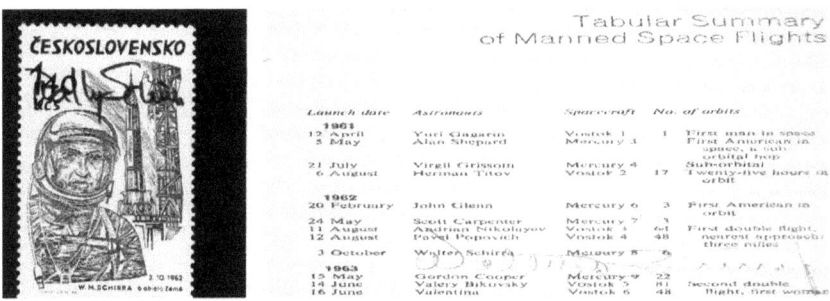

Figure 4.3: Two autograph souvenirs from the meeting with spaceman Walter Schirra.
Source: Author's collection.

Mr Schirra was booked on an early flight back to Houston as a commentator for the Apollo 13 mission, and back at the hotel I watched him consume vast amounts of black coffee to get himself in shape to travel to the US. He left the hotel at something like 4.30 am, by which time I was pleased to get the chance of some sleep before the next day's activities. It was a good event, and when our wives met us at Manchester airport, all rather the worse for wear, we were able to hand over leather briefcases containing sherry and brandy. Walking through customs, we must have looked like refugees from the Freemasons, or even the Mafia, all carrying similar cases containing booze rather than guns.

We experienced a tragedy during the Hygena program conversion exercise when, after an all-night session on the 9400 equipment, an engineer died on his early morning trip home. He had a wife and very young family. I was proud of the way that Barry Aiken, the human resources manager in Altrincham, handled the situation. I thought that it was great that he had been able to visit the widow that same morning and hand her a cheque for 10 times our engineer's annual salary. But he had made a mistake. Had he read the HR manual correctly, he would have seen that the company did insure its employees for accidental death at the rate of 10 times the individual's annual salary, but kept to itself the option of deciding how much of the insurance money would be paid to the family. Barry had made a mistake in doing what everyone else in the office believed was the right thing. Barry was good though. He survived his mistake and was transferred shortly afterwards to London head office. As many as 20 of us attended the funeral. This was a time when it was fashionable to wear photochromic lenses in spectacles and I was very conscious that the company representatives could have been mistaken for a Mafia outing — we were all short, wearing black suits and dark glasses.

Alan Campbell came good on his anticipated 'vertical marketing' organisation. I had an interest in the manufacturing sector since looking after Bibby's and Hygena's accounts. Alan recruited Bob Devine as my knowledgeable pre-sales engineer, and we got ourselves ready to do battle. Tom Williams from Bibby's was allocated to my small group. Sperry had acquired a software system — Universal Manufacturing Information System — that was managed at the UK level by Alan Bellinger, a most conscientious engineer.

As an additional responsibility, Alan asked me to supervise the in-house development of the sales database. Bernard Place, the ex-Shell project manager, was the lead technician for the development, and he had recruited two young trainee software engineers. I made the decision to structure the hierarchical database around the UK postal codes — originally based upon established postmen's walks — some of which were granted the postmen's initials when they were defined. Alan Campbell wanted a system that monitored his three golden rules of salesmanship. He was also convinced, by market research conducted by Honeywell, that computer salesmen did not fulfil 80 per cent of the obligations they made to prospective customers to maintain contact with them. The number of calls made to any prospect, time spent, and expenses incurred were also entered into the database. Putting a salesman in charge of the project gave

4. A TASTE OF NORTHERN BITTER

it a higher profile. We used computer time bought back as a part of the James Neill business for database development and I even construed an acronym for the system — TOPSY: territory-oriented planning system — and developed a formal presentation of its capabilities. We were testing the system. Alan Stevens, by now the sales manager of the Midlands branch, had volunteered his sales team as reporting guinea pigs when Des Pitcher, the UK managing director, learned about TOPSY. Des also had a scheme under construction. He told Alan to suspend development of TOPSY. We did not, but we did adopt a lower profile. Terry Duffy, the UK technical director, also had an interest in TOPSY and was looking to use it as a platform for a skills database for his department.

Interestingly, it was through TOPSY that I was introduced to Eddie French, the managing director of a new service bureau customer in Galway to which I was seconded. That secondment was a life-changing event that took me from Altrincham at very short notice, and I never worked from that office again.

5
Eddie French's rainbow

Like everyone else in the Altrincham, northern region office of Sperry, I was aware of the sale of a Sperry 1106 to a joint venture between a Dublin-based accountant and entrepreneur, Eddie French, and the Irish Government. The successful salesmen had been Alan Campbell, the regional director, and Pat Cullen, the sales manager. Indeed, one of my system specialists, Bob Devine, our manufacturing systems manager, had been seconded to this project. It made sense. Bob was an Irishman from Achill Island on the West Coast of Ireland.

I had spent a couple of months languishing in the office as team leader of an in-house computerised sales management system that was Alan Campbell's baby; a baby I knew was in competition with a system being developed by the UK managing director. It did not come as much of a surprise to be asked by Alan to present the status of this project to Mr French one afternoon. During the slideshow presentation, Mr French asked me a couple of times how easily the system could be transferred to another computer system and adapted to another organisation. It was not an easy transfer in an Irish context, because I had decided to use the UK postcode as the prime sort key to lead us to the assigned Sperry salesman and the list of businesses assigned as that salesman's territory. I had to tell Mr French that, as the Republic of Ireland did not have a similar general area and postman's walk coding system, we should have to think of another coding strategy and database structure. I also surmised that Alan might have been keen to use the new Irish computer site as the operational computer. Up until that point in time, we had been developing and running TOPSY using the time we had agreed to buy back from James Neill and Company in Sheffield.

It was a shock to be called into Alan Campbell's office after the end of our working day that same afternoon. Mr French was there. Alan asked me to take responsibility as the project manager for Riomhaire Teoranta — starting today — and asked if it would be convenient for me to catch the ferry from Liverpool to Dublin with Mr French that night. This was a surprise. I had enjoyed talking to Mr French that afternoon and he seemed confident of his business plan. TOPSY was hardly the love of my life, so I agreed.

Eddie and I caught the overnight ferry, breakfasted at his Leopardstown home in Dublin, and we drove across Ireland, stopping for a bacon and cabbage luncheon at Hayden's of Ballinasloe, in the Midlands, on our way to Galway. In the late afternoon at the Ardilaun Hotel in Galway, we met my new team and colleagues. A meal at Hayden's Hotel at Ballinasloe became a regular treat during this project in Ireland, and each subsequent visit, although they now have gone upmarket with the huge influx of tourism to Ireland; you are lucky to get bacon and cabbage these days, and even then only as a special.

During that first full day spent with Eddie, I learned that he had a 50 per cent share of the company Riomhaire Teoranta — Riomhaire is the Irish word for 'computer' and Teoranta is a company title, the equivalent of 'limited'. We also traded under the name of Datacom Limited in the UK and Ireland. The other 50 per cent of the company was held by the Irish Government, through the Irish Development Authority. Our project was within the purview of Gaeltarra Eireann, the Irish Government department set up to encourage and promote the continuing use of the Irish language where it was still the indigenous tongue. The computer centre was nearing completion in Na Forbacha (Furbo), next to the Gaeltarra Eireann Ardoifig (head office) close to the village of Bearna (Barna). Our mission was to bring third-level technology to the County Galway Gaeltacht, an Irish-speaking part of Ireland, and operate a money-making service. This would be no mean feat.

Eddie was an accountant. I asked who was backing him in this venture. He suggested that it was the data processing head at Littlewoods Pools in Liverpool, a friend of Alan Campbell. I did not think to pursue this, as his response made sense. He was proud to tell me that Riomhaire had been able to recruit returning Irishmen for the project and that the computer centre was almost ready for our occupation. Eddie had agreed with Alan Campbell that I would be appointed general manager of Riomhaire Teoranta, reporting directly to Eddie and interfacing with Gaeltarra Eireann on his behalf, as he was to stay in Dublin. These days we would have called this an outsourcing/facilities management deal in which the supplier also took responsibility for infrastructure management. The company had three offices: the computer centre at Furbo; a sales office in Harcourt Street, Dublin; and a sales office in Manchester in the UK.

The technical staff in Galway, from where I would manage the company, included Tony Johnstone, who was recruited to return to Galway from Tandy Corporation in San Francisco where he had been the programming manager. Joe Whitston joined Riomhaire from the operations section of Shell Centre in London and was experienced in the operation and management of a Sperry 1100 system. Eddie had appointed Joe as operations supervisor. One of the best decisions I made was that as Joe was doing the operations manager's job, that was how he would be recognised. Joe still thanks me for that decision when we meet. His staff were all local, raw recruits, and included lads who had been fishermen, farmers, and even policemen. We were bringing third-level technology to the Gaeltacht. Two of Tony's programming staff, four of Joe's operators, and six Irish-speaking young girls who were trained as card punch operators were included as part of the training plan.

The Sperry 1106 system had been installed and was being put through its acceptance tests when I arrived. I did not realise until 29 years later that it was all second-hand equipment that had been staged through the Altrincham office and tested operationally before being shipped to Galway.

At the time, we believed the Sperry 1106 to be the most powerful computer system in Ireland. The plan had been that Bob Devine would fill the role of general manager. He had already performed Herculean tasks in getting the computer centre ready for the housing of staff and the computer itself. However, he had also rediscovered fishing and his Irish heritage — so much so that it was decided he had lost the plot. I replaced Bob and he returned to his job in Altrincham. I felt very sorry for him. It was known that his wife was not at all keen to relocate to Galway. Bob was devastated. He died a short while after.

ALSO INNOVATORS

My introduction to the computer centre was an eye-opener. Although the equipment was unpacked and positioned for installation in the computer room, the room was not ready for occupation. The building was a single-storey construction with a flat roof. It had good big windows, with the exception of the computer room, which for security reasons had disguised slits high in the wall that allowed in a minimum of light. The necessary air conditioning units for the computer room sat outside the building on a concrete platform which we would later need to enclose, again for security reasons. The transformer to convert the Irish electricity supply to drive the US-built computer system had not been planned and was eventually housed in a wooden shed from the local hardware store, which was the cause of an environmental pollution complaint from local homeowners. The foundations for the centre had been blasted out of the granite that comprises the coast above Galway Bay to the north of the city.

The Gaeltarra head office had magnificent views of Galway Bay across to the Burren and the Aran Islands to the west. I was delighted to view the plans and see that my office would have floor-to-ceiling glass for me to enjoy that view. The centre was a few weeks away from completion, but with a most definite completion date. On 11 October the centre was to be officially opened by the Prime Minister of Ireland (locally referred to as Taoiseach), Mr Liam Cosgrave. We took our lives — ankles anyway — in our own hands on our regular visits to the new offices, scrambling over the granite chips and blocks that were the surrounds, until the afternoon before the prime minister's visit, when tarmac was laid and we acquired parking spaces. For several weeks, Riomhaire Teoranta operated from the conference room of Gaeltarra Eireann Ardoifig. It was not particularly satisfactory, although we did have access to the excellent dining room, which we continued to use for some time after we moved into our own building.

Figure 5.1: The Riomhaire Teoranta Computer Centre in September 1974.
Source: Author's collection. Computer room photographer: Neil Warner of Galway. Site photographer: Jimmy Washe of Galway.

The market we were entering was dominated by University Computing Company (UCC) of Dallas, who was already offering remote job entry services for jobs to run on Sperry 1100 systems. UCC had taken over Computer Services (Birmingham) and had a European presence in addition to a very successful operation in the US. UCC sold computer time at the rate of £400 per hour of 1108 processor time. The Riomhaire basic price was £200 per hour for our 1106 processor time. The Sperry 1106 was designed as a cut-down, slowed-down, more affordable model of the 1100 family of processors. Our prime suspect list was those organisations using the UCC service, particularly if they were government departments, who could be cajoled to switch to our service, which was government sponsored. The UCC users already had programs that were written and running on our competitor's compatible system, it would cost our prospective customers half of what they were currently paying to UCC, to run the same job, on the Riomhaire computer system. The work and revenue would stay in Ireland. This was the marketing model that Alan Campbell and Pat Cullen had sold to Eddie French, who, in turn, sold it to his backers, including the Irish Government.

We needed to be in our own premises with ready access to the 1106, as our pricing structure only made sense if the 1106 ran a job in less than twice the time it would take to run on the UCC 1108. We could find no definitive benchmarks published by Sperry to prove the case one way or the other. UCC had other charges: for the use of mass storage, tape storage, punched cards read or punched as output, and the number of lines of output printed. We wanted to be able to keep our algorithm simple. I had several heated sessions with Eddie and Derek McHugh to thrash out what it was we wanted to sell and how to achieve this. Working against us was the fact most commercial users do not want to understand an algorithm that described something as obscure as 'time to run a program on a computer' — time being divided into and recorded as processing time and input/output processor time. As our sales encompassed local Galway commercial businesses, we eventually simplified our pricing. Our users could better comprehend paying 50 pence per invoice or payroll slip.

I was initially a great source of mirth to my colleagues. I was told my pronunciation of Riomhaire Teoranta, when I picked up the telephone, sounded rather like a cat sneezing. I hope I did not dissuade too many customers. I wanted the telephone answered immediately. We were in the service business and I was not going to countenance any laziness in answering the telephone.

We moved into the computer centre about four weeks before the official opening. We did not have enough furniture to make the centre look even habitable. One area that had been beautifully equipped, however, was the general manager's office, which had been laid out in conventional public service fashion to have me sitting with my back to one of the best views in the world. I needed to change that. I had a most successful excursion to a local second-hand office furniture store and caused considerable concern by equipping my office with a long settee which would allow me and two guests to look over Galway Bay, resting our feet on the low window sill. I also acquired a large conference table, placed behind the settee with drawers, for formal meetings, and a flat area for other work. This caused great consternation among the public servants from next door, a government department head office who had shown their set ideas about what should be contained in the general manager's office, but our new style eventually met with approval after the tour parties subsided because it was purely functional.

I had a telephone call the day before the opening from the Prime Minister's office to ask:

'What will you be providing by way of refreshment tomorrow?'
'Champagne and finger food. We did not think to be different. Is that OK?'
'Sure. But could we ask you to get some Crested Ten whiskey? Mr Cosgrave does not like champagne.'
'Of course.'
'Thank you, enjoy the day.'

The management of Gaeltarra Eireann and local invited dignitaries descended upon the centre and were in place before our guest of honour's fleet of vehicles arrived on the brand new driveway. The opening was a grand affair, but was partly spoilt for Eddie French because the attention of the *Connacht Tribune* was focused on a small group of protesters who had taken advantage of the prime minister's attendance. Eddie and I had purchased a superb oil painting by a Galway artist, embellished with an engraved silver plaque celebrating the date and event. Tony's wife, Ita, made a small curtain with a pulley to disclose the painting — it was very much a do-it-yourself event.

Figure 5.2: The Riomhaire Computer Centre at dawn, 11 October 1974.
Source: Author's collection.

Prime Minister Cosgrave was accompanied by his wife and the Minister for the Gaeltacht, Tom O'Donnell. We would see quite a bit of Tom O'Donnell, whose portfolio included our enterprise.

We initially met in the computer room, for the photo opportunity. Mr and Mrs Cosgrave were super, and stood and sat where asked for a whole series of photographs of the interested parties, including the Sperry group, the politicians with the Gaeltarra management, Joe Whitston and his team of operators, and more. We then removed to the large open plan area — designated for systems and programming— for speeches, champagne and nibbles. For the most part, the ceremony was conducted in Irish. Not wishing to draw attention to my inability to participate in Irish conversation, I hid at the back.

After speeches by Messrs French, Pitcher, McGabhann and Cosgrave, and the official opening, I was flattered to be sought out by Mr Cosgrave, who approached me with the suggestion: 'I hear you have got some whiskey for us. Let's go to your office.' So we did. We talked about all sorts of things for long enough to have two good measures of Crested Ten each, before Cathal McGabhann knocked on the office door and found us. The Taoiseach was a quiet, modest man. I enjoyed talking to him. We had talked family rather than politics, and had sat on the settee with feet on the low window frame looking at the view. After the crowds had left, I was teased unmercifully about the way I had marshalled our important guests through the photo shoot. It was not something we had planned, but someone had to do it.

Figure 5.3: The Sperry sales and management representatives at the Riomhaire opening.

Left to right: Geoff Barton (the northern region technical support manager and my nominal Sperry boss) standing in for Alan Campbell; myself; Ted Jones (UK marketing director); Graham Morgan; Prime Minister Liam Cosgrave sits at the main computer console in the computer room; and Des Pitcher (the UK managing director).

Source: Author's collection. Photograph by Neil Warner.

5. EDDIE FRENCH'S RAINBOW

Figure 5.4: The general manager has two minutes to explain computing to Mr and Mrs Cosgrave. Meanwhile, in the background, Eddie French is busy selling.
Source: Author's collection. Photograph by Neil Warner.

Figure 5.5: The Riomhaire Teoranta management team pose with the Taoiseach.
Left to right: Mike Nevin (finance manager), Joe Whitston (operations manager), Tony Johnstone (systems and programming manager), Vic Saunders (Dublin manager), myself (general manager), Derek McHugh (sales manager), Eddie French (managing director), and the very patient Liam Cosgrave.
Source: Author's collection. Photograph by Neil Warner.

It was during the opening that local environmentalists raised their concerns about the continual hum from the motor alternator in the gorse between the Riomhaire and Gaeltarra offices. They were quite right, and we had few excuses for the noise which resonated from the hut at all times. The local television channel became interested, and I was approached several times by an interviewer who preferred to speak Irish. Eventually we soundproofed our shed, leaving little room for air circulation around the machinery, which created another ongoing maintenance concern for Joe Whitston.

More important to the continuity and standard of service we were offering was the build-up of static electricity in the computer room. The design of the room had included the installation of a grid of copper plates underneath the false floor on which each piece of equipment was earthed. We were experiencing unusual intermittent faults. The installation specialists established that their original earthing design was not working. They recommended we adopt a more robust earthing policy, sinking long copper rods into the ground outside of the computer centre. This exercise caused us great mirth. Rather cruelly, we watched one afternoon when two workmen appeared with several long copper rods. One climbed his stepladder while the other held the rod in a vertical position. The higher man proceeded to drive the rod into the ground with a heavy hammer. Our amusement was in watching the rod penetrate perhaps six inches into the ground before turning 180 degrees and emerging a few inches to the side, threatening to wound one or the other of them. You cannot drive copper rods into granite.

The next solution we attempted was the installation of a huge copper plate. A hole, perhaps 6 by 10 feet, was blasted in the granite some 20 feet away from the main building. This itself caused great consternation in the computer room, as we knew that our rotating drum storage equipment was most susceptible to vibration. We had no warning of the blasting and I dashed to the computer room screaming: 'Lift the recording heads!' Fortunately, minimum damage was caused to the polished surface of the drum, although we had to take the unit out of operation for a few hours for Bill and his guys to check, and wait for the dynamiting to stop. That afternoon — Murphy's Law again — Alan Campbell was demonstrating the system from Manchester; I had shut the system down. Such things happen, but should not. Alan was on the telephone by the time I was back in my office. How do you explain the machinations of Irish workmen to your boss in another country? It was not easy. Eventually, a hole of sufficient size to accommodate the copper plate was manufactured in the streambed, in a trickle of water flowing down in to the bay. It was connected to the internal earth grid and the intermittent faults we had been experiencing were minimised.

The year 1975 was a glorious one on the West Coast of Ireland. Lough Corrib, the lake on which we were living at Oughterard, was at its lowest level within living history. It occurred to me that we should perhaps take a look at our copper plate to see how it was surviving the drought. Joe and I eventually found it by tracing the stream. We knew where it entered the grounds. The gorse and ferns had recovered to hide the demolition and there was still a trickle of water, obviously sufficient, running over the plate. The water was warm and there on the down side of the plate sat several of the largest, most contented-looking frogs I have ever seen. We had created the perfect ecology for them.

Another natural hazard was the loss of electricity to the centre. Brownouts were a fairly common occurrence, caused by seabirds flying into power lines and shorting them out. It made for an interesting life.

In planning for the computer centre, the Sperry pre-installation engineers had allowed for a sophisticated burglar-alarm system. Any sensed disturbance in the centre created an automated telephone call to the local Garda Síochána (police) station with a prerecorded message saying who we were and that our alarm had sensed something unusual. My home number was given as the second referral, after Joe Whitston's. Joe took the occasional call. Initially, we had placed our computer room movement monitors incorrectly and the remotely initiated printing on the computer room prompted a warning. We eventually got this right.

I took a call in the small hours one morning.

> 'Hello there. Is that Mr Yardley? This is the Sergeant from the Spiddal Garda here. The alarm has gone off in your factory in Bearna.'
> 'Thank you, Sergeant. Will you be going to see what the problem is?'
> 'Not us, sir. We are not going anywhere near that place.'

Not terribly helpful. I think on that occasion I drove the 24 miles to Furbo to find everything in good order. We were certainly an unknown quantity to the local populace, although we had previously invited the police and the fire service to come and see us.

Letters between Riomhaire and Gaeltarra were written in Irish. I was so lucky that Brid McDonnagh, our receptionist, was confident in the business language of Irish and English. I had every confidence that I would not be offending anyone through the written word. I would also occasionally need to create documents as the on-site Sperry project manager, such as milestone payments, to send to the manager of Riomhaire. As I was fulfilling both roles, it made for some interesting forms, but the accountants never queried the anomaly. I also had Bill Leahy to witness these documents.

Sales were slow. UCC had its customers locked into solid contracts and it took attrition of those contracts to bring in the easy customers. The sales team, including Graham Morgan, were in Dublin, but the largest group of us were in residence in Galway, so we felt obliged to look to local customers for business. Tony Johnstone had done his first degree at University College, Galway (UCG), and his previous lecturer, Bobby Curren, was head of computing when Riomhaire opened its doors. I met Bobby with Tony Johnstone during a Galway pub crawl. Tony viewed every new pint of Guinness with an obvious delight: 'The first today, and badly wanted.' I eventually questioned his numeracy: 'Tony, we have had six pints already.' Unabashedly, he viewed the next drink with even more relish: 'The first seventh pint today, and badly wanted.' We still use that salutation to one another today.

Bobby Curren was really supportive and encouraged his users to try our service. They would arrive with trays of punched cards, and at the time we were able to run most jobs there and then. The Sperry 1100 family of computers was well blessed with software languages, and UCG tested us and our support capabilities. We needed to implement a proper local job acceptance procedure, but we were doing real work and were billing real money. Eventually, UCG installed a purpose-built remote job entry terminal, the Distributed Computer Terminal 2000, which was another unique piece of equipment in the country.

We looked for commercial software that we might offer in Galway. We wanted simple sounding applications, such as a general ledger and payroll. But although we searched high and low, we could not find general application software packages we might localise and use to provide the facilities that we needed. Tony and his team wrote the software from scratch. To help with this endeavour, we recruited another returning Irishman, from the Sperry UK Training Centre in Acton, London. 1 had known the man from my time in London, but I had not known he was an alcoholic. I only discovered he had the disease when exposed to him on a day-to-day basis. We were not able to predict a reliable output from him.

The on-site Sperry engineer in charge was Bill Leahy. He and I developed a friendship that has lasted until today. At the start, our relationship was a little strained as Bill came to terms with our both being paid by Sperry and my assumption of the role of general manager for our customer. There were times when, representing Riomhaire, I would have to hassle Bill. He would also need to tell me a few home truths about limitations on the service he could provide — mainly equipment support — and that, because of geography, only a few simple mechanisms were put in place that eased the situation. We agreed that I would never enter the engineers' office or spare parts storeroom without their permission. I also sought Bill's input to my regularly monthly report to Sperry UK. I could understand Bill's concern, although I did not discover that Bill believed his appointment might be precarious until years later. He had very little interface with managers, back in Manchester, who were his line bosses.

One day, when Bill and I were at the local hostelry for lunch, rather than my usual pint of Guinness, I opted for a gin and tonic. When Bill questioned my change of habit, I responded: 'We have visitors this afternoon, Bill. I shall have to do the selling and I do not want my breath to smell of beer.'

He thought this through and said, 'In which case, I'll have one as well'.

That evening, our wives, who were also pals (the two boys in both our families were about the same age), joined us at the Twelve Pins pub — named after the Twelve Bens hills that feature in the Connemara landscape. Bill was beginning to enjoy his first experiences with gin and tonic. Theresa, Bill's wife, asked what he was drinking. When told, she exploded, 'Bill Leahy, you stop drinking that gin and tonic. Drink beer like a proper man.' Theresa has always been a fun person, used to speaking her mind.

I commuted to and from Altrincham for five months. Initially it would be a weekly trip, but as we became busier it would be fortnightly. Eventually, I took my car to Ireland, but I did use rental cars for a while, during which time I had a sequence of three mishaps.

Week one: A driver who had been in the Twelve Pins pub ran into the back of me when I was turning into a friend's driveway for dinner. The other driver was very much the worse for wear. On the Saturday morning I returned the car to Dublin Airport and completed the formal accident form. No real fuss.

Week two: I was driving in the country when I hit a rook. The impact broke the windscreen and dented the roof. On the Saturday morning I returned the car to Dublin Airport and completed the formal accident form. No real fuss.

Week three: Saturday morning I was again headed for Dublin on a wet and windy morning before sunrise when I hit a cow on the road. Although it was drizzling, we had not had much rain, and it was known that the farmers were putting their animals on the long acre to feed on the grass verges of the road. The penalties for damaging a beast on the roads in Ireland were severe. I saw the animal too late to avoid hitting it. The animal travelled up and over the bonnet in slow motion. I stopped to see it drag itself off the road trailing its back legs. As luck would have it, a police car came from the opposite direction almost immediately. I flagged it down and the policeman listened to my explanation of what had happened. He was sympathetic. He got a crowbar from his car and somehow we managed to lever the front left wheel arch off the tyre so that my car might move again. That done, he asked where the animal had gone. He drew his revolver and suggested I drive on: 'We do not want any bother now, do we?' I returned the car to Dublin Airport and completed the formal accident form. No real fuss.

Somehow, when I left Altrincham the next day for the return trip I did not pick up my wallet and credit cards. A passport was not necessary for the flight. Shamefacedly, I approached the Avis desk to explain my predicament.

> 'Do not worry, Mr Yardley. Of course you can take another car. We know you. You are one of our best customers.'

Thank you, Avis, and thank you, the Irish sense of reality. Lovely people.

It was eventually decided that my wife Audrey and the boys would close the house in Hale Barns and come to Ireland. I travelled to Galway on 27 December 1974, and Audrey and the boys came in her car by ferry a couple of days later. Audrey came in time for the Gaeltarra New Year's

Eve party. My work colleagues set me up to make a fool of myself with an Irish New Year's salutation that was not what I thought it was, but no offence was taken. It was interesting to Audrey and I that the Gaeltarra management were most solicitous with Audrey and assured her: 'Do not worry. No harm will come to Chris.'

When we questioned this, we were told that the Irish Republican Army, the IRA, had kidnapped a Ferenka factory manager, an expatriate who was doing, we supposed, a job in Ballyvarra that was similar to mine. The victim, a Mr Tiede Herrema, was car-jacked outside his home in Castletroy. The Garda Síochána searched for him for 18 days before information painfully extracted from two IRA men led them to a council house in Monasterevin, County Kildare. The ensuing siege lasted a further 17 days. Barricaded in an upstairs bedroom, Herrema was tied to a chair and wired to explosives. The kidnappers were demanding the release of three notorious IRA prisoners in exchange for Herrema. Eventually, the siege broke and Herrema walked away a free man. I had travelled through Monasterevin a few times on my way between Galway and Dublin and recognised, on the television, the terrace where Herrema had been held captive.

As all this was happening, I was stopped on the road a few times, during the countrywide search for Mr Herrema, close to Oughterard, the village where we now lived. On one occasion when I was flagged down, the policeman approached me.

> 'Good morning, Mr Yardley. Would you be identifying yourself, please.'
> 'But, Gard. You know who I am.'
> 'Of course I do, but I still need to see some form of identity.'

I felt quite safe.

I feel obliged to make note of 'The Troubles' in Northern Ireland. We had got to the republic shortly after the time when political leaders from North and South had announced at Stormont in November 1973 that they would form a new government, with power to be shared, for the first time, with Catholics. The (Protestant) Loyalist paramilitaries immediately announced their opposition, and the IRA set off a series of explosions to show its disapproval. The government caved in after the Loyalist-dominated unions called a general strike, shutting down the province for more than two weeks, and scrapped the agreement. Galway did not appear to be overtly interested or involved. We were aware of rumours that Teach Furbo, the hotel opposite our office, was used as a rest and recreation centre for IRA soldiers. It was not a particularly good inn, and we seldom used it except for a quick lunch. IRA songs were a part of the spontaneous music-making that would ignite the pubs of Galway. I learned the words, but did not join in. My Riomhaire workmates were not in any way so constrained, and we enjoyed many a good craic. Once or twice, Ma Cullen, the proprietor of Cullen's Bar in Station Road, would shake her head when Audrey and I went in. So we did not venture past the front door.

Tony Johnstone's father died while we were there. Audrey and I were invited to the funeral to be held in Limerick. We met up with Tony at the Durty Nelly's hostelry on the outskirts of the city for lunch and several pints of Guinness before going to the cathedral. The celebration of Tony's father's life included a full funeral mass, and there were many anxious glances when, after the two-hour ceremony, we lined up to follow the hearse to the cemetery — the boys lined up, the ladies followed in cars. Good as gold, the cortège stopped outside the first bar on our route and half of the male mourners rushed in to relieve their bladders. The other half left when we stopped again outside the second bar. The mood of the event was a true celebration, until unexpectedly a darkly dressed, bereted man in dark glasses came to the front of the crowd and fired a revolver over the open grave. He dissolved into the crowd just as quickly, but Audrey and I sensed an immediate change in mood and removed ourselves to the back. As family guests, we had been invited back to Tony's home and we went there, but were left alone in the front room. Tony was most concerned, but we decided discretion was the best course, and I took off for Dublin by train as planned. I was so pleased that Joe and Florence were there to take Audrey back to Galway. The only explanation we received was that Tony's father had been a member of the Irish Republican Brotherhood, an organisation that evolved into the IRA, and that permission had been obtained for the soldier's farewell. In retrospect, that was the only time we felt uncomfortable. I have subsequently had a great interest in the history of Ireland in the twentieth century. Understanding has to be key.

Audrey and I were stopped when the Garda Síochána had their regular purges against the manufacture and distribution of poteen, the illegally home-brewed whiskey. If only they had known: I was stopped possibly half a dozen times with a couple of crates of poteen in the boot of the car. I had guessed it was an initiation test. When Paddy Clancy, my farmer neighbour in Rinnerroon, Glann, discovered I was working with Gaelgories (a slang term for Irish speakers) from the Gaeltacht, he suggested: 'You should be able to get some of the good stuff from them.' I asked Joe and Tony at work and, of course, the younger lads were able to provide it for a few shillings per bottle. Paddy seemed to have his own sources as well, and we soon recognised poteen as a cure-all for any problem. Paddy would even give it to sick animals. We also saw the Gardaí motor boats patrolling Lough Corrib, which we overlooked from our lounge. We never gauged the seriousness of these purges, and the smell of the illicit brew was one we learned to recognise and accept in the countryside.

Audrey and our two boys joined me in Galway. Audrey had found us a rented cottage beyond the fishing village of Oughterard. The house was in Glann. It was approached through a gateway, partly hidden by wild fuchsia bush, across a cattle grid, and round the edges of three or four cattle- or sheep-filled fields onto a track where a group of half a dozen cottages were widely scattered at the end of a peninsula in Lough Corrib. Lough Corrib was reputedly the best salmon and trout lake in Ireland. The view from the cottage, the summer fishing home of Lady Barrington-Ward, was 180 degrees of water, and we had a boat in the stone jetty off the garden. We put the boys, then seven and eight years old, into the Oughterard Catholic school. We knew that they would receive schooling in Irish, but that was why we were there. They coped wonderfully. I had been travelling during their first week at the new school. Pat, the village mechanic, picked them up in the school bus along with the other Glann boys for the six-mile ride to Oughterard.

We were breakfasting on the Saturday morning when I asked:

'How are you getting on at school?'

Adam, the elder, looked at me with a puzzled expression and asked:

'Dad, what's a Protestant?'
'You are, son. Why do you ask?'
'Well, dad. The boys at school are hitting us because we are Protestants.'
'So what are you doing?'
'Hitting them back, of course.'
'Good boy.'

ALSO INNOVATORS

The younger lad, Jason, was also perplexed.

'Dad, I think you might get cross with this school.'
'Why, Jason?'
'Well, dad, at the start and finish of every lesson we all have to do this.'

He quickly genuflected.

Audrey and I kept straight faces and assured them that they would get used to the school, and they did. In days they changed from being the polite, smart, school-uniformed pupils we had loved in Altrincham to the casual, roughly dressed country lads they needed to be to survive in the two-class village schoolhouse. Audrey had to wash their clothes every day, as they brought back rural smells and muck into Lady Barrington-Ward's house. The boys would even help Paddy's youngest son, Michael, with farm chores on their way back home from where the school bus driver, Pat, had dropped them. The young (village) priest was a regular contact with the lads at school and took it upon himself to keep us advised of the school activities that were announced in church. He had sought advice after Adam had argued 'The Creation' with him during catechism classes.

Our boys did us proud and continued with the full Catholic schooling curriculum. Interestingly, they were able to revert straight back into the Cheshire system when we returned to the UK a few months later.

Business was slow. But it did give us the opportunity to get on with the training of the new recruits, who were most willing pupils. We were very proud of them all. Our approach was that trained people would produce more, reduce costs, eliminate costly errors, and generate new worthwhile efficiencies, and we looked to create reusable code wherever possible. Gaeltarra management were excellent and allowed Riomhaire to make a claim for training expenses, including payroll, in addition to whatever other grants we were taking. This money kept us going through a most difficult period.

We also had time for Eddie French's continuing training and computer orientation. He came to Galway every other week to see us. I went to Dublin most weeks that Eddie stayed there. We developed a good working relationship, but it was occasionally strained. We had agreed to participate in a Gaeltarra exhibition in Limerick and sent Tony Leonard and Jim Butler off with a computer terminal in the boot of the car to

5. EDDIE FRENCH'S RAINBOW

help demonstrate our wares. Eddie met them at the Limerick Conference Centre. He anxiously called me by telephone. As he was a quick speaker, I initially had trouble deciphering his concern until he slowed down.

> 'Tony Leonard has gone mad! I could see that the display was not responding as it should. He has taken a hammer from his toolkit and is hitting the back of the terminal. He will ruin it and it cost us a lot of money.'

Not to mention the fact we needed it for the show.

All sorts of images went through my mind. Tony Leonard was a bit mad, we all knew that. Then I realised: the UTS 200 was a new device and reputedly did not travel well. The printed circuit boards tended to loosen and had to be reseated with a large rubber-headed mallet, provided in the engineer's toolkit, especially for that purpose. Tony was just reseating the boards. Phew! None the less, I thought it wise to travel to Limerick to placate Eddie.

I had some additional contact from Sperry UK as well as my regular sales visits to Manchester, in order to assist with and close business from the UK. I would try and see Geoff Barton on these trips. I was sending Geoff a copy of my monthly general manager's report, which was written for Mr French, so he was quite well advised of successes and problems. Charles Pigden, the Sperry UK training manager, visited us in Galway, both at home and in the office during the time we were developing the Riomhaire training plan. He was most taken with the fact that I was carrying a fly fishing rod and my waders in the boot of my car, and that we had such easy access to fishing rivers. One day he even managed to cajole me into donning the waders over my suit pants and waving the rod over the stream that went through the grounds at Furbo — the stream that kept the earth-plate wet. He had organised a photographer, but I am pleased to say that I never did see the resulting photo in any Sperry documents. That particular stream was never going to contain a worthwhile trout.

Peter Jackson, the specialist central computer unit regional support engineer, was Manchester-based and visited us twice, coming during the two times when Bill and his lads were not able to fix a specific problem. That did not necessarily mean that we had to suspend our service, but we were aware of a problem. Peter immediately impressed us all. He would fly from Manchester to Dublin in the late afternoon and drive across the country to reach us late evening, around 11.00 pm. With minimum fuss, he would stand at the engineer's panel, where he was able to manipulate the contents of registers in the processor, and would play the machine like a piano. Every few moments he would ask for a different printed circuit board, which one of the lads would get from the spares holding, until he had diagnosed the problem and determined its resolution. It was inspiring stuff, made all the more impressive as Peter would have purchased two half-bottles of Scotch at the duty free shop on his trip, one of which he would sample as he worked. If the job took him three hours, that was probably the two half-bottles. We would then convey him back to the Ardilaun Hotel for a beer, where they obliged, no matter how late it might be.

I enjoyed being a general manager. I had a good team and could effectively leave a clean desk of an evening, having gained acceptance from Tony, Joe, Mike Nevin, or Bill Leahy for a resolution of any of the day's outstanding issues. I would then try and get back across the bogs to Oughterard in time to see Audrey and the boys before the boys went to bed. I would often spend a couple of hours on the Lough, alone in the boat, enjoying being in such a fabulous place. I would drown flies, but the actual catching of fish was not necessary for complete enjoyment and relaxation. I could not have imagined, had I not experienced it, the thrill of being aware of salmon leaping from the water as they travelled up the lake, or knowing the delight of being splashed by them.

Late one Friday evening, at home in Glann, I had a most surprising telephone call from Graham Morgan in Manchester. He had been to the Altrincham office where the rumour was that Alan Campbell had left Sperry. Graham said that the story was most confused, but seemed to be Riomhaire/Datacom related, and that it concerned the commissions that had been paid to Pat Cullen and Alan Campbell at the time of the sale of the 1106.

There was a knock on the door very early the next morning. It was Alan Campbell, who came into the house while I dressed and had a quick breakfast. He asked me to take him to the computer centre, which he had never seen. I never did discover how he found me — the postal address gave no clue as to the actual whereabouts of the house. Glann was such a small village that the postman knew all our names or used house names rather than street names or numbers.

In the car to the computer centre, Alan told me he was the owner of Riomhaire — he was Eddie French's backer. Ever the salesman, he elaborated upon the point that my appointment had been about placing the best man in the region for the job. Now I would understand why he had me, back in Altrincham, in a technical holding role to develop my software understanding. I took him to the centre using the scenic route, across the peat bogs along farm tracks, and he was surprised to see how rural our location was. He liked the centre. Alan could not believe, however, that I did not have the keys to the actual computer room, and was quite dismissive of my reasoning that I had never had cause (until now) to want to enter that area.

I called Joe Whitston. While we waited for him to arrive, I tried to explain our full complement of equipment. Alan was amazed that he had sold and had been expected to run a bureau service with so many single points of failure, and so little random-access storage. He had to believe it. Joe left his keys with us. Alan and I spoke for most of the day and went through the company's business from my point of view — but only that material that I had already provided to Geoff Barton and that which Eddie French knew that I had shared. I left Alan at a Galway hotel and spent Sunday with the family.

On Monday morning I had a call from Alan Wightman, who had been appointed the replacement Sperry regional director on Friday. His advice was for me to quit Riomhaire at once and to get back to Altrincham lest I be tarred with the same brush as Alan Campbell. I was never given an official version of what caused Alan Campbell's dismissal from Sperry. Was it the double commissions as Graham Morgan had said, or was it discovered that Alan Campbell owned the company to whom he had sold equipment? The commission rumour was partly substantiated when it was discovered that there were two sales entries of the same Sperry 1106 in the branch records, one to Aer Lingus, and the other to Riomhaire Teoranta.

I took Alan Wightman's advice. What a bloody shame. It was all coming right. We had created a technical and support team that worked, and I was disappointed to leave it. I discussed what had occurred with Gaeltarra Eireann management, who very kindly offered me a position with Gaeltarra. I discussed this with Audrey, but by then she had had enough of the chauvinistic society that she perceived that was Ireland in the mid-1970s, and we headed back for the UK.

6

The brewer's assistant

Our retreat from Galway and Riomhaire Teoranta cannot have been that hasty, as we would have had to terminate the lease on the cottage at Gortdrishagh and arrange for the ferry to get two cars, loaded to the gunwales with stuff, from Dun Laoghaire to Liverpool. Audrey was also going to have to open a house that had been empty for nine months. More importantly, we had to get the boys back into Elmridge Junior School.

So it was about two weeks after initially speaking to Alan Wightman, who had been appointed the replacement Sperry regional director, that I met him in the Altrincham office. I was really lucky. He had an immediate, two-year project assignment for me. The Sperry Corporation (our name at the time) was introducing the role of account manager into Europe, and Alan was keen that I take this role at Bass Charrington. Alan was a big, energetic man who was quickly promoted from salesman to regional director in order to replace Alan Campbell.

Alan Wightman had done superb work with Bass Charrington, reputedly the largest brewery group and pub operator in Europe, selling them a real-time order processing and stock control system. Being in Galway, I had missed the excitement of the sale and submission of tender, but was told that the sales clincher had been a film (this was long before videos) taken to show a Bass Charrington order-processing clerk, with telephonist earphones and mouthpiece, sitting at a visual display terminal, ringing the pub for its regular weekly order:

'Good morning, Mr Lloyd. This is Jackie from Bass Charrington. I am calling to ask for your order this week. If it helps, your order last week was [read from the screen]. Shall we restock the Black Bull this week with the same order? … How did the cider special go last week? Shall we include five crates of the dry cider? … Our specials this week are [read from the screen] … Can I put you down for an extra crate of the Johnnie Walker whisky and an extra crate of the Old Ruby port?'

The film as a concept demonstration was super. If I had been on the Bass Charrington selection panel, with lots of ready cash, I would have bought as well. The viewer also heard Mr Lloyd's replies, and needless to say the order clerk was very pretty and was wearing a short skirt at the terminal as she confirmed Mr Lloyd's order. Our filmstar was Merilyn McHard, one of several outstanding young sales ladies taken on specifically to sell Sperry card punches.

Alan showed me the film in his office when he asked me to take the Bass job. That same afternoon, he drove me down to West Bromwich to introduce me to John Henderson, the Bass Charrington Computer Centre director, and I was off and running.

The new account manager role was an extension of the Sperry matrix management philosophy and the mixed discipline team I joined, comprised of approximately 25 persons, including software engineers and the on-site customer engineers in the computer sites at West Bromwich and Glasgow. Alan Wightman retained a lively interest in the sales situation. The West Bromwich staff was drawn from the Midlands Birmingham regional office and the Glasgow staff from the Scottish branch office. This arrangement worked perfectly, although the Bass project would occasionally lose staff needed for other quick jobs, in which instance it was a simple case of negotiation with the requesting manager. An informal ledger of man-days owed one way or the other worked well. My appointment was at the time when the hardware had been installed in the West Bromwich office. It was running some of the programs from the Honeywell 200 computer system it was partly replacing. The project to that date had been concentrating on converting the Honeywell written code to run on the Sperry 1110. Having reached that point in the plan, the second Sperry 1110 system was to be delivered and installed in the Bass offices in Glasgow. Alan admitted the software development was stalled, hence the company's decision to appoint an account manager.

6. THE BREWER'S ASSISTANT

During the drive to West Bromwich, Alan and I worked through an incentive plan for a UK account manager. Alan wanted the available money to be allocated at his discretion. I negotiated for a scheme that had both a qualitative and a quantitative element. We agreed on an annual basic £1,000 to be available on a discretionary basis from the regional director – was the account manager doing a good job from his perspective? — and £1,000, divided into 10 parcels of £100, would be paid subject to the number of warranted complaints to senior Sperry management about the performance of Sperry on the project, team behaviour, and/or complaints about the account manager. In other words, a Bass complaint might cost me £100. The mathematics was simple. I would tell the Bass management about the plan and suggest any concerns be addressed with me over a lunch and that recourse to Sperry management should only happen if the project team did not react sensibly to the situation.

I was quickly brought up to speed by Vijay Avasti, the Sperry real-time programming manager, who was based in the Bass office at West Bromwich. This was not going to be an easy project. We did not have a written system specification. But Bass knew what it wanted: it was recorded on film. I did not meet any of the Bass clerical staff for a few months, but I knew instinctively that none of them would be as young, pretty, or as personable as Merilyn McHard. The Sperry 1110s were the first of that model to be installed in the UK, the largest of the systems available from the company at that time. The system included a new communications/symbiont processor, the programmable forerunner of what we have come to know as a file server. As the name implies, it took the processing responsibility for communicating with terminals and printing from the main processor. This saved a huge processing load from the main processor, as it would present complete terminal messages where previously every terminal character would have prompted an interrupt in the main processor and a delay to any jobs being run. The plan was that Bass would share the database between the two processing centres. The Sperry world was watching to see how we handled the split database. This was to be another first.

The available telecommunications links between the two centres would be stretched by the requirement to keep the database synchronised between the two centres. In the event that one centre was not available for any reason, the other had to take the full processing load of both. We would also need a switching mechanism to transfer the southern sales order clerks to connect to the Glasgow computer centre if West Bromwich was not available, and vice versa. This was all leading-edge stuff at the time.

The technical teams in place were excellent, but they had long been in report mode on what was such a visible project to both Bass and Sperry. My role was simple: to relieve them of that obligation so that they could get on with the job at which they were best. The first task was to get a written specification of the system that was agreed on by both parties. Without this we would never get a sign-off that the project was complete. This was still being finalised 18 months into my time with the project, alongside with the development, which was going really well. I have to admit that I exacerbated the development task through the fascination Alan Wightman and I had for the new intelligent terminal that Sperry had introduced: the Universal Terminal System (UTS) 400. The UTS 400 was programmable (the forerunner of the PC that was to appear three years later) via the Microprocessor Control Program (MCP) language, and had its own in-built storage — a seven-inch diskette, if memory serves me correctly.

Figure 6.1: Here I pretend to understand the UTS 400, beyond which is pictured the standard (non-intelligent) UTS 200 terminal.
Source: Author's collection.

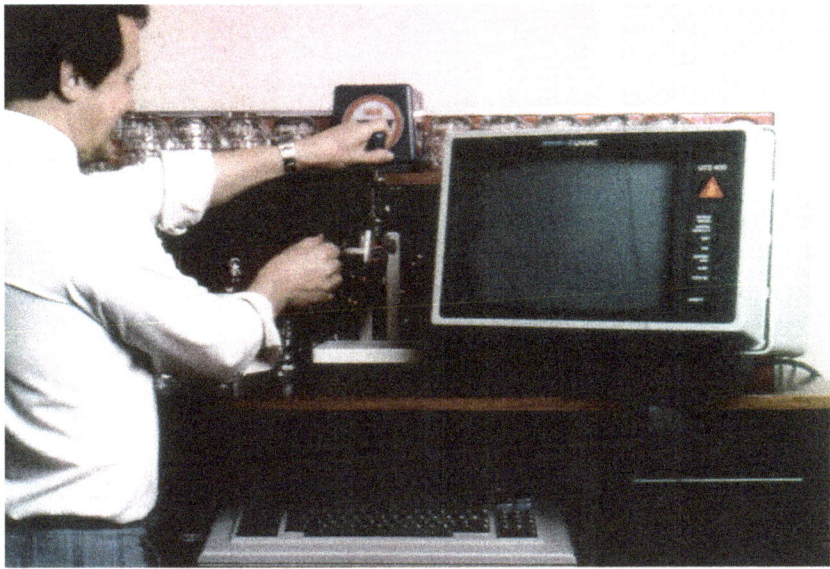

Figure 6.2: An unrealistic juxtapositioning of the UTS 400 next to the beer tap in the office.
Source: Author's collection.

The potential of the UTS 400 took us towards a PC-style operation and would be of value in ensuring that the sales order clerks would always be able to function. (We did not know that Bill Gates was also working with MCP language at this time in Seattle.) Bass accepted our recommendation that the system be developed to use the potential of the UTS 400. For a while we had a continual stream of visitors to see how we were getting on with the new terminals, the new mainframes, and the communication processors.

There was another reason, perhaps, that we were able to encourage visitors. The Bass clerical staff, across the company, had the same facility made available to them as their co-workers on the brewing side of the business: beer on tap in the office. At West Bromwich, a barrel of beer on tap was accessible in our team office. Bill Huntley was the Midlands regional director at the time and Alan Stevens was the sales manager. They would request regular update meetings at Bass, normally in the late afternoon, and, fortified by Bass Bitter, the meeting would be a good start to an evening out. The Midlands engineering manager was another frequent visitor to see how his team was getting on with the new equipment, and somehow his meetings tended to move from the computer room to the development office.

My day-to-day contact was John Henderson, the Bass Computer Centre director. We did not actually meet on a daily basis, as I was spending quite a lot of time in Glasgow. We made a habit of meeting every Wednesday morning to discuss matters of mutual interest and if it so happened that we were still talking at lunch time, we would continue over lunch. These meetings were not minuted, but were invaluable and covered all the common interest aspects of the project. John was under pressure from Harry Burton, the Bass data processing director, who was based at the Burton Brewery in Shropshire, some 30 miles from West Bromwich. Harry Burton had been one of the original Bass decision makers for the project, but he and his technical support team were, because of geography, out of the loop. Vijay Avasti and I made sure that we kept them abreast of progress and solicited their input about development direction.

One of the innovations Alan Wightman had introduced during the sales process was a Bass–Sperry golf day. As the Sperry account manager, it fell to me to organise an annual golf day and competition. The venues were easily arranged, as Bass owned a number of the best courses. In 1977, we played Turnberry, two days before the British Open Golf Championship. The course was magnificent. The opportunity to play at such a venue was too good for Sperry management, and we had far too many folk wanting to play than we could cater for. We played 10-a-side and the ideal result would be a win by five-and-a-half games to four-and-a-half to either team. Team selection was difficult, as I had telexes reminding me of everyone's willingness to participate. The after match dinner was infamously boozy, and it seemed that also appealed as much as the athletic component of our day.

Driving off first as captain of the Sperry team, on a championship course with the other players watching, was more than off-putting. I had played some social golf in Ireland, on the best courses with the Gaeltarra Eireann Golf Society, but it was still a relief to get my first drive down the fairway. It mattered not that I took another 19 shots to get on that first green. I was determined to have a good day. Bass was generous on such days and had refreshment stops at the sixth and twelfth greens. No player or supporter was going to be allowed to end the round thirsty. The last

I heard, the Bass Charrington company, which has now evolved into the InterContinental Hotels Group and Mitchells & Butlers (reverting to a name from history), are still using Unisys point-of-sale technologies.

Bass Charrington was not the only brewer in the Sperry stable. We also provided the computer system to Robinsons Brewery in Stockport and the John Smith's Brewery in Tadcaster. They both allowed the local office to buy drinks at wholesale prices, so it was not really a surprise when John Henderson asked if I and the Sperry project team wanted to avail of Bass wholesale drink prices at Christmas time. We did. It was a nice gesture from Bass. The following year, we had the same offer and this time I faxed the wholesale price list to team members in Glasgow and members working from the Birmingham office. I thought no more about it, until sometime in February 1977 when I was summoned to John Henderson's office to be told that the Sperry project office was the highest spending Bass wholesale outlet in the UK that Christmas period. We were awarded a nice cuckoo clock with Bass badging as a memento, one that perhaps we should not have earned. It was actually embarrassing. I did some research, but stopped short when I learned that Bill Read, the UK managing director, had ordered big on behalf of the company and himself, and that the order was in the tens of crates for spirits and fortified wines. Better to take the award and keep my head down. The splendid clock is still in the UK on the wall of the living room of my brother-in-law and his wife in Kirkleatham, Yorkshire, and is much admired.

If I had an average week, it was to fly to Glasgow on Monday morning to visit the computer centre, which was housed in the Tennent Caledonian Brewery. Coincidentally, that computer centre was managed by Bill Glasgow. Bill was a bit crusty, but he had taken hard knocks and ran a disciplined computer site. His operations manager was Sandy McNeill, and he and I became friends. Sandy would later join Sperry International Division as an operations consultant, and we shared an apartment in Singapore for a time when Sandy came to town for an assignment with Singapore Telecom.

I expected to stay overnight on the Monday to be able to brief the Sperry Glasgow management on the project's progress, as it was their people we were using as the on-site engineering team. I flew back to Altrincham on the Tuesday evening. Wednesday morning would see me on the road early, on the M6 Manchester to Birmingham Motorway, to be in West

Bromwich to meet with Mr Henderson at 9.00 am. Most weeks I would stay two nights in West Bromwich before venturing back on the motorway to be home for the weekend.

Travelling that motorway twice a week was by far the most harrowing aspect of the Bass project. The three-lane motorway had a designated slow lane, fast lane, and an overtaking lane with a top speed limit of 70 mph. The average speed, however, was 100 mph. If you were travelling even the slow lane at 70 mph you would be hooted and bullied onto the hard shoulder by the sheer volume and speed of the traffic that tailgated you until you got out of the way. Where practical, I would take the A roads, which would be marginally less stressful. I upgraded my car to the biggest Alfa Romeo just to have the grunt under the bonnet to survive undertaking that trip on a regular basis. My programmer pal David Miller was not so fortunate. He called in at our house on his way home after an accident in his Toyota Celica on the M6. His car was a write-off, but the Volvo that was involved was fine. The next time we saw David he was driving his own Volvo. The M6 really was that bad.

More often than not, one evening a week in Birmingham I would have a few drinks with Alan Stevens — of the infamous stutter — who by now was sales manager in the Birmingham office. His wife, Jean, was not well, and we would spend the later part of the evening over a nightcap at Alan's home so he was there if Jean required attention.

Figure 6.3: Some of the team at the Bass Charrington Computer Centre at West Bromwich.
Source: Author's collection. A photograph commissioned for the Sperry publication *Punchline*.

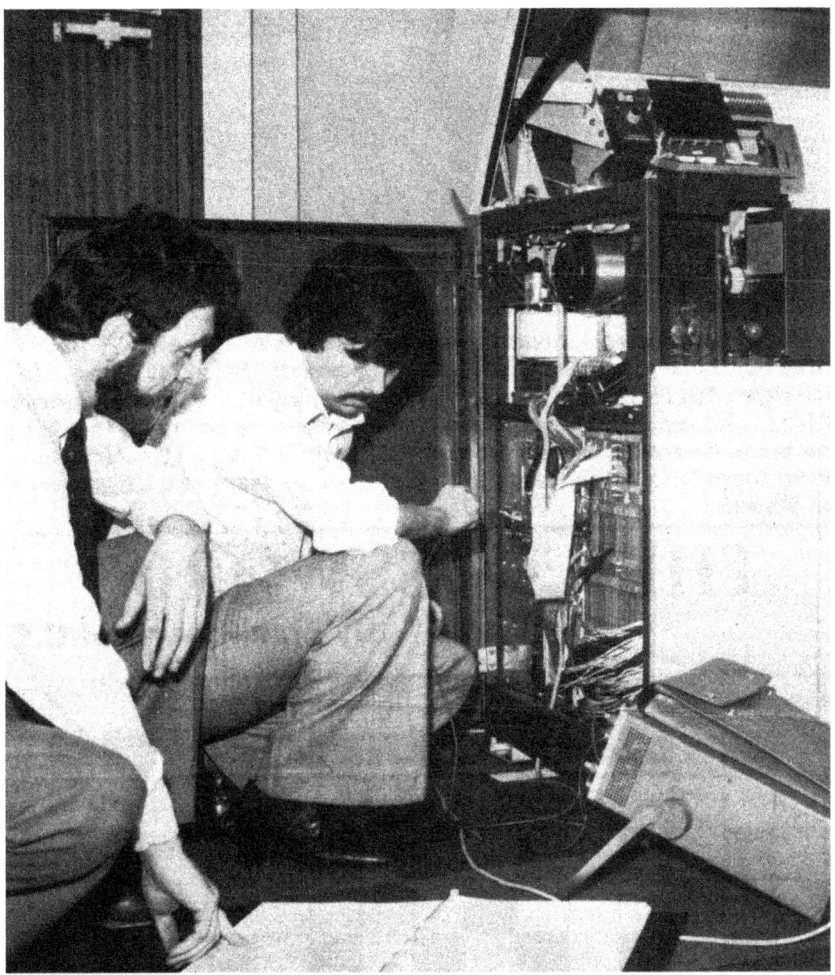

Figure 6.4: In the Glasgow Computer Centre, chief engineer Ken O'Brien and Walter Dixon follow the wiring diagram for the new 0770 printer system — 2,000 lines per minute.
Source: Author's collection. A photograph commissioned for the Sperry publication *Punchline*.

Alan Stevens asked if I would also take responsibility for the Queen Elizabeth Hospital account in Birmingham. This was not an arduous task. It was a highly proficient installation, one of three hospital projects funded by the UK Government to explore the uses of computer technologies in hospitals. The Queen Elizabeth Hospital had been wired so that access was available for a computer terminal on a trolley, via a plug in the ward wall. The demonstration proved that the average in-hospital stay period could be reduced from seven days to five if the doctor could have patient history and test results instantly available. The demonstration also proved that any patient was likely to receive incorrect medication during their hospital stay. Funding for the project was discontinued after the trial period, which was a huge disappointment.

Towards the start of my Bass appointment, I had written a paper and formulated a presentation for in-house Sperry use that I called 'A View from the Other Side'. As impartially as possible, I reviewed the difficulties I had encountered as a Sperry customer, as the manager of the Riomhaire Teoranta computer service bureau in the 18 months preceding my joining the Bass project. Alan Wightman asked me to present this twice within the Northern region and I unwittingly generated a deal of personal antagonism from colleagues for whom the company could do no wrong. Alan was concerned that my message be heard in the UK head office, but that I not be exposed to prejudicing my career. My paper and presentation was sent to Terry Duffy, the technical director, and he and I had a couple of conversations. My biggest concern had been the lack of relevant application software that we could easily use to generate revenue. The tyranny of distance from support staff was also a concern. This initiative was rewarded by my being asked, at the conclusion of the successful two-year Bass assignment, to return to Ireland again. I was keen. My wife was not. I was able to negotiate a deal whereby I was given set targets that did not carry a time constraint.

7

Pursuing my own rainbow's end

As the regional director and the original salesman to Bass Charrington, Alan Wightman had kept in close contact with me during my two years working with Bass. My assignment to the project was acknowledged by Alan and Sperry management to have been successful and, when the two years were up, Alan asked if I would like to return to Ireland to assist the established general manager of Remington Rand in setting up a Sperry country office. I was really pleased to have this recognition. I had enjoyed the Galway experience and there were unanswered questions as to what had really happened with Riomhaire Teoranta, University Computing Company, and the equipment we had so lovingly looked after.

Alan Wightman wanted two things: for the new Irish office to make its first-year sales target — a modest US$500,000 — and for me to train Gerry Maher and two recently recruited salesmen. That did not sound too hard. I knew that my pal Bill Leahy was back in his native Dublin and was the technical support manager for the new branch. He was looking after the systems and engineering sides of the business and I anticipated that Bill would have been able to retain the group of engineers from the Galway Riomhaire days.

For the first few weeks of the assignment, the office was still based in the old Remington Rand office on the Naas Road, in West Dublin. The building, I am sure, had been fine for the 1950s and 1960s, when Remington was a force to be reckoned with in office equipment. A new office, in town, had been Gerry Maher's achievement to date and was a great improvement. We moved in after I had worked with him for four or five months.

Gerry Maher, whose hand I was to hold, was as established in his habits and attitude as the Remington building was decrepit. He was a small, dark man with an aquiline nose, a receding hairline, a snarling speech habit, and suits that were too big. He drove an ancient Mercedes, aggressively, with one arm and shoulder out of the window ready to hurl abuse at other road users. Thank goodness Bill Leahy had got Gerry started on the path to acceptable behaviour before I got there. I might not have had the patience to cope with the original Gerry. He expected autocratic obedience from his staff. His habit of requiring his secretary, Margaret Parkinson, who was a lovely girl, to take shorthand notes whilst he used the ensuite in his office was his worst excess, and was only cured after the move to the newer premises. Gerry did not know how to take me. I believe he only tolerated me because I had the Riomhaire experience of selling computer services in Ireland. He accepted that selling computers would be different to selling Kardex filing systems, filing cabinets, and typewriters. Bill and I had to show him that selling was still a people business, especially as he could expect to be dealing with people that were younger and with a higher intellect than he had become used to.

Gerry's two salesmen were Bob Sinott, a precise, slim, moustached, pipe-smoking man who was ambitiously determined to impress his Sperry colleagues, and Bernard Flanagan, a jovial young man who looked overweight and was content to let things happen, until we showed him how to make things happen and why our approach to our market had to be disciplined.

Of the Riomhaire on-site engineers, Bill Leahy, Jim Butler, and Tony Leonard were back in Dublin. Bill had purchased a home in Galway, which he sold well and moved himself and the family to Terenure, where he had been brought up. John O'Callaghan was back home in the family O'Callaghan suburbs of Cork, looking after the Sperry 90/30 system installed as a part of the Ford Motor Company worldwide network. John also supervised Martin Daley, who was resident in Shannon, with a system installed for Burlington Warehouses Limited, again part of a worldwide network. The only one of the Galway-based engineers who had moved on was 'little' John Caughlan, who had returned to an expatriate engineer lifestyle in the Middle East.

7. PURSUING MY OWN RAINBOW'S END

Tony Leonard was not a considerate person. I remembered an awful evening with him in Galway three years previously. He wanted me to experience rabbit shooting. I was really scared that evening when he started to drive across the countryside with his rifle out of the window, taking pot-shots at ravens and gulls on the telephone lines. We killed a few rabbits, but I did not enjoy that either. He had not mellowed. He was due to drive from Dublin one morning with spare parts required by Bill in Cork, and they had agreed to meet somewhere in the middle. But before he left, he read the newspaper, had his lunch, and a snooze. When I remonstrated with him, he observed it would do Bill good to be able to sit and relax while he waited for him. Tony was not all bad. He could be very funny at times. He had no sense of urgency.

Gerry Maher knew his market and had targeted two organisations: Dan Morrissey Limited of Carlow, County Carlow, and the Mitchelstown Creamery of Mitchelstown, County Cork. The sooner we had these two signed up, the sooner the branch would make its quota and the sooner Gerry would be left alone. These were two accounts in businesses I had never looked at, so it was going to be interesting. I was looking forward to it.

With more than 10 years of Sperry experience, I had got used to preparing artwork for 35 mm slides used in visual presentations. Before we visited Gerry's prospects, I had slides made with the Morrissey and Mitchelstown logos for inclusion in a standard set of the 'Introduction to Sperry Computer Systems' slide show. Gerry's obvious delight and the faces of our prospects when they saw these showed that I was starting out on the correct foot.

Dan Morrissey was a most interesting company. The founder of the dynasty had set up the company as a builders' merchant. With five sons available, he had been able to diversify into building in his own right, and had developed a large pit on his land to provide sand and gravel in County Wicklow and surrounds. Carlow at the time was becoming a dormitory town of Dublin, but most people worked in agriculture or at the nearby sugar factory. Gerry Maher had provided office equipment to Morrissey and had watched the Morrissey boys grow up. Sperry was not the only company to have recognised a potential sale to this high-profile and growing enterprise. The family had an interest in horses and all of the boys had private pilot licences. The boys all lived on the family land and each had a department of the company to run. Our main contact was with the youngest lad, Phil, who was assigned to run the office.

We sought pre-sales technical support to assist with the sales to Morrissey and were blessed to have Peter Stewart assigned. I knew Peter as a salesman who had been working the commercial accounts in the East Anglia region. Peter had had success as a salesman, selling to Dixons Photographic, and had a high-profile in the company as a fly fisherman and fly-tier — we knew that much from the Sperry company newsletter, *Punchline*. Peter took to the Morrissey family and they took to him. Peter was appointed bid manager for the technical aspects of our proposal. He was also the unofficial technical consultant to the Morrisseys as they evaluated the alternate vendor tenders and proposals they had received. We were also assisted by Terry Duffy, the technical director in London, an Irishman who returned home every year and was more than happy to call in to Carlow. Gerry was advised by Phil Morrissey that we would win this business, subject to a final negotiation.

We were asked to attend the final negotiation at 6.00 pm on a weekday evening. We asked Bill Huntley, the sales director from London, to attend. We wanted Bill to see how business was done in Ireland and to understand how different the rural requirements were from the requirements he was used to in the UK. Sperry was represented by Bill Huntley, Gerry Maher, Peter Stewart, and myself. We sat in the front room of the original farmhouse with the five brothers and started to drink bottled Guinness. We were made very aware that 'Mother' was going to be an attentive participant in the discussions, although she was in and out of the lounge room as she prepared dinner for us. We sat down to dinner at about 8.00 pm. And what a fabulous dinner it was — a roast with all the trimmings, followed by apple pie, ice cream, and custard. The (seemingly inexhaustible) crates of Guinness had followed us into the kitchen and our glasses were topped up whenever they started to look empty. Dinner took us through to about 10.30 pm, when the table was cleared, and out came coffee and a couple of bottles of whiskey. Mother came and sat with us.

When Phil Morrissey, the youngest brother and administration director, brought out his list of questions, Mother and the boys moved their chairs closer to the table, and Gerry Maher and Bill Huntley tried to push their chairs back out of the line of fire of questioning, which was OK until the major support issues came out, literally on the table. We expected that they would want to negotiate on price. We wanted, as ever, to leave price until last. Were there any other concerns? We were not ready to be asked if Peter could be assigned full-time until Morrissey-defined milestones were achieved. Our project plan had included using Bill Leahy's technical staff in training and indirect hand-holding. We withdrew to the lounge to discuss this. The Morrissey strategy worked. We were already in the small hours of the next day and wanted a positive resolution. Peter was keen to take the assignment but wanted to know the terms and conditions of any secondment before he would agree, as this would mean moving his family to Carlow. Peter obviously knew beforehand that the Morrisseys would ask for him and he was prepared with his requirements. Price was also negotiated. It was a long session, but we staggered out of the family kitchen with a signed contract, having typed out the new clauses on a typewriter on the kitchen table with the family still in attendance.

I have never learned if Bill Huntley had any problems with the contract back at head office, or even if the contract made money. I do know that Peter Stewart put in a huge effort to make the system a real showcase. He moved his family to Carlow, no harm came to his two lads in the local school, and Maureen (Peter's wife) seemed happy with her lot. I was happy to have Peter in Carlow. It was a good spot to stop on the drive to Mitchelstown or Cork, and he made me a really nice fishing rod from a blank I had acquired in Cork where we were selling to Mitchelstown Creamery.

My first visit to the creamery was memorable. Gerry and I drove to Mitchelstown from Dublin to meet Padraic O'Murray, the newly appointed data processing manager. Padraic had been recruited from a London job, where he had been known as Pat or Paddy Murray. A big man with a florid complexion, he was delighted to be back home in Ireland. His Irish accent was very thick, but I could not place it. The creamery was already a computer user, having a magnetic tape-based IBM installation with which it was basically satisfied. We spent the first morning going through the standard sales presentations and getting to know one another. At noon, we asked Padraic if he wanted lunch and asked if we should go to a local pub. Padraic pointed to a pin he was wearing on his jacket lapel and explained: 'We can go to the pub for lunch, but I shall not drink. I am a Pioneer and I do not drink. Why don't we have lunch in the creamery canteen?' The canteen it was. The food was magnificent. The creamery kitchen laid out a leg of ham, roast pork, baked jacket potatoes, and a selection of cheeses. The baked potatoes were the Irish finest, with thick skins and a very floury centre, and butter was necessary to soften the spuds. The milk was very creamy. It was super. We got to meet the creamery management who were most attentive. After lunch, Padraic walked us around the creamery and attempted to define what he wanted from his new computer system.

We followed the course of the milk collection lorry through the weighbridge, the recording process, and where the decision was made as to whether milk was destined for the manufacture of butter or cheese. The operations man at the weighbridge would make that decision on the anticipated butter-fat content of the milk, knowing the milk tanker collection route that had been made. Samples of the milk and the butter-fat measure followed through the process control mechanisms as they became household milk, butter, and cheese, or were processed into dried milk. We toured the cheese and butter making sections of the creamery, which covered a vast area. We also visited the farm and were shown the pedigree animals whose progeny would improve the stock quality of the local farmers who belonged to the cooperative — we were reminded the company name was the Mitchelstown Wholesale Cooperative Society Limited. In 1977, it was the largest cooperative in Europe. The animals we inspected included bulls of various breeds, pigs, and sheep. It was a real eye-opener for a town boy such as myself. At the conclusion of the tour, Gerry again asked Padraic if he would like a drink. Padraic pointed to the pin he was wearing on his jacket lapel and again explained, 'I am wearing the pin. I am a Pioneer and I do not drink!' We went back to Padraic's office. I wanted to find out what IBM was offering to meet Padraic's wishlist. Following its usual practice, IBM had not made a definitive proposal, but was asking Padraic to make a decision between two expensive alternatives, neither of which was what he wanted, as I pointed out to him.

At 4.30 pm, Gerry again asked Padraic if he would like a drink. I thought that Padraic might get angry, but Gerry instinctively knew his man much better than I did. Padraic removed his pin and put it in the top drawer of his desk: 'We could have a drink in the Royal Hotel in Fermoy.' We drove in two cars to the Royal Hotel, where Padraic prevailed upon me to try Murphy's Stout: 'If you like Guinness, you will enjoy Murphy's.' I did. It was very smooth and moreish. I should have watched Gerry Maher, who was drinking coffee, with an occasional Irish coffee. It was a good job that we had enjoyed such a big lunch. Once Padraic got a taste for the Murphy's, he kept them coming — fast. Gerry had removed himself from what was developing into a binge.

I cannot remember what time I eventually left Padraic. I cannot even remember leaving the Royal Hotel, but learned the next day that I had hailed a Garda Síochána (police) car and prevailed upon them to take me to the hotel. Gerry had not left my bag, which had my sleeping wear and a change of clothes, out for me. I presumed it was still in the boot of his car. I had a most restless night, during which, running around the hotel corridors looking for a toilet, I had fallen through a fire door and descended the metal fire-escape, one landing at a time. On the first landing my body exploded from the excesses of the day. During the subsequent descent, I knocked chunks of skin from every sharp bit of my body. It would not have been a pretty sight, I imagine, when I was found naked and bleeding, with excrement falling through the landing lattice, at the bottom of the fire escape in the kitchen garden. The hall porter and night manager found me. They did their best to stem the flow of blood and clean me up. They dressed me in a roll of kitchen towel and put me back into bed. I am not sure what time I was up, but it was early. I found Gerry's room, demanded my change of clothes, showered, breakfasted, and was back at the creamery by cab at 8.30 am to see Padraic. That was the start of my developing relationship with Padraic. He was adamant that no other sales representative had been able to hold their own with him in the pub as I had done. He was impressed, and so was Gerry Maher when he heard the story. But I had to swear the two of them to secrecy. From that time on, Padraic was keen to work with Sperry, but we could consider him only as a prime recommender, not the decision maker who would carry total weight with the full cooperative.

One reason I had wanted to see Padraic quickly that morning was because I had the germ of an idea that might meet his system needs. At the time, the only system that we could offer that would have not been too costly was the Sperry 90/30. The real-time Sperry 90/40 had not been announced, and we had to find a way of making the 90/30 into a pseudo real-time machine. We had a good start, as it handled terminal communications well enough. My thought had been to find a terminal that could accumulate real-time data and present it as a communications message for processing. I had seen the advantages of analogue data collection when selling process control to Shell for Control Data Corporation. Sperry did not make or understand process control systems, but I thought we could handle data if we could collect it.

It took a few weeks to find Feedback Limited, a Home Counties supplier. I met with Feedback Limited in London and it was able to make a substantial case that it could handle the weighbridge system and present the milk weight data on a Sperry screen in a specific form. The operative would add other variables such as date, time, driver, collection route, and the initial milk-fat measurement. A similar system could be used for the weighing of cheeses travelling down a conveyor belt when the retail price tag associated with that block of cheese would be printed, and an accumulation of data collected for submission as batch data to the main production system. The prices and feedback support commitments were OK, and were presented to Mitchelstown and included in the full proposal that was accepted by the Mitchelstown board of directors. In parallel, we processed the contract acceptance paperwork through Sperry UK and got sign-off from the interested managers — with the exception of Bill Huntley, the technical director. But the deal went through.

By this time I had brought my car to Ireland and was no longer dependent upon being driven everywhere by Gerry Maher. As we proceeded towards the business with Morrissey and Mitchelstown, Gerry became more confident in allowing me to visit his prospects without him needing to be there. Gerry was now able to spend time with his salesmen and train them in his sales methods. The Sperry 90/30 systems were on quite a short lead time, and were quickly installed. Peter took control of the Morrissey account, but Mitchelstown was slower, and from my perspective allowed to drift. The first job was to convert the IBM system to operate on the 90/30, which required one skill set. The design and implementation of the new system needed a different approach and personnel, but support staff from the UK were loath to give up their initial assignments, as they were having too good a time.

I visited Mitchelstown quite frequently and stayed in the Royal Hotel at Fermoy. I was able to indulge in my fascination for fly fishing on the Blackwater River beyond Fermoy. One of the creamery computer operator's family farmed land through which this most famous river flowed, and I was given a free run of the family's access to the water. I made my contact with the water bailiff and thoroughly enjoyed the activity. My favourite beat was where the river ran over pebbles at the foot of a high cliff and where the trout were accessible at most times. The Sperry project team who were assisting Mitchelstown, mostly on secondment from the UK, found a family guest house in Fermoy and had a great time in Ireland. We regularly lunched as a project team in a pub beyond Fermoy which provided excellent bar food. The smoked herring was special.

I'd try to get to Carlow and Mitchelstown once a week to offer project support. I was probably left on this assignment a month or two longer than was necessary. We had achieved the initial sales target, and shown that Ireland could be a sustainable branch in its own right. Gerry Maher had his own confidence levels, and wanted to run his own shop. We tried to reference sell off the back of Mitchelstown to the other creameries, but it was too early for this. The other creameries wanted to see results from Mitchelstown. Gerry and I had allowed the two salesmen too much licence in terms of reference selling. In this, we were embarrassed by a mistake made by Bernard Flanagan, who had taken a photocopy of the proposal I had submitted to Mitchelstown Wholesale Cooperative Society Limited and used Wite-Out to remove the typed name and the logo which appeared on every page of the original document. A typist then typed over that long 50-character space the name of the prospect creamery — 'ABC Dairy', for instance, a much shorter, eight-character name. This was then photocopied again, and submitted as a unique reasoned proposal. It was so obvious that the Mitchelstown paperwork had been plagiarised that we had to apologise to the cooperative and afterwards were treated with suspicion in the cooperative market.

It did not help that I had a car accident on my way to another cooperative presentation. After passing a car on a country road, I overcompensated getting back into my lane, hit the ditch and rolled the car. I can remember the roof hit the road twice. I was OK, but agonised over two broken fly fishing rods in the boot. The driver and passenger in the car following were very kind and took me into Wexford. The police took notes and we pushed the vehicle into a field — it was a write-off. I never saw the car again. The next day during the presentation, I put my hand into my jacket pocket and removed chippings from broken windshield and windows from the car. I can still hear the sound of the tinkle of the glass as I dropped it into an ash tray. The amazing thing was that the jacket had been in a suitcase in the boot of the car.

Not having a car restricted my freedom in Ireland, and head office requested that I return to the UK to project manage the Sperry presence at the Provident Management Services Limited installation in Halifax, Yorkshire.

Before I left Ireland after this second assignment, Audrey came across the North Sea and I enjoyed showing her Carlow, Mitchelstown, Fermoy, and Cork, before we headed to Galway for a short break. We got a great welcome from the Mitchelstown Hotel where I had disgraced myself some six months previously. Hotel staff had fun reminding me and it was not too embarrassing after Audrey got over the shock of the initial announcement shouted from the reception desk to the hall porters: 'It's him. He's back!' I still look forward to getting back to Ireland, principally to the West coast. It is a great place and I must have been to Galway 30 times for holidays since then.

8

The tallyman and other endeavours

I returned from Ireland, for the second time, in late 1978 to project manage the Provident Management Services Limited (PMSL) account. It did not sound a promising career move, and I was concerned with being used again as a troubleshooter.

David Holroyd had sold PMSL a dual-Sperry 1106 system some 18 months previously. The Sperry system was to have replaced a number of smaller International Computers Limited (ICL) systems, but the project had faltered, only one of the processors had been installed, and PMSL had announced an order for the latest ICL medium range system. I was briefed on the situation by the northern region director, Alan Wightman, and the regional technical support manager, Philip Good. Phil was also very much involved with the system implementation of the 1106 at J. D. Williams in Manchester, a major direct mail operator. My unwritten brief was to establish a presence at PMSL and minimise Sperry's exposure to the potential loss of this prestigious account.

Pat Cullen was now the Manchester sales manager and a friend of Mike Samuels, the Leeds sales manager. Mike had a more gentle demeanour and casual approach than the average sales manager, although he had the reputation of being a tough nut under pressure. David Holroyd had been the previous ICL salesman to PMSL and had joined Sperry Computers to sell the Sperry solution that had been described to him by Mike Samuels.

David was dark, with slicked-back hair, a deep speaking voice, and was always very well groomed. A salesman's salesman, David earned a lot of commission.

PMSL was based in Colonnade, Bradford, and the new computer centre was nearing completion in the village of Mixenden, near Halifax, West Yorkshire — magnificent in local sandstone. The computer centre was 80 miles from my home in Altrincham — a 60-minute journey using the M56 and M62 motorways to cross the Pennines.

PMSL had been founded in 1880 to provide responsible lending to working class families in industrialised West Yorkshire. Its speciality was home credit, and local agents were lending small, short-term, unsecured loans to people in all walks of life, delivering cash and calling every week to collect the repayments. PMSL admitted this was moneylending, and its aggressive salesmen were known as tallymen. The salesmen sold PMSL cheques against a deferred payment. The cheques were redeemable in most shops and stores in Yorkshire and an area extending towards the UK Midlands. The computer system being developed by PMSL was the overall control system for this operation. We were anticipating a database of 2.5 million customers at any one time. PMSL believed themselves to be the biggest moneylenders in Europe in terms of number of clients.

The PMSL team with whom we had a regular interface included Derek Whitehead, the charismatic managing director; John Walker, the operations director for both the ICL and Sperry systems, with an office in both Bradford and Mixenden; Ian Chippendale, the Mixenden operations director, who was young and thought to be the protégé of Derek Whitehead, the Mixenden operations director, with an office overlooking a huge (and very empty) computer room; Peter Hughes, bearded, diffident and loose-limbed, was operations manager, and had the office next to Ian at the end of the viewing balcony above the computer room; and John Clegg, the PMSL systems manager, an ex-ICL user rapidly coming to terms with Exec 8 (the Sperry 1100 operating system) and DMS 1100 (the hierarchical database system implementation).

When I first arrived at Mixenden, I sat in an open-plan area close to John Clegg and his team, which was a valuable introduction to the problems they were having. I eventually had a separate Sperry office across from the computer suite and overlooking the trout pond, the centrepiece of

8. THE TALLYMAN AND OTHER ENDEAVOURS

the complex. (When the complex was finished, trout were introduced into the lake in anticipation of a future fishing opportunity, but they did not prosper. It was eventually discovered that wild mink were inhabiting the pond, and they were enjoying the trout even as they were being replenished. The mink, obviously escapees from local mink farms, were occasionally seen but never trapped.) The Sperry problems with the installation occurred because only half the proposed equipment had been installed. Every hardware hiccup was a disaster that would have been mitigated if the fail-safe complete hardware complement had been in use. Once the contracted hardware was available, we were able to address the database software issues that imposed almost daily constraints upon what we were doing. The equipment was mostly second-hand, although refurbished, which had somewhat of a negative effect on the morale at Mixenden.

I was happy, as was PMSL, with the on-site Sperry engineering team, which included Duncan Read, the engineer-in-chief, who had a very strong Yorkshire accent and a tall, lean body, and a confidence in his computer system that was always reassuring. However, in repose we recognised our Duncan as lugubrious, and, if I understand the word, 'gloomy'. Keith Woodhouse was another local boy. Keith had an endearing enthusiasm for every task he undertook. Terry McGee, who I knew as the Glasgow field engineering manager during the Bass project, was the engineering manager in the new Leeds branch and was project friendly when it came to providing specialist support should we need it.

I was not the lone technical support representative for long. Charles Dickinson, an operating systems engineer and software generalist, joined the Leeds branch after having been a support programmer at the Open University. Charles was seeking the opportunity to live and bring his family up in West Yorkshire. He was assigned full-time and the timing of his appointment could not have been better. Always well dressed, Charles presented well, if somewhat formally, but if you looked there was a twinkle of mischief in his eye. He was a good work colleague and a great ally of John Clegg, and he made a positive contribution to the work we were doing. Although not designated a database management system expert, Charles's advice was invaluable in this area. Database problems were initially taking far too long to resolve, and we initiated a fairly basic, but stringent, set of rules to be followed by a fault-resolution team to speed up and document resolution. It was a matter of understanding and documenting what we thought we should do, and recognising the fact that something must have changed to introduce a fault in to what was once working. Charles and I were members of that team.

I had very little day-to-day rapport with Mike Samuels or David Holroyd, but an on-site presence obviously helped them off site and they were able to persuade PMSL to install the second-half of the originally contracted equipment. PMSL was always open to a bargain and accepted proposals to replace the now dual Sperry 1106 with the 3×2 Sperry 1110 that had been installed at Shell-Mex and BP, and the two original Sperry 1108s from Shell Centre London and Shell Wythenshawe. These systems came with complements of peripherals, and suddenly we had a very full computer room. The Sperry 1110, as I had used at Bass, was a faster, bigger and later model in the Sperry 1100 family in a three central processor, two input/output processor configuration.

The pending delivery of different hardware brought another decision. Neither Shell-Mex and BP or Shell Petroleum had been updating the operating system software. It was my responsibility to make sure that we simplified the operations. Charles Dickinson and I talked this through with John Clegg, and we decided to recommend that we run all our hardware on the very latest Sperry 1100 operating system. We had opposition from our own salespeople and the PMSL operations department also had reservations.

I put the arguments into a presentation into which I put a lot of effort. I used Letraset, rub-down lettering, and pictures on A4 cardboard. This artwork was converted into 35 mm slides and black and white set of photocopies that were bound together for distribution. At the time, this created a favourable impression, although it looks primitive compared to today's Microsoft-assisted artwork.

I had to give the presentation in its various forms quite a few times. Phil Good endorsed our decision to move the software forward and allocated Ivan Roy, an engineer from the Shell account, to assist us with preparation and testing. It all worked perfectly.

8. THE TALLYMAN AND OTHER ENDEAVOURS

UNIVAC AMBITION WITH INSTALLATION OF 1110 SAME AS PMSL'S.

→ PMSL user satisfaction is key.

→ Univac will (also) have to live with the decision.

→ The final decision as to the most suitable, stable sub-level can be left to mid-January. Will probably be Level 36 R2b.

Figure 8.1: Artwork used in the PMSL selling situation. (After 25 years, the Letraset appears to be holding out.)
Source: Author's collection.

I eventually encouraged PMSL to buy something new. PMSL ordered and we delivered a new disk subsystem that was installed over a weekend. What a disappointment to view the equipment on the computer room floor on the Monday to see that the metal exterior of the units was damaged. Easily discernible boot and fist impressions scarred the units. PMSL was not at all amused. We investigated and learnt that these units came off the production line in the US the day that redundancies were announced in the factory and our units bore the brunt and marks of the workers' frustrations. We had to have new skins specially made. It did not help. Matching the paint was a real concern.

PMSL was most innovative in one aspect of its interface with the computer vendors. John Walker let it be known that he would be in the Crown and Anchor, also known as 'Ronnie's pub', at the gates of the Mixenden Centre for his lunch every Friday, and that if vendors wanted to speak or to socialise with him they were welcome to join us. Pink gins were traditionally the Friday drink, although I do not know why. It was fun to meet the other vendors and swap stories and technical exaggerations with them. At the time Sperry was the winning team, which might have made it easier for us to enjoy our participation.

Figure 8.2: The PMSL computer room at Mixenden, Halifax.
So much wonderful Sperry 1100 equipment.
Source: Author's collection.

PMSL was a young and sociable lot. We joined them to play soccer and knock-about cricket. Charles and I were invited to their management badminton evening, which helped cement relationships. I generally stopped over one night a week to participate in PMSL-based activities.

In time, there was less and less for me to do at PMSL. My days became the drive across the Pennines, checking with Charles Dickinson and Duncan Read that we had no major concerns, and confirming this with John Walker and Ian Chippendale. Lunch and a few beers with whoever was in Ronnie's was next on the schedule, a look into my office after lunch, and a leisurely drive back to Cheshire. There was excitement one Friday evening when a blizzard closed the M62 (Manchester–Leeds motorway) and I was marooned on the road overnight until the snowploughs opened a path for us. I was warm enough in the car, and a yellow-ringed hole in the snow drift that built up against the car marked where I had spent those hours.

I was left on site and on the project too long. It was possibly my fault. During the two years I attended Mixenden I did not have cause to go into either the Leeds or Altrincham Sperry offices. I did attend a sales kick-off meeting. Bill Read had succeeded Des Pitcher as managing director when Des took up a European marketing role with the company. Bill was an ex-National Cash Register employee and, true to form, brought in other recruits. One such was John Pascoe, who was supposed to have political connections, including with the Isle of Man Government, whose computer system we provided. Bill Read decided that the capital, Douglas, would be a good venue for one of the annual marketing meetings at which the sales and pre-sales engineers expected to be inspired to achieve ever increasing sales targets. It being an island venue, we had to fly into Douglas. There must have been about 200 participants, and arrival times were staggered during the morning as aeroplanes arrived from all over the UK. Somehow the hotel bar was persuaded that an open bar mandate existed and a lot of booze had been consumed before we sat down to a late lunch in the hotel. The guest speaker was the Secretary of the Tynwald, and he gave a perfectly acceptable speech of welcome, extolling the virtues of the island as a holiday resort and saying good things about Sperry and the uses to which its computer system was being put.

When Bill Read got up to speak, the background noise level in the restaurant rose two or three levels. Suddenly the whole ambience changed from one of well-being to open aggression against the boss, who was unable to make himself heard above the general din, despite the use of the microphone. John Pascoe leapt to his feet but was greeted with disdain and verbal abuse. I hope never to experience such a situation again. It was weird. Normality was restored when Bill Read and John Pascoe obviously abandoned trying to be heard during the meal. The group then went about its scheduled business for the rest of the day. Dinner passed without event and the outburst of hostility was forgotten. The general feeling was one of apology and contriteness. We did have one situation. Calvert Douglas, who was sharing a room with another loud Scot, Ken Struthers, fell off the room's balcony and had to be taken to hospital overnight. They were obviously clowning about. I was quite relieved that Calvert was no longer my immediate responsibility. He had been my salesman in Scotland previously. The next day, the Altrincham and Leeds office personnel enjoyed a tour of the island before heading back home.

Although I had no occasion to go into a Sperry office, I had an excellent rapport with Phil Good to whom I submitted a monthly progress report. I met Phil socially to talk out support or minor personal difficulties, and Phil attended, on request, meetings on site. Phil endorsed my plan to talk with other Sperry locations about finding something else for me to do, with three results: a one month human resources assignment; co-option into a project management training exercise; and an eventual assignment that took me to Southeast Asia, from which I never returned to the UK to work again.

The human resources assignment was to recruit salesmen for a new product line for Sperry in the UK. Sperry had acquired the BC/7 range of mid-range business computers from the Singer Corporation of the US, and the plan was to have a separate organisation to sell and support them. My task was to find the first 36 salespeople. The assignment was one month in duration and was the only time I worked at the new Stonebridge Park office, 20 minutes by train north of Euston Station. I commuted Monday through Friday and got used to being spoilt on the London Pullman from Wilmslow, Cheshire, to Euston, and return. It was a gracious way to travel, so long as you did not have to drive at the end of the trip. Champagne and kippers was an ideal breakfast to start the week, and a steak dinner would help finish off before the weekend (and a game of rugby or cricket). The company had briefed several recruitment houses of our needs and made shortlists of candidates. In 20 days at Stonebridge Park I must have interviewed 120 people. Surprisingly, I was not given any help by the human resources department, and had to very quickly draw up my own list of things to look for and quiz the candidate about. Perhaps more importantly, I derived a scale of marks for me to score potential and as a way of remembering so many people. I was exhausted at the end of that job. I had to avoid the tendency to talk too much as an interviewer; I understood how important it was to listen.

The second divertissement was to join three other European project managers and for us to work with a US industrial psychologist for one week to prepare an updated project manager's handbook, which became UNIVAC publication UP4166. The three of us were selected as having installed the highest value of Sperry 1100s outside of the US. Most of the work was done and we were more proofreaders in terms of custom and culture than having to author the manual from scratch. We worked quite well together and were also able to contribute thoughts as to an associated project management course. We determined that the essential value of a course would be in working with a real project. We also put forward the idea of working with the actual documents from a project, as well as the changing requirements during a contract negotiation and challenging the course students to accept (or not) the project and come up with a project plan. This seemed to make sense.

8. THE TALLYMAN AND OTHER ENDEAVOURS

I was pleasantly surprised to be asked by Charles Pigden, the UK training manager, to work with Geoff Munday to see if we could put such a course together and teach it in the UK. The key to the course, from my perspective, would be the case study. The case study we found from Holland regarded a Honeywell H200 batch system replacement of a small Sperry 1106 with online enhancements. We were provided with the prospect's original request for proposal, and the Sperry sales response, which included an outline project and software development plan in English. We also had access to the meeting notes from two top-level prospect Sperry meetings, in which project requirements were refined. Best of all, the Dutch project manager, who was part way through the actual implementation, was available to us for questions. Geoff and I spoke to him and he was keen to participate. We agreed to run the course over one week. Another tool available to us was a half-day management game in which teams competed against one another to make paper boxes in a simulated real-life situation where facilities were unexpectedly changed and which prejudiced the planning options. We decided to share the front-of-class duties. I would release and detail the project and Geoff would teach and remind our students of specific project tools and techniques. At the end of day one, we would release the prospect request for proposal; day two, the Sperry response; and, at the end of days three and four, the two sets of meeting notes and changes to requirements and schedules agreed to by the company. Each day, the real-life project manager was available for questions from the entire group or individual teams. On day five, four teams of four students would present their decision as to whether they accepted the project, along with their project plans or reasons why they would not accept the project. The presentation was made to Bill Huntley, the UK technical director, who travelled to Birmingham for the end of the class.

At 9.00 am on the Monday morning, I was extremely nervous standing up in front of 16 of my peer project managers, some of whom were friends and were facing greater and more urgent challenges than I was at PMSL. The main thing working in my favour was that I expected to get some sleep on the Wednesday and Thursday nights. I knew that if Geoff and I were successful in leading the class, our students would be working through these nights to complete their documented plans. That is what happened. It worked beautifully.

ALSO INNOVATORS

Bill Huntley raised one issue with me: 'Did you teach these people to look for a confrontation as a defined point in a project plan?' I had to admit to Bill that I did. Project implementation marks a change in emphasis for the supplier. You move from pre-sales mode and wanting to say 'yes' to every request, to the situation where you have to define what it is the project will achieve. A moving target does not allow for a project finalisation. The project manager chooses the point of confrontation to emphasise that change of perspective. Bill partly accepted the argument, but was at great pains to state to the students that it was not company policy. The feedback from the students, according to Charles Pigden, was the best from any course of which he had had oversight. This was very flattering. I did not get the chance to assist with any other similar classes, but I understand that Geoff Munday ran it again.

My third venture to gain release from PMSL was to announce to past colleagues that I was looking for a new assignment. Al Harvey, who I had met in Glasgow during the Bass project, called me from Hong Kong to ask if I would be interested in a three-month pre-sales assignment in Singapore. As an overseas assignment, there was home leave once a month. Al said that if I was prepared to forgo the home leave, I could use those travel credits to invite my wife and two boys to join me in Singapore for Christmas and the New Year. That sounded like a great deal.

I had one task to finish before leaving the PMSL team. The previous weekend we had attended a parachuting course in Sheffield, but had not been able to jump because of high winds. We attended again and achieved jump status after a quick refresher. Audrey was aghast that I was going to do the jump knowing I was to go to Singapore the next week. But it went well. In fact, we all enjoyed the experience, even the girl whose hands were forcibly removed from the open door frame by the instructor. She had frozen on her egress to the wing of the aeroplane, from which we had been drilled to cast off into space. Once on the ground, she could not have been more pleased with herself. The target, a red cross in the field below, looked very small from the aeroplane. The drill into which we had been disciplined required we shout a count of one to 10, and, should the parachute not open by that time, release the stand-by parachute. Our instructor told us that he would be able to hear us shout from the ground. The next instruction was to enjoy the experience, but not for long. We had been taught how to fly, to direct the descent, and I was delighted to have landed within 25 metres of the marker, the only problem being my decision to land in front of the barbed wire fence rather than risk falling through it.

9

Adventures in Southeast Asia

I had been stranded at Provident Management Services Limited at Mixenden too long. Its development cycle was in place, and it had more computing power than you could shake a stick at. I had done one or two odd jobs in the UK, but was not enjoying not having anything real to do. Nothing for the troubleshooter, as I had become, was my impression. I made a real effort to seek a move within the company for the next challenge. It came from an unexpected direction. I had spoken to Peter Evans at the international division in London, and I had flagged a wish to move to Terry Duffy, by then the technical director in the UK.

The rescuing telephone call came direct from Al Harvey in Hong Kong. I had met Al four years earlier during the Bass Charrington project in Glasgow. At that time, he was the customer engineering manager for Scotland. Big Al had the reputation of being a bit of a hard man. Now, he was the Asia-Pacific technical director. His offer was immediately attractive. Was I prepared to accept a three-month assignment as a pre-sales technician in Singapore? The total package included the option for the family to join me in Singapore for Christmas and the New Year at the end of the assignment. Could I be in Singapore next week? It was a well thought out package, and I instinctively said 'yes'.

As I travelled to Singapore for the first time in 1980, I pondered what I knew about the place. It was not much. I knew about the Federation of Malaysia, which originally included Singapore, and I knew about the conflict with the communists, as a Daily Mirror Group colleague had fought against the insurgents during his national service. Singapore had left the federation as a separate state and Prime Minister Lee Kuan Yew had a burgeoning reputation as a statesman and a benign dictator of the city-state. The images from my stamp collection were the substantiation of my sparse knowledge of Singapore's location and customs. It was exciting. I was not used to the constant heat, of course, and the clothes I had with me were unsuitable, but I became easily used to not having to wear a jacket and tie. Tailoring was cheap. I obtained lightweight trousers without difficulty.

The city was bustling. Everywhere were streams of people of mixed race, all seemingly with a purpose. Pedestrians created flows on the crowded pathways that spilled into roadways when necessary, around foodstalls and artisans, such as letter writers and shoe repairers, working on the pavements. My daily walk to the office was a delight. Before 8.00 am it was busy, with people breakfasting on the street, clustered on rickety stools around their food provider of choice. There were a few tables where the food was provided from a building. At lunchtime, and on the way home at night, I learned which stalls provided the food that took my fancy. Living and working in Singapore and Southeast Asia for almost five years would be a privilege.

I arrived in Singapore on Wednesday. I had a reservation at the Stamford Hotel on Orchard Road. The Sperry office was on the fifteenth floor of the Oversea-Chinese Banking Corporation (OCBC) Building, Chulia Street, in the centre of the central business district. Located on the very edge of Chinatown, the office block is an icon of Singapore, designed after the fashion of a modern, newfangled calculator of its day. It stood very tall at 50 storeys and was the most modern building I had ever been in. After five days in the hotel, anticipating a three month stay, I leased an apartment within easy walking distance — through Chinatown — of the Sperry office. I moved into its spartan interior expecting to be the lone occupant, despite the fact it was a three-bedroom facility. It was not to be. Frank Dorrian, the local Sperry manager, moved in within days (in order to be able to lease out his own apartment), and we were shortly joined by Sandy McNeil. Sandy and I had been pals for a few years and enjoyed one another's company when I managed the Bass Charrington account. At the weekend, Sandy and I regularly went to Sentosa Island to swim and jog. The more health-conscious Sandy also equipped the kitchen with tools such as a toaster and a toasted sandwich maker.

9. ADVENTURES IN SOUTHEAST ASIA

Figure 9.1: My walk through Chinatown to the office. The bustling, colourful atmosphere was not spoilt for me, even on a rainy day.
Source: Author's collection.

My assignment was to assist a local salesman, Alfred Tong, in his endeavours to sell another Sperry 1100 system in Singapore. Our immediate team included two other super Singaporeans, both technicians, Tan How Choon and Nanette Westerhout, who, along with Alfred, could not have made me feel more welcome. Tan How Choon, whose habit was to introduce himself as 'Tan How Choon, you can remember my name by thinking hot and cold', was to become my ideal Singaporean. He was very bright, pragmatic, and eager to learn. Somewhat thickset, he knew he would have trouble every year in his role as a Singapore Army Reservist, as he had to prove he was in shape by running a kilometre in eight minutes. Nanette, a stunning looking Eurasian, had been providing ad hoc pre-sales assistance to Alfred, along with How Choon, while undertaking real support to our major customer in the island state, the Telecommunications Authority of Singapore (TAS). Alfred was outstanding. He was prepared to study any aspect of what it was we had to offer our prospective customers to find the key benefits we might have over our principal competitor, IBM. A business studies graduate of the National University of Singapore, and having completed two-and-a-half years of national service, Alfred did not need to be advised what to do — he just needed guidance on how to do it.

I was to learn what it was like to be a Singaporean from Alfred, How Choon, and Nanette, and could not have been happier with them as mentors and colleagues. I was submitted to an informal, but crucial, aptitude test my first lunchtime in the office. The four of us removed to Keppel Harbour for a local favourite, fish head curry. It was delicious, and I realised the honour and the challenge when How Choon expertly removed one of the eyes from the fish head in curry juices with his chopsticks and placed it reverently on my plate in a nest of rice. This was it. I was not sure. Fortunately, I had been given a fork and spoon as well as chopsticks, and picked up my treat. Was I supposed to chew or swallow? Did it really matter? It did. That test passed, I was one of the team.

9. ADVENTURES IN SOUTHEAST ASIA

Figure 9.2: Left to right: Alfred Tong, myself, and Gene Risso working late in the Singapore office.
Source: Author's collection.

Figure 9.3: At the Sperry Singapore 1980 Christmas party. Left to right: Tan How Choon, Frank Dorrian behind Joseph the jaga (office odd-job man), and big Al Harvey from Hong Kong.
Source: Author's collection.

Figure 9.4: Lovely ladies. Left to right: Jennifer Lim, Nanette Westerhout, Audrey, and Alfred's wife, Dorothy.
Source: Author's collection.

My first two days went quickly. The weekend was to have a profound impact on the rest of my life. I wanted to walk the length of Orchard Road during the Saturday, and I had even been into a number of shops. At the southern end of Orchard Road was the Padang, a luxuriously green sports field, which at 4.00 pm was a hive of activity. Hockey was being played at the Singapore Recreational Club east end of the Padang, and rugby on the Singapore Cricket Club main pitch. Walking the footpath between the two pitches, local Singaporeans went resolutely and disinterestedly about their business. I was one of very few spectators who watched the conclusion of the rugby game. It was followed quickly by a second game, with players who were enormous. I had not seen 30 such big men before, except when watching very good rugby. This rugby was of a good standard and was played with a passion and a pattern. I watched and got into conversation with the players from the first game, who shortly emerged from showers, still hot and perspiring, and carrying cans of beer in ice in plastic bags to help support the first team, as I was to learn. The club was playing one of the New Zealand Infantry Regiment teams in the First Division of the Singapore League. I liked the look of this. I was offered a can of beer, and then another, and then another. I spent the evening with the Club Rugby Section, mostly expatriates, in the men's bar of the club and elicited the invitation to play with them the next day if I fancied it. The invitation was to turn up at 3.00 pm with the expectation I would get a game: 'Just bring along your own boots and jock strap.' This I did, and played against a visiting side from the Royal Bangkok Sports Club. The Thai side were a mixture of tough-as-teak Thais and expatriates and although it was very hot I enjoyed the game. The club and its members welcomed and somehow absorbed me. The club was to become the focal point of my life in Singapore.

I appreciated I was in Singapore for the technology transfer of whatever sales skills I could pass on to Alfred. Sperry Singapore was a small entity. The main customer was the Telecommunications Authority of Singapore, who had bought a Sperry 1100/60 to run the Swedish Telecommunications Company (Swedcom) software, which incorporated a database of installed copper circuits under the ground matched to a sophisticated mapping system. But first Sperry had to convert files from an IBM system to work with the new Sperry system. Alfred was the salesman to the Telecommunications Authority.

Before I had left the UK, Sperry was promoting its 'we understand how important it is to listen' advertising and promotional message. This message was included on letterheads and envelopes. The company distributed audio cassettes on learning how important it is to listen and training officers carried the message across the company. Thinking laterally, Alfred offered the course to TAS and it was very successful. One or two of the other state organisations also had the course.

At every TAS meeting, whatever the time of day or the length of the session, plates of green cake would appear with hot and cold soft drinks. The green cake took some getting used to, but became a part of the ritual of our meetings. Singaporeans can be very direct. Miss Lim Beng Choo was the systems and programming manager. Her main experience had been in using IBM equipment. She was not used to the Sperry 1100 hardware and software, and could be very aggressive in her approach: 'This is not the way we did things with IBM.' I should have listened. One day I went too far in defending the Sperry position, attacking 'IBM monkeys and their limited abilities in doing much more than peel bananas'. This was a crude, attempted analogy to suggest that Sperry systems did some things better or differently to IBM systems. Beng Choo did not appear to be too put out by my response, but Raoul Fischer, the Hong Kong company regional vice president, received a letter of complaint from the CEO about my attitude. Raoul replied nicely and asked that I drop a note of apology for any offence caused to Beng Choo. This done, I was well received during my next technical meeting and believe I was given an extra large piece of green cake. I am not sure if this was good or bad.

Alfred Tong was a delight to work with. He was prepared to tackle anything, and if that meant learning, for example, a new computer language, he would have set about that. As it was, the most significant business opportunity was that being pursued at the Housing and Development Board. In 1980, the board housed well over 80 per cent of the Singapore population and its policies were a strict implementation of Lee Kuan Yew's People's Action Party government policy. The board, known by its initials, HDB, was very visible everywhere in Singapore. Alfred had already developed an easy relationship with chief architect Dr Saw Boo Chan, who had the responsibility to take HDB computer policy into the 1980s. Dr Saw was open to any and all ideas of moving forward. We looked to Sperry to find application software that we might move into HDB, but at the time it had not been compiled into a directory we could easily use. We spent time following up on existing users of the Sperry Integrated Civil Engineering System (ICES) software package, but were not able to find another government authority using Sperry equipment with a cradle to grave responsibility. We were also restricted by government mandate, at the time, from being able to recommend an extension of the TAS database to encompass a property database for HDB, although the project team had every HDB property in their files. As a part of the bidding process, after submission of a full proposal we were invited to make a formal presentation of our recommendations to the HDB directors. I spent a number of weekends with Letraset and photographs putting together a 35 mm slide show to tell our story. Our presentation was very slick and professional looking. We brought the big guns in from Hong Kong and the US to participate in the presentation and to review our competencies. Working in pre-sales was back to basics for me, but it was a rewarding and a positive experience, which was why I was there. A tangible weakness in our story was a past local successful conversion from an IBM system. The work at TAS had not been completed and IBM made sure that HDB was aware that conversion was as much art as simple recompilation of the original IBM programs. We did not win the HDB business, but were in good shape to tackle the next big one.

The next big one was the Public Utilities Board, whose head office was opposite the Telecommunications Tower, and whose staff had the opportunity to mix in both work canteens and the hawker stalls at the back of Orchard Road. Once again, it would have made sense for us to sell on the back of the geographic infrastructure of the telecommunications network, but again we ran up against the government restrictions placed upon us and the politics between the two organisations.

The government was discussing its options on the development of a service-based economy. The country's recognised greatest asset was its well-educated, hard-working, and young population. Government wanted to discuss the viability of a national computer policy with the computer industry. Sperry worldwide had a large number of university users, but no real whole-of-government reference sites that we could identify and sell from. International Computers Limited (ICL) was in Singapore and saw a national policy incentive as a worthwhile investment on its part, and placed consultants in Ngee Ann Polytechnic, which was the designated lead establishment to look at the policy. Alfred, Frank, and I were able to develop a relationship with policy advisors, but we never got as close as the full-time ICL consultants.

In no time it was Christmas, and Audrey and the two boys joined me for their holiday. They found living at International Plaza rather spartan. I had to ask my two lodgers to find other lodgings in order to accommodate my family.

Figure 9.5: The view from my International Plaza apartment looking towards the OCBC Tower at back left.
Source: Author's collection.

I was walking with Audrey and the boys along Shenton Way to the Esplanade, the first Saturday she was there, as I was to play rugby. I had an admission to make:

> 'I have something to tell you. If you think that perhaps my approach to you has been less than aggressive, it is because, I have to admit … I have lost my front teeth. They were knocked out in a game against the Singapore Armed Forces side. I now have a bridge for the four missing teeth.'

Audrey almost guffawed in relief.

> 'I am so pleased. I have been worrying about how I was going to tell you that I have had accidents in both of the cars at home.'

Such is life.

I also had to tell the family that Al Harvey had asked me to extend the assignment for a further three months, to the end of March 1981, with the expectation I would be home for Easter.

I was given another general administration task. The rate of movement of staff from one computer company to another was hurting the users and the suppliers. It seemed as if the Singaporean technicians, mainly young women, would change jobs for even the smallest of salary increases. Under the chairmanship of Robert Iau, the president of the Singapore Computer Society and a deputy secretary of one of the government departments, we met to discuss the problem. I represented Sperry. All the computer companies sent a representative. Mr Iau is a forceful personality. Under his direction, we formulated a policy of using the US Hays Grade to define tasks and levels of responsibility for computer-related activities and set an upper and lower salary band for that level, one we could all agree to. We met some months after setting the policy and agreed it was working: staff were doing less job-hopping and productivity was better.

Robert Iau ran the Singapore Computer Society with a firm hand. I thought him far too authoritarian, and wrote unsolicited, published articles for the local computer press about the meetings with the byline of Bee C–Y. Robert was also a member of the Singapore Cricket Club. I subsequently came to learn and appreciate Robert's style. He was also very generous. We met on an aeroplane to Bangkok and he took me out on the town that night. I regretted I had ever written those articles, in ignorance of his competences.

9. ADVENTURES IN SOUTHEAST ASIA

During February in the New Year, I was working with Richard Hawkins in Kuala Lumpur when Sperry had a change of management for its Asia-Pacific region. I was in ignorance of the change, and had not seen Frank Dorrian when I got back to International Plaza on Friday night. I was sleeping in on the Saturday when the telephone rang. It was Frank.

> 'We have a new boss and he wants to see you. We are all waiting for you at the office.'

I tried to sneak into the back of the conference room without making a fuss, perhaps 40 minutes later. The man in the dark brown suit at the front saw me come in.

> 'Hello! Don't I know you?'
> 'Yes, Rom. I was working for John Woods at Remington House when you came in as UK managing director a few years ago now.'
> 'Yes, I thought so. What are you doing here?'
> 'Well, I'm sorry I am late, Rom. I was In Kuala Lumpur last week. I am working on assignment from the UK in pre-sales with the Singapore branch.'

Rom looked at me for a moment. He then looked up and wrote my name into an empty box on an organisation chart on the whiteboard.

> 'That fills that gap. Chris will take up the role of technical director.'

Gulp!

> 'Of what, Rom?'
> 'We are creating a new Asia region of the company.'

I sat down and listened. I was probably still in shock even after a game of rugby that afternoon and an evening at the cricket club when I met up with Rom again on the Sunday.

It was a dynamic reorganisation, and by no means cast in concrete, which was a good thing. For a brief while, Al Harvey and his team worked for me, as did the other worthies in the Hong Kong office. Everyone took the change pretty much in their stride. It did mean that a new Southeast Asia region had been recognised, which consisted of Singapore, where we sold directly in to the market, and included six countries where we sold via a distributor network: India, Indonesia, Malaysia, Philippines, Taiwan, and Thailand. These were perceived as being the hard countries.

ALSO INNOVATORS

Romuald A. Slimak was an American of Polish birth. Rom's appointment was as a vice president, which was a role he took very seriously. He immediately tried to get additional floor space at the OCBC Centre, but none was to be had. That forced a move to the Octagon in Robinson Road, a building close to completion. Rom delighted in the chance to influence the style and decoration of the eighth floor — we took the whole floor. Rom's *pièce de résistance* was the marble entrance foyer, which was re-laid three times before he was satisfied — but it did keep him occupied. He also took time to find a nice new Mercedes and a suitable residence for himself and Mrs Slimak. The house was a classic black-and-white mansion, after the style of an English Tudor house in huge grounds in Cornwall Gardens, very exclusive and at SGD$12,500 per month it needed to be good. Rom expanded the staff for the Singapore regional office and branch office.

Figure 9.6: Rom was fine with me using his image in light-hearted fashion for internal meetings. On other occasions, I put Frank Dorrian's head into the picture.
Source: Author's collection.

Rom was good at many facets of the job. He surprised us with his observation that he had been at the London School of Economics at the same time as the then Deputy Prime Minister of Singapore, Dr Goh Keng Swee. Rom took Frank Dorrian with him to meet Dr Goh. Rom's approach to Dr Goh was to ask if the Singapore Government would find it of value to place one or several of its favoured sons with us to give them experience of working with a multinational company in a sales role. We recruited Henry

Lau through Dr Goh Keng Swee. Sperry being the company it was, we went through the process of asking Henry to complete an application form and interview. Frank and I separately interviewed Henry. At 23, Henry was a Presidential Scholar who had attended Bath University in the UK, was Secretary of the Department of Defence with responsibility for 300,000 staff, chairman of the Singapore Symphony Orchestra, and Dr Goh's political advisor.

Frank and I recommended Henry for a sales job: 'Very suitable.' Here was someone of very high calibre and the government helped fulfil Henry's promise. As a Sperry salesman he was credited with sales to the Ministry of Education, the Singapore Internal Security Organisation, and the Singapore External Security Organisation, and some other sales contributions to round out his credentials. Henry became the chairman of Amdahl Computers in Singapore before he was 30 years of age.

The government of Singapore, under founding Prime Minister Lee Kuan Yew, was totally pragmatic. Mr Lee's National Day address in 1981 highlighted Singapore's strengths as its educated population, who were blessed with a fierce work ethic, and Singapore's key geographic position at the crossroads of Asia. The government made the decision to educate Singaporeans in the use of computers and, through the education minister, we were given every opportunity to be a part of and contributor to this policy. Henry had joined us by the time we were putting together some final thoughts to answer the opportunity. We proposed a European visit for ministry of education representatives. Another of the outstanding young Singaporeans, Tan Chin Nam, tall and confident, was appointed to lead the team. We expected Henry would accompany the team on this trip. Henry was hesitant and recommended that someone else might be more suitable — someone with more Sperry experience. I naively agreed to accompany the team. Selfishly, it made sense for me. I was due to spend Easter back with the family and discuss the extension of my tenure in Singapore with them, and maybe I'd be able to meet with Sperry UK.

The Singapore education study team and I did four or five excellent customer visits in Europe over 10 days, during which we saw Sperry computer systems involved in university and city infrastructure applications. We were not, however, able to show the visiting Singaporeans what they were hoping to see — another country developing a cadre of computer professionals upon whose skills an export market would be developed. I was able to brief Alan Stevens, 'the Bishop', now Birmingham branch manager, and Charles Pigden, still UK training manager. Through a round-table conference, we started to develop with our visitors the nucleus of an idea based upon the UK National Computer Centre model — they were looking at standardisation and training as key elements of a UK policy. Tan Chin Nam was warming to the direction our discussions were taking, and the meeting concluded with a positive feeling. That evening, Alan, Charles, and I tried to work out ways and means from the Sperry perspective. It was going to be very difficult. The Singapore Government wanted a computer manufacturer to take responsibility for setting up a training centre, with a team of experienced lecturers in Singapore, at the manufacturer's expense. We doubted that Sperry would buy that idea. (It did not. ICL did, providing nine senior lecturers for up to five years.) My trip with the team taught me a few things. When travelling with Singaporeans, expect to eat Chinese food for breakfast, lunch, and dinner. I understood and appreciated Henry Lau's grasp on the politics of reality. There was no way he was going to accompany the team without knowing he would come back with the order.

Shopping in Singapore for consumer goods in the 1980s was cheap. It was not just rumour. We found that the Chinese shopkeeper expected you to try to barter with him. Whatever price he quoted, the experienced shopper would offer 50 per cent. After haggling a price, when both parties were satisfied, you paid 70 to 80 per cent of the original asking price. This was the custom and it became a way of interfacing with the shopkeeper. The only drawback to this process was that visitors seemed to want to spend all day haggling with several shopkeepers for the same article to save a few dollars. We knew how the pricing worked. For example, the Japanese camera manufacturers were offering the retailer 11 units for the price of 10, so it was stock turnover that was driving the price.

Everything in Singapore had a reason. The People's Action Party Government under Lee Kuan Yew had been in power for 15 years and was pragmatic in its approach. It perhaps helped that all members of that parliament were from the People's Action Party. When I arrived, public offices were still showing a government notice to the effect that 'Males with long hair will be attended to last'.

Figure 9.7: A common sign in government offices in Singapore in the early 1980s.
Source: Wikipedia Commons.

As Singapore has four official languages — Chinese (Mandarin), English (sometimes referred to as Singlish), Malay (Bahasa), and Indian (Tamil) — most official signs carry the message in four languages, although not the 'no long hair' message. We lived through the process for the banning of betel nuts, chewed by Indians, colouring their teeth and mouths and spittle a bright red. I initially wondered what was adorning the pavements. Next came the 'do not spit' campaign. The 'one is enough' family planning policy was also current. This was partly rescinded, but it did have some unexpected consequences.

In the 1980s, Singaporean men were obliged to undertake National Service for two-and-a-half years, and serve on the National Reserve for a further 10 years. A dramatic result of this policy was fascinating and obvious as we went about doing business: young Singaporean women were the drivers of business and were entering the professions. Chinese culture prevented a young man from being able to work for a female his junior in years and status. All men effectively lost that two-and-a-half years of career opportunity. What was left for them? Becoming a salesman was one option.

Terry Thompson joined the office from the United States airlines group, where he had been working as financial controller, and was appointed director of distributor operations. These were the 'difficult' countries in which we sold through a local distributor. Rom endorsed the plan that I join Terry as technical director. From my perspective, this was six super jobs in one, concentrating on developing our business in India, Indonesia, Malaysia, Philippines, Taiwan and Thailand. We basically handled the pre-sales effort with and for the distributor, who took a margin on the sale — as did Sperry, of course — and handled the post-sales activities as best we could. Each country was culturally different, which determined how business would be done. Each country was so different I shall talk about my experiences with each of them as a separate entity.

What do I mean by 'difficult'? Another word might be 'corrupt' by the standards Sperry accepted. We sold through local distributors to isolate the company from any suggestion that our business practices were anything other than competitive. The distributor functioned independently and isolated Sperry from whatever business practices were prevalent in the country.

As a Sperry employee my contract forbade me from indulging in corrupt practice. Depending on the relationship I developed with each distributor, they might explain their business relationships with their customers or not. My role was to provide the technical interface. The Sperry relationship and contract to provide equipment and technical support was with the local distributor.

Terry appreciated the added value that the Singaporean office staff gave to our work, although he was never at ease with them. He invited the whole office to a Christmas party at his apartment, which was easily large enough to accommodate 50 party-goers. He called me on the telephone early the next morning in an agitated state and told me that the local engineers had thrown his barbells from the apartment balcony into the car park below, and the Singapore police were at his place. I must have enjoyed the party, within walking distance from where we lived, but I did not put the facts together as I should have: 'So what if barbells had gone over the balcony?' I was picturing a small stand with miniscule tinkling bells on it. It was only when I got to the Wing on Life Tower and saw the crater that Terry's exercise weights had made in the concrete below that I appreciated his concern. The police suspected that it must have taken a team effort to lift the actual bar, as all the weights were on it. The customer engineers were suspected, but no action was taken.

9. ADVENTURES IN SOUTHEAST ASIA

Rom Slimak stayed with us long enough to effect the move to the Octagon and begin to enjoy his life in Singapore. He left Singapore in September 1983. I cannot remember that Rom did much travelling, and neither Terry Thompson nor I forgave him for one trip to India to meet the management of ORG Systems, our Indian distributor. Rom insisted that the meeting take place at Delhi Airport, so that he need not leave the airport before returning directly to Singapore. This example did not encourage our Singaporean-Chinese support staff, who had an aversion to going to India anyway. If they travelled there at all, they carried their own rice and water for the duration of their stay.

One story about Rom that I have told many times involves the visit of Gerry Probst, the (Mormon) CEO of Sperry Corporation, who had attended Harvard Business School at the same time as President Suharto of Indonesia. It was President Suharto's turn to host an alumni gathering, which Mr Probst decided to attend. Sperry representatives were lining up to accompany Mr Probst to Jakarta as protocol demanded. I thought it really big of both Mr Probst and Rom Slimak to decide I should have that honour, as it was I who had the most interface with the Soedarpo Corporation, our Indonesian distributor.

I had spent the week in Taiwan. On the Friday morning I left the Taipei hotel very early, as getting through Taipei Customs could be very difficult. Taiwan at that time had no recognition of copyright, but its customs could be ruthless in removing the title pages of plagiarised books to maintain face to the outside world. If the day was a 'search all luggage for locally printed books and tear out the title pages' day, the queues in customs could cause one to miss the flight. It was not going to happen to me. It was a quiet day, and I was clear of customs and in the first-class lounge at 4.30 am awaiting the 6.30 am flight to Singapore. I mixed myself a couple of fiendish Bloody Marys and was in fine form when the champagne was distributed in first-class during the flight. I got back to Changi Airport about midday and went straight to the Octagon. The place was deserted. Rom was entertaining Mr Probst and the staff at lunch prior to a barbecue at his home in the evening. I did whatever work was instantly apparent and went for my own lunch in the Ship, an English-style pub in Robinson Road, where I met up with my banker pal, Euan Ansley. I stayed in the pub until I had an early evening call from Audrey reminding me that we were due at Rom's.

Audrey brought a change of clothes for me and I changed at Rom's house. It was a swinging party — I have to admit that I was swinging. I had been drinking, albeit slowly, for some 14 or 15 hours before getting to the party. It was obvious, even to me, that discretion was to be the better part of valour, and that it would not be appropriate for me to enter into conversation with Mr Probst. It must have been a bit obvious, because Mrs Probst managed to corner me to ask that I talk to her husband, as 'Gerry is keen to meet you, as he wants to know what subjects will be raised in Jakarta'. Mr Probst did not drink at all, so I thought it better that we talk in the garden. I could not remember the conversation. My colleagues said that it was a long conversation that appeared animated from a distance. I learned later, when the company policy with regard to the cost of spare parts — which had always been a real problem for the distributors — was changed, that I had been able to make at least one point. The cost of spares was halved. Something else I learned later happened at the end of the evening. A few of us, including Audrey, myself, and Richard Hawkins, stripped down to our underwear to use Rom's swimming pool. Messrs Slimak and Probst were apparently watching with binoculars from the house. I accompanied Mr and Mrs Probst to Jakarta and to the palace, where the Harvard class reunion was taking place, and got to shake the president's hand before leaving.

Uruguayan-born Gus Sichero replaced Rom as vice president of the region. Gus had a successful sales and management career with Sperry in South America and the US. Gus was ready for the rough and tumble of the distributor world, and was a great support in deriving aggressive pricing strategies for targeted accounts. He and Terry Thompson would spend hours with their yellow accountant's pads honing in on a winning number. Gus was an inspired user of 3M Post-it notes. He insisted on noting action items and dates for completion as a result of every discussion, writing these down on the yellow stickers. These were placed in his desk diary on the targeted completion date. You could be very sure that, come the day, Gus or Albina (Rom Slimak's secretary) would telephone to ask for confirmation of the completed task. Gus never missed a deadline. It soon taught us the importance of getting his jobs done on time.

On the following pages I show a few photographs from the distributor conference we put on in 1984. It was the first such regional conference Sperry had initiated. It was a huge success.

9. ADVENTURES IN SOUTHEAST ASIA

Figure 9.8: We were able to publicise our conference on the front of the Hilton Hotel, the venue for our meeting. This excited our distributors and demonstrated our commitment to the business. This banner was photographed and shown in *The Straits Times*.
Source: Author's collection.

Figure 9.9: What a good-looking lot. Gus Sichero in the centre sits between Terry Thompson and Mr Soedarpo. Richard Hawkins is the beanpole at the back.
Source: Author's collection.

Figure 9.10: The leaders of a successful sales grouping, from eight different nations.
Source: Author's collection.

Figure 9.11: The conference party at Terry's apartment. Sumra Manning tries out the first Sperry PC in Southeast Asia (actually made by Mitsubishi), while Richard and Marion Hawkins watch from the back.
Source: Author's collection.

9. ADVENTURES IN SOUTHEAST ASIA

Gus left Singapore after a gruelling session with Mr Soedarpo of the Soedarpo Corporation (recounted below), and was replaced by Tom Yam, another Sperry stalwart, from the US. Tom was Hong Kong Chinese and his appointment occurred at a most appropriate time. The Singaporean Government was beginning to question the continued employment of expatriates who had been encouraged to the island state to help effect a technology transfer. The government was asking if the transfer had been effective and if it was time for locals to take more responsibility. Tom was determined to be seen to make a difference. That determination led to Terry Thompson's dismissal and my wish to look for a different challenge. The timing for my change was perfect. Our two boys had left Singapore for the UK (rather than having to serve two-and-a-half years of Singapore National Service), and Audrey was no longer keen to be alone for the 250 nights a year that my job demanded I be away from Singapore.

Although I have written positively about the timing of my completion of tasks in Singapore there were a few negative experiences.

I had a rugby accident in early 1985. The Singapore Cricket Club was playing the New Zealand Infantry Regiment at Sembawang Barracks and, as ever, it was a close game. I was playing hooker between two of the strongest men I have ever known, but we had been pinned down into a sequence of scrums under our own posts. On perhaps the sixth attempt, Andy Martin, a future New Zealand All Blacks manager, did not go down straight. I was badly bent. The problem was diagnosed some months later as an exploded disc. Part of the disc between the fourth and fifth vertebrae had disintegrated. Final diagnosis was made during an operation at Gleneagles Hospital, and kept me out of the office for two weeks. The surgeon wanted me to have three months bed rest, and I had to explain to him that, while working for an US company, three months leave was not an option. Only twice in my working life have I had cause not to be in the office, other than for an agreed vacation. Both times saw me needing to look for another job.

Who said business was easy?

On the following pages I recount my experiences working and travelling throughout Southeast Asia for the Sperry Corporation.

ALSO INNOVATORS

India

I thoroughly enjoyed the opportunity to work and travel extensively in India.

Our Indian distributor was ORG Systems of Baroda. ORG was originally the acronym for Operations Research Group, which described the origins of this division of the Ambalal Sarabhai Enterprises Limited, at the time one of the top 10 Indian family-owned and operated consortiums.

India was regarded by Sperry as a hardship posting and the company offered to pay a hardship allowance of US$30 per day for time spent there. I do not think it made any difference, but it was an anomaly. It also caused accounting problems with the payroll departments at home, as most of us were on assignments from a home country. The compromise offer was that, travelling from Singapore, we were encouraged to stay over in Bangkok for a day on the outward and return trips to recover. This was never a problem, as I always had tasks to do with Summit Computer Company there.

Figure 9.12: The street in which ORG Systems had its New Delhi office, 'near the Priya Cinema' as I learnt to ask the taxi driver.
Source: Author's collection.

India is a fascinating, vibrant place. You know you are somewhere different when the aeroplane doors open and the air conditioning is replaced by a warm, moist, and spicy embrace. It is a mixture of people, animals and dust. Immediately leaving the aeroplane, you notice what appear to be piles of rubbish swept against the wall — these are people asleep in the terminal. You cannot tell if they are staff or visitors in waiting. People are everywhere. Once outside of the confines of the terminal, there is the noise of living people, traffic and machinery. The roads are packed with people — so many people.

I worked most closely with Hari Dave (pronounced Dar-vay), the ORG sales manager, and V. K. Malhotra, the ORG software and support manager.

Hari was probably in his late 30s, running towards being plump. Hari's safari suits never seemed quite full enough around his waist. He moved from one crisis to the next and was always in a hurry between assignments. He was a shrewd and skilled computer generalist, a good man to have around in the Indian marketplace that had been abandoned by IBM in 1977 when the Indian Government would not permit IBM to retain a controlling interest in its Indian subsidiary. V. K. M. Sharma was ORG executive director. A slender, small, slightly hunched man with grey hair, we would see him at the ORG office of an evening. His interjections were always insightful, and it was a pleasure to do business with him. I never got to the head office at Baroda, but Terry Thompson did, and was impressed with the top management of ORG.

Figure 9.13: ORG representatives at the Sperry Singapore distributor conference. Left to right: Hari Dave, D. N. Jetley, and V. K. Malhotra.
Source: Author's collection.

V. K. Malhotra was technically very competent, although somewhat academic in his approach. The Indians were gifted programmers whose education (and comparative lack of resources) made them most disciplined analysts and programmers — they actually read and understood the manuals. This did not happen anywhere else in my experience — and still does not. D. N. Jetley, the ORG marketing manager, was the political mover and shaker, and he used his role as president of one of the branches of the Indian Professional Engineering Association as a part of his selling technique. Bringhi Dev was a young, scholarly looking, energetic ORG salesman in Bangalore, the Garden City. He had reason for his enthusiasm, as we eventually had a number of installations along the main thoroughfare in prestigious organisations, including Bharat Heavy Electricals Limited, Hindustan Aeronautics Limited, the National Aeronautical Laboratory, and the Indian Space Research Organisation.

We did not meet many of the ORG workers. We only came across them on customer sites, when our focus was generally on talking to customers. ORG did a good job. Customer complaints, if they were raised and were not easily resolved by ORG, would need a Sperry intervention, which was my responsibility.

We never got really close to our Indian colleagues. They were work friends, but the social aspect was largely ignored. Delhi was dry at this time, although occasionally ORG senior management would meet us at the Maurya Sheraton in Delhi for a drink or two. But apart from Hari sometimes dropping me off at a hotel, we did not meet outside of working hours. D. N. Jetley was an exception. He invited Audrey and me to his house for dinner on one occasion that Audrey was in Delhi. We went to the family compound and met the extended family supported by D. N. We had a wonderful evening, and were particularly taken by the younger children, who seemed fascinated by our fair complexions and hair. We had received the invitation before leaving Singapore and asked if there was anything we could bring as a gift. We were asked to bring a foodmixer. We thought Mrs Jetley would want a big Kenwood Chef electric device but her ambition was much more modest. A battery-driven whisk would be wonderful. Her concern was the availability of spares should there ever be a problem. India in the early 1980s was without the extensive use of plastic utensils we were used to in Singapore, and even simple gifts of nesting plastic boxes were ideal gifts for our colleagues. Once they

9. ADVENTURES IN SOUTHEAST ASIA

knew we were OK to bring small items, we would receive long pleading requests for the most mundane of items, which would bring the promise of 'everlasting gratitude and fulsome thanks for your kindness'.

A noteworthy problem in India was the availability of systems and programming manuals. Sperry did not generally expect to provide many copies of manuals for the 1100 systems, and these were subject to continual update. The US Government stipulated that Sperry only supply one copy of technical manuals to our Indian customers. At the same time, India had a ban upon the import of foreign copier machines, so it was not easy for the user to reproduce manuals for the large number of programmers who needed to consult them. The single copy of manuals we provided were copied by hand at desks under strict control. I suspect also that management tended to keep the printed set of the manuals in their offices as a status symbol. The manuals on the shop floor were in constant use and quickly became soiled and dog-eared. Despite all the material things that the Indians might have asked us for, we were always asked for extra copies of technical documentation. Paper is heavy, but we all did our best to meet these needs.

There were a number of significant installations in India which interested Terry and me. Air India in Bombay was the most prestigious, and was a reference site of world status. Bharat Heavy Electricals Limited (BHEL) had Sperry 1108 large computer system installations at Hardwar and at Bangalore. Indian Airlines, the government-owned domestic carrier, had indicated its wish to use the UNIVAC Standard Airline System, but never had enough clout to be able to convince government to allow them to budget and buy the system. We also had a large number of Varian installations from the Sperry takeover of Varian, who we saw as potential customers for upgrade to the current Sperry range of equipment. ORG Systems expected Sperry to help with the sale of the computer system and the inevitable negotiations about price and margins, but ORG would undertake the installation and all the post-sale support.

Indira Gandhi was enjoying a second term in office with its non-aligned government policy. The US Government was unhappy with this, as India's 'non-alignment' was slanted towards Russia in order to gain access to military technology and weapons. Prior to the escalation of the Cold War in the 1970s, Russia had purchased an airline system for Aeroflot from Sperry UNIVAC. Before I ever got to India the rumour was rife, even back in the UK, that Aeroflot was being supplied with spare parts and support through India. I never saw any indication of that. The Indian Government computer acquisition policies controlled by the Department of Electronics mandated spares holding for five years within the one-off purchase price, and ORG always bought the Sperry recommended spares. It was unlikely that any ORG customer would want to see his spares being re-exported. The Indian Government was not on the approved US list of favoured customers, and with each potential sale we had to make application to the US Department of Commerce for permission to sell a Sperry system. Terry and I used long aeroplane trips to put together the words to convince the US Department of Commerce that the sale of equipment to Indian Space Research Organisation did not infringe its rules about the uses US manufactured computers could be put to. We emphasised potential administrative functions — payroll, for example, or library inventory. As it was, the systems we were selling, other than to the airlines, were for manufacturing purposes and particularly for computer-aided design (CAD), and all our systems included advanced graphics terminals from a third-party supplier, usually Tektronix. BHEL told us privately that it manufactured electric transformers, under licence from Russia, and that they were so superior to the Russian equivalents that the Indian-built units were used in key installations. It told us a similar story about the MiG-23 fighter aircraft later manufactured by Hindustan Aeronautics Limited.

Under ORG's direction, a sale took a prescribed path. ORG waited for publication of the list of systems that the Department of Electronics was to purchase in the next year. We did not meet all the potential customers prior to tender submission. The department would issue its request for tender, with very specific requirements covering all elements of hardware and software. Memory size and speed, and the instruction set were specified, as were basic units such as card readers, card punches and software levels to prescribed standards. We met many of the department technicians, as they were assigned to a particular system requirement, but at all times were very aware of the overriding influence of Dr Seshegari, the head of the Department of Electronics in Bombay.

ORG collected the tender request from the Department of Electronics. I would draft the response if it was to be anything other than straightforward. Terry or I would derive a price to ORG, including the five year spares complement. The department would have specified its buy price, and more times than not Hari Dave would try and negotiate our price down. The hardware was often sold by ORG at very small margins, as it had the capacity to make money through technical support, project management, program development, and the mandatory five-year maintenance agreement. In 1980–1984, Sperry was still providing software within the hardware price, with the exception of CAD software, which we onsold without margin.

The department's tender request followed a proforma, with the first 12 pages listing the specific hardware and software components of what it wanted. The 12 pages were publicly exhibited at the department for a few days after the tender submission. ORG sent a suitably qualified engineer to make a written note of every response. The selection criteria was based upon how closely the vendor was able to match the stated requirement. Occasionally, a vendor would announce a new product to the Indian Government before it was announced elsewhere in the world, which was valuable market intelligence. Importantly, ORG would challenge the other vendor's capability statements, verbally and in writing, and expect to win the tender through discrediting of another vendor's solution. Burroughs always had problems as it did not have a standard 200 cards per minute card punch. This was a real Achilles heel for it, and often left the field clear for ORG and Sperry.

A typical week in India for Terry or me involved leaving Singapore late evening Sunday to meet with the Department of Electronics for a day and a half in Bombay. We presented the latest Sperry product slide sets as a precursor to a general discussion about our company's latest and greatest developments. IBM had withdrawn from India. We expected some competition from Burroughs, and perhaps ICL, although occasionally IBM would bid direct to maintain a technical presence. Our visits to the department were not only to push the knowledge barriers. We were also asked to help with the drafting of the next set of requests for tender. If we did not state what we had to sell, the department would not know to ask for it. Wednesday and Thursday of the week would be spent in Bangalore, Ranchi, or Calcutta talking to customers. Friday would be spent in Delhi before catching the overnight flight back to Singapore. Terry would sometimes stop over to play golf, but I invariably had a game of rugby or cricket (or both) in which to participate in Singapore.

The US Department of Commerce had concerns about our selling technology that might be used for unfriendly applications. Sperry also had a concern about our selling the latest technology because of a fear that it would be copied. Our distributor, ORG Systems, also manufactured hardware, which it barely disguised as a copy of a Sperry original when it was designated with the same type number. Six months after we delivered the first of the Uniservo VIC magnetic tape drives to India, ORG announced its own, similarly specified ORG 6C tape drive, which even looked the same as ours. Interestingly, there were no restrictions imposed upon our releasing the latest versions of software.

The Indian Department of Electronics prohibited our bidding of a programmable communications front-end processor, and we were left to bid an old but highly reliable hardware switch. It was our belief that the department wanted Indian manufacturers to develop their own communications solution, as it was obvious that communication networks were going to be a big thing in the future.

We did not always get it right, even if we had a good relationship with a prospective customer and an understanding of what was required to provide the application support he was looking for. D. N. Jetley was keen we should make a good showing at the Steel Authority of India Limited (SAIL) Research and Development Centre at Bhilai. We were due to meet Dr Detna of SAIL in Delhi, after the submission of our formal proposal and presentation to the Department of Electronics. The day before we met him, he advised that the competition was fierce. Although the three tenderers were answering a request for a defined hardware capability and software, the situation was as appears below:

Technical ranking by SAIL	Supplier's response	Price to SAIL (US$)
1	ORG/Sperry 1100/72	2.8 million
2	ICL 2996/7	1.2 million
3	Honeywell	2.2 million

In such a situation, I was obligated to report to Sperry that price was a problem. Given time, we might have been able to challenge the Honeywell price, but not the relatively low ICL bid price. We never really knew if ICL had determined SAIL was a strategic account it had to have.

I got it into my head that I wanted to visit the BHEL installation in Hardwar, in the Uttar Pradesh province in the north-east. The name of the town was one that Sperry never spelt correctly (and Microsoft Word is still prompting me that it is typed wrongly). As a computer company, everyone added the extra 'e' and spelled it 'Hardware'. I told Hari Dave that I wanted to make this visit. He had never been there, nor had anyone from Sperry. Hari hired a taxi from the Delhi street for me and told the driver I would need the car for three days. The drive to Hardwar was long and dusty, going into the foothills of the Himalayas. Hardwar is an important religious centre for Hindus, and is regarded as the birthplace of Mother Ganga, being the first town on the Ganges River. It took perhaps eight hours to drive there. Having arrived, photographs were taken by the company sign to prove we had arrived at the BHEL enclave.

Figure 9.14: My picture of the taxi driver at our destination.
Source: Author's collection.

We approached the factory down a long drive, and were conscious of a crowd of people about the entrance area, but they showed no concern when we drove up. I went in the main entrance to announce myself. A manager came out to see me. I was expected. But I was not expected to arrive in a taxi. Would I mind going back to the main gate and coming back again? Nothing surprised me in India, so I did as I was bid. When we drove back to the main entrance again, the crowds had been formed into a group with musical instruments. As I got out of the taxi, I was greeted by a discordant rendition of 'Rule, Britannia' — 'Britons never will be slaves' — played by the BHEL Works Band. It was a lovely compliment and still brings a smile. I wonder who warned them I was an Englishman.

Having made the trip, it was inevitable that I should be asked to look around the computer room. This required removal of shoes and socks and rolling trouser legs up to walk through a disinfectant pool at the entrance and over a drying mat. The operations staff were wearing thongs in the centre. Presumably the pool was to remove the threat of dust. I recognised the Sperry 1108 hardware, but commented on the fact that two operators were writing down all the console messages on pads. I also saw that they were writing alternate lines. Exec 8, the 1100 operating system, could produce a lot of console messages. I asked why the console printer was not being used and learned another unforeseen obstacle to Indian use of the latest technology: the Indian Government prohibited the import of printer ribbons, expecting they could manufacture their own. This console requires a unique 13-inch-wide ribbon. BHEL staff had been copying the console messages in longhand, which had to be written out again in correct sequence for years. I did not say anything, but was able to find a Sperry source, and the next time one of us visited India he carried six of the correct ribbons destined for Hardwar. A used ribbon might again be impregnated with ink to extend its usefulness. (As Westerners we did not expect to be impeded by customs when entering India, but Indians returning home would be expected to empty every bit of baggage they were carrying and even empty their pockets. Some of the bags the locals carried back were huge and looked heavy. In observing activity in customs, you could see that people were indeed bringing in the consumer goods that were not available on the subcontinent.)

I stayed two nights in Hardwar at the BHEL company house, which was basic but very clean. After dinner with D. N. Sud, the BHEL deputy manager, I asked the taxi driver to take me into town and had a fascinating evening absorbing the spectacle. Hardwar is a religious centre, and the devout were bathing in the Ganges from constructed ghats along the banks on both sides of the river, seemingly from every available access point.

Sperry generally had success selling in India. The competitor we met the most frequently was the Burroughs Corporation. Burroughs's reputation was based upon the banking and finance sectors, not the airline or engineering sectors where we were winning orders. In the four years that Terry Thompson and I were involved, we won most of the medium to large scale computer business in competition with them. We would also compete against ICL, CDC, Honeywell, and Data General. We were, however, concerned at ORG's 'wait and see' approach to future orders, and we initiated a rapport with companies we thought significant. Terry put in several months of hard bargaining to convince S. K. Sengupta,

9. ADVENTURES IN SOUTHEAST ASIA

who was consulting to Indian Airlines as its deputy director of finance, that a submission to the Department of Electronics would be successful. It was. Sperry had been waiting for a number of years to fulfil that need.

Indian Rail was another organisation to whom we believed we could sell without ORG initiative. Indian Rail used IBM 1401 systems, some with magnetic tape storage, and with the withdrawal of IBM from India was maintaining its own equipment. As the rest of the world grew out of vintage IBM 1401 technologies, Indian Rail purchased them for additional installations and spare parts. We did not know whether to believe Indian Rail when it claimed to have over 100 IBM 1401s in service — it probably did. We knew that railway travel in India was not only a practical way to get about, but was also a recognised tourist attraction. We approached the rail company on the back of our UNIVAC Standard Airline System (USAS) reservation systems, and there was an immediate enthusiasm. The railway requirement was for a reservation system that would also record personal details of the purchaser. We had only to see the queues at the main Delhi stations to see the reason they needed a system. The queues were horrendous and people with money would employ professional queuers to wait in line for the hours it took to get to the head of the queue. Indian Railways wanted to stop this proxy purchasing by having the ticket carry a form of purchaser identity. Its argument was related to the value it perceived of the ticket. At this time we were working with the Malaysian Government's Department of Roads for a licence with a portrait of the driver for the same reason: in Malaysia, the wealthy would employ test-takers to pass their mandatory on-road tests. This sort of photo-image technology was impractical and too expensive to consider for railway tickets. We opened a good dialogue with Indian Railways, but were not able to come up with an affordable solution.

The post and telegraphs organisation was also targeted. We knew post and telegraphs business first-hand through our work with Telecom in Singapore, and were able to talk sensible applications. I met N. T. Sinha, a posts and telegraphs director, half a dozen times in the hope that when the Department of Electronics worked with it to define its computing needs it would prejudice its requirements towards us. Indian Post and Telegraphs was huge, operating over 150,000 post offices.

I did a lot of work with the Oil and Natural Gas Corporation (ONGC), which was based in the Dehradun chemical engineering enclave. ONGC was looking for oil and petroleum application packages at the same time as PETRONAS, the Malaysian oil and exploration enterprise, so it was handy to be able to share information with both. IBM was fighting for the ONGC contract, looking for a way back into India that was not as the junior partner of an Indian joint venture, and was a formidable competitor. As it was flying in everybody who spoke to ONGC, it was able to bring in the real experts from its worldwide petroleum industry customer base. But flying people in is not as effective as being in-country, as ORG and Sperry were able to prove. There is no doubt that we did not have the applications portfolio of IBM, but the solutions we were putting forward to PETRONAS were equally applicable to ONGC. Another factor in Sperry's advantage was that we were still mainly a bundled supplier. IBM had separate price lists for hardware, software and support, whereas we still provided a total inclusive price. However, this was about to change with a deal we were negotiating with Air India.

We won orders and the ongoing potential was high. Richard Hawkins, who had been our man in Malaysia, moved his family to Singapore and took prime sales responsibility for India. Richard commuted to India one week in two and was able to cement our good relationships with the Department of Electronics, ORG Systems, and our increasing customer base. Richard's appointment reduced the need for Terry and me to travel there quite so much. Richard was a natural for India, and soon set up his sideline business based upon the barter of fake watches from Singapore for antique scientific instruments he would find in Indian antique shops, which he then sold to finance the purchase of vintage car parts from London or Melbourne for shipment to Singapore and his vintage car interests. Richard would later hone this business to the extent it threatened to overwhelm his real job.

We had enough business and interest to hold an Indian user group meeting. The role of chairman of the group fell naturally to Mr Jayant of Air India, who was a legend within Sperry Corporation — as we were called at the time. Mr Jayant was assistant director of data processing at Air India in Bombay. Although the word 'assistant' featured in his job title, his was a government appointment, and Mr Jayant was definitely in charge of the department. Mr Jayant not only frightened Sperry staff, I have subsequently learned that even his senior staff would avoid walking past his open office door in dread of being seen and asked in to 'explain'. I had heard that Jayant — we always pronounced it as 'giant' — delighted in terrorising Sperry senior staff. I had met Jayant several times and quite liked the man. We did our technical work with K. K. Venkateswaran and S. Ranganathan, but it was Jayant who controlled the relationship.

Getting to the Air India Santacruz, Bombay, offices was pretty dreadful. The verge of the road on both sides was used as a public toilet by the residents of the shanty town — men in the morning and the ladies in the afternoon, and playing in the mess were children, white egrets, and hogs. Even the taxi driver would request that the car windows be closed as we approached or left the airport surrounds.

At the beginning of February 1983, Sperry and ORG participated in the three-day Electronics USA 1983 exhibition, held at the Maurya Sheraton in Delhi. We imported new terminal equipment from the US, and support staff to operate the equipment and demonstrate the Mapper product from the UK. We used the event for formal presentations to teams from Indian Railways and Indian Airlines. The UK people, Terry and I attended and enjoyed US Ambassador Hallock R. Lucius's cocktail party, and I was pleased to meet a Singapore Cricket Club rugby-playing pal, who I normally found in Bangkok. Kevin Payne was representing Geophysical Sciences Incorporated at the exhibition.

Figure 9.15: People queuing to look at the ORG display at the Electronics USA 1983 exhibition in the Maurya Sheraton.
Source: Author's collection.

We held the Sperry Users Association India meeting in Delhi on the Thursday and Friday of that week. Terry had left for a meeting with Air India and returned to Delhi with Mr Jayant. Most of the user meeting attendees had been able to see a new Sperry PC at the exhibition, and we kept it for the extra two days for one-on-one demonstrations. The meeting went well. Mr Jayant vigorously pursued his theme of the developing country — India — being held back by the First World — Sperry — in refusing to provide adequate numbers of programming and systems manuals, or share design philosophies from the research laboratories. This was Jayant at his politicking best. To an extent, we agreed with him. But it was nothing new. We had invited Department of Electronics people to participate in the afternoon's Mapper presentation and demonstration to the user group. This was successful. Jayant told the Department of Electronics, within the hearing range of Mr Sengupta of Indian Airlines, that, as the international carrier and experienced Sperry USAS user, Air India should be appointed to supervise the domestic airline's use of computing. This was another theme we were used to, as was Sengupta.

After the Sperry users' meeting, I took the ORG team to Bangalore to pursue more business there. Bangalore was the centre of computer and aerospace activity in India. Perhaps it was because I had ORG personnel away from their homes that on the Monday evening we all went out to the Talk of the Town nightclub. The atmosphere was more like a UK working man's club than a nightclub. When young women came on to the stage to strip, I did wonder if the boys had brought me here because of a misguided idea it was what I wanted. That worry was soon dispelled. I believe I was the only foreigner present. The first young lady — who was quite slim — disrobed from her sari to stand before us in a formidable bikini. I suspect I was the only person to applaud, even politely. Ten ladies danced for us, one at a time. By the time the tenth lady disrobed, the audience was noisy, ecstatically enthusiastic, and calling for more. This last lady was enormous. This was a real culture shock.

Other orders for Sperry 1100/61 systems were taken from the Uttar Pradesh Government, and MECON in Ranchi, South India. MECON (Metallurgical Engineering Consultants) and Ranchi would come to haunt me. It took several months for ORG to install the equipment so that I could provide Sperry with a signed customer acceptance certificate. The problem was the uncertainty of the public power supply in Ranchi. Once we had the hardware installed, we needed to run extensive software tests on the individual hardware components before we set about installing the operating software. We needed something like 30 hours of uninterrupted running to tailor the software for the particular hardware set. Daily

9. ADVENTURES IN SOUTHEAST ASIA

brownouts prevented completion of the software installation. MECON had ordered a no-fail power backup system from an Indian supplier, but it was not yet available.

In early 1984, I forecasted that Air India would acquire the cargo reservation system of the UNIVAC Standard Airline System (USAS), along with message switching. These two items would just about complete the set of USAS software modules, which was seen as a tremendous opportunity. The timing was also such that Air India would be the first Southeast Asian Airline that would be expected to pay the real price for the software. Sperry was belatedly unbundling the hardware, software, and support charges. We were a market follower in this respect. The cargo proposal also included a substantial hardware element and would be by far the biggest order in our region for that fiscal year.

The big potential order attracted the attention of the new vice president of sales in the airline division, Pehr Leufven, a Swede who had been responsible for the sale of the Scandinavian Airlines System in the Nordic countries. We tried to put Pehr off wanting to visit India. Terry Thompson was very possessive of our relationship with Indian Airlines, the domestic carrier, and Air India, the international carrier. After several years of promising to do so, Indian Airlines had signed up for the USAS Passenger Reservation System hardware and software the previous year, and was in the process of implementation. Mr Jayant was politicking for a merger of the two airlines' data processing activities. Pehr would not be put off. Terry agreed to convene a meeting with Mr Jayant on the basis that we accompany Pehr and get a three-day opportunity to brief him before we saw Mr Jayant.

Pehr Leufven was a couple of days late arriving at the first-class Ambassador hotel where we were staying in Bombay. When he arrived, he was tired and angry and not at all interested in the dire warnings we addressed to him to be very, very careful in his initial approach to Mr Jayant. He knew better, and was content to go through the technical aspects of our proposals, but not the personal relationship aspects.

At the appointed hour we piled into a taxi, which was too small for five people. As 'locals', we took our coats off and loosened our ties. Pehr did not. We dressed again at Air India's reception from where we were shown into the visitor's broom cupboard. There were not enough chairs for five people, so someone had to stand. It was very hot so we disrobed again, as much as was practical. Again, Pehr did not take the advantage we suggested. Eventually, we were ushered in to Mr Jayant's presence. Another obvious sign of Mr Jayant's status was the fact that he had a lady secretary who was very pretty. In Mr Jayant's office the air conditioning units were performing at maximum capacity. We locals were better off, as we were able to put our jackets back on, but poor Pehr, whose suit was wet and hanging disconsolately from his shoulders by this time, had no such relief. In no time, he was shivering violently and looked most unhappy.

Mr Jayant was dressed in an elegant, pale blue safari suit and was quite at ease behind his big desk. He enquired about the health of the home team, one at a time, and showed his familiarity with us all. Terry was questioned about his wife's piano lessons. Wayne answered questions about the large amount of travel that was his life. I discussed my wife's and children's activities in Singapore. Frank was asked if he was enjoying his transfer to Terry's group, having relinquished the role of Singapore branch manager. Mr Jayant then turned to Pehr:

> 'And you, Mr Leufven. Welcome to Air India. Any number of other senior Sperry people have visited me and sat where you are now. They only ever come the one time. Do you think it is because they lose interest in us after we have signed a new contract, or is it because as a Third World country we make more demands upon Sperry support than other users?'

This was a good Jayant leading question. We held our breath. We had warned Pehr.

> 'Mr Jayant, thank you for your welcome. Of course, there is truth in both parts of your question.'

At this, Jayant leapt from his chair.

> 'Mr Leufven, please leave. I do not think we can have a relationship if that is the preconceived attitude you bring to this meeting. Goodbye!'

Pehr had no option but to leave. He waited outside the office during the time that we spent with Mr Jayant. He was not a happy person, but did have the good grace to admit that we had tried to warn him. Pehr bought us a really good meal that evening. As Mr Jayant predicted, Pehr was never seen in Bombay again.

Frank Dorrian took over Richard Hawkins's Indian territory, after Richard returned to Melbourne, in time to close the Air India upgrade order, which was far and away Sperry's largest single order through its distributor

9. ADVENTURES IN SOUTHEAST ASIA

operations in 1984. The overall price was US$5.8 million, plus an ORG Systems service fee of 1,52,87,000 rupees.[1] This included a software charge of US$781,000 — the first time we charged for software in India or the region. It was a difficult project for Frank to have to assume. He had to build a relationship with Mr Jayant and stick firmly to the agreed price schedule, which had been lodged 12 months earlier with the Department of Electronics. It was not an easy project from which to extricate myself, as this proposal was the culmination of 30 months of work with Jayant and his team. We had evaluated almost every word that was written in the business case section of the bid. It was undoubtedly a good order to get.

I was afforded the opportunity to say goodbye, after five years, to the friends I had made within the Department of Electronics, our customers, and ORG Systems. ORG was very gracious, and took me out for lunch at the Maurya Sheraton Hotel. During lunch, Hari Dave stood and said:

'Thank you, Chris. You have been a very special friend to India.'

I had to interrupt.

'Hari, I have done nothing special. As you know, I have enjoyed every visit.'

'No, Chris. You have been very special. You are the only Westerner who has drunk the water.'

Whoops! My life flashed before my eyes. On my first morning in Delhi, I had almost gagged drinking a tea that had been brewing on the stove for days; it would have been pure tannin had a substantial amount of condensed milk not been added. It was as awful as Irish tea, also brewed constantly. After this, I always asked for water. I realised in that instant that the ORG guys had been going on to the street to stop a water carrier, using the handleless chipped cup to scoop the warmish water from the tin panniers either side of the back wheel. There was no running water in ORG's office. That is what I had been enjoying. Nothing ventured, nothing gained. I drank water at lunch rather than beer, as no one else would have joined me. What a mistake. I spent the next three days in bed in Bangkok on my way back to Singapore.

---

1 I am perhaps showing off here in introducing a touch of local colour, but I have a copy of the formal proposal to Air India and these were the prices accepted. India has a different numbering system to the Arabic system, using commas every two figures for numbers above 9,999. The ORG service figure was the equivalent of another US$5 million.

ALSO INNOVATORS

Indonesia

The Soedarpo Corporation was our distributor in Indonesia. Mr Soedarpo Sastrosatomo, who, like many of his generation, used his given name, omitting the need for the family name, was an extremely well-respected businessman with a finger in any number of pies. In the computer business, he had the distribution rights for the Sperry computer systems. He was a founder and part-owner of Bank Niaga. He had a share in the Samudera Shipping Line, and was a major player in the timber business. His history had it that, in 1947, when General Sukarno expelled the Dutch from Indonesia and became president, he promoted a 23-year-old guerilla fighter, Soedarpo, as part of an envoy team to the United Nations to seek UN representation. He was not appointed the ambassador, and returned home. While in the US, Mr Soedarpo had recognised the impact that computers would have, and when he returned home he brought with him the sales rights to the UNIVAC, IBM, and Data General product lines, and — although IBM eventually opened its own office in Indonesia — the rest is history.

Like India, business in Indonesia is operated on family lines. The flagship of Soedarpo's business empire was the Samudera Indonesia Shipping Group. In 1955, Mr Soedarpo set up Bank Niaga and at the time I worked with the bank it was the second-largest private bank in the country. The group also had insurance, engineering, and advertising interests. The boss, who was dark and tended to favour safari suits, was known to fall asleep in technical meetings and did so a few times at the bank when we were discussing hardware configurations. Mr Soedarpo's daughter, Shanti Poesposoetjipto, was undoubtedly his confidante, although I did not initially have very much to do with her. Shanti became a major player in the Indonesian tech business.

9. ADVENTURES IN SOUTHEAST ASIA

Figure 9.16: Mr Soedarpo and his daughter, Shanti: 'I had a different way of doing things.'
Source: Author's collection.

Shanti's husband, Usmawi Saleh, was the sales director of the Soedarpo Divisi Sistem Komputer (Computer System Division). He was not very interested in computers and was eventually relegated to the family chicken farm business. Pandji S. Choesin was the marketing and sales manager of the computer division. Pandji is the son of the ex-Indonesian ambassador to Russia and the United States. Pandji carried himself very well, and dressed in suits most of the time. He was dark, heavy jowled, and of average height. He spoke excellent English, as you would expect, having been schooled in the US. Both Pandji and Shanti undertook their higher level education in Germany and graduated in engineering. Pandji was always an excellent host in Jakarta, but our everyday entertainment became somewhat curtailed when he took on the role of principal interviewer and newsreader on the new Indonesian English-language television channel over weekends. He was recognised when we ate out in downtown Jakarta, which made being out and about difficult for him. He became quite adept at deflecting enthusiastic fans in my direction by stating I was a foreign television executive seeking talent.

The Soedarpo Corporation worked its diplomatic ties. When the time came for Pandji to marry, a wife was found for him from within the diplomatic tier of society. He now has two sons.

Figure 9.17: The Soedarpo team from Jakarta at the 1984 distributor conference in Singapore. From left to right: Pandji Choesin, Soedarpo Sastrosatomo, and Usmawi Saleh.
Source: Author's collection.

The Soedarpo staff were generally competent, but non-demonstrative. They did not contribute to discussions. It was obvious that the corporation had a social responsibility and employed a number of disabled staff, including an American, married to another Soedarpo employee, who was the office dogsbody, although his demeanour suggested a position of authority.

We had a reasonably large systems presence in Jakarta, with Sperry 1100s installed at two out of the five major military installations — the Department of Defence, army, navy, air force, and police — and eventually two System 80s. Government legislation during the period of my interest prevented the import of computer systems above the relatively small threshold of US$150K, which restricted what we could sell. This did mean, however, that Soedarpo staff became very competent in working the Sperry System 80s to their practical limit. From early 1982, Bank Niaga operated a two-processor System 80, providing full online counter services and achieving very creditable response times. I always felt that the Indonesian engineers were better at hardware than software, but they certainly combined these skills on this bank project.

9. ADVENTURES IN SOUTHEAST ASIA

As Sperry representatives, we got to meet the Indonesian customers and have a chance to develop a rapport with them. As was common at this stage in the life of the computer industry, the vendor was expected to have a mirror image computer system in their home office in the event of failure of the customer equipment. Soedarpo used its stand-by Sperry 1100 and 90-series equipment to provide a service bureau business, and its office always seemed to be busy.

Another company that came under the Soedarpo sphere of influence was P. T. Jasa Insuransi, who in 1982 also installed a System 80. Wahjono became the electronic data processing manager, promoted from head of the Planning and Statistics Division with the installation. I was keen to promote software written by Jasa Insuransi and Soedarpo for inclusion in a regional applications software directory, but it never happened quickly enough.

Pandji generally negotiated price with us. We were seldom asked for too much. I have details of one negotiation. Don Ramble or the regional boss had the final say in our pricings, but I had enough knowledge of the company's requirements to be able to recommend a price to Don that I believed would be acceptable to us. One such agreement (for a police system 80 upgrade) is shown below.

Component of bid	Sperry list price	Soedarpo wish	Agreed bid price
System 80 hardware	US$150K	US$135K	US$150K
4 x Uniservo 16 tape units (not standard)	US$50K	US$25K	US$10K
Spare parts	US$6K	0	0
Total	US$206K	US$160K	US$160K

In this instance, when the order came in, we should be able to show a list price for the essential hardware component, which was what Sperry head office needed to see. The tape units and the spares were probably zero transfer cost items to the Singapore region, for which we should receive US$10K. You will note that software still played no part in the pricing algorithm. Sperry resisted charging for software for a long time after it became a part of other manufacturers' price, following the lead set by IBM.

With the increased level of interest being shown in them from Singapore, who were a lot closer geographically than when the regional office had been located in Hong Kong, Soedarpo and Pandji raised the company's sales profile. I worked with Toro Yudo and Ungang Prijadi on the practical sales campaigns that they hoped to put in practice.

Once a month, Mr Soedarpo organised a Friday afternoon golf round for the senior generals of the five defence organisations. Terry Thompson was brave enough to play golf with them. Occasionally, Terry was not available and I would volunteer my services as a caddy. I know that our direct involvement with these Soedarpo customers helped with the relationships, and we got to see some excellent golf courses where we were thoroughly spoiled. Mr Soedarpo quite liked the idea of a presentable and amenable caddy who was employed by a major US corporation.

I never saw any hint of corruption in my dealings with Soedarpo Corporation. I did avail myself of the Soedarpo influence on one occasion. When the government restricted the number of entries to the country on an Indonesian visitor visa, I left my passport with Soedarpo Corporation and was rewarded with a multiple entry visa. I did not do much travel within Indonesia — it was only a one-hour flight from Singapore, although getting through customs and immigration at Jakarta could take another hour, and the cab into town just as long. Through rugby at the Singapore Cricket Club, I had access to the International Sports Club of Indonesia (ISCI). I knew where to find the boys after their training sessions on a Tuesday and Thursday evening, and so was never at a loss for activity when staying over during the week. Blok M (a shopping quarter with expatriate bars) was an ISCI favourite haunt and was not that far from the Jakarta Hilton where I stayed, reputedly one of the finest hotels in the world.

It became a tradition that Soedarpo Corporation and Sperry would present a vendor profile on an annual basis to the Department of Defence. I think it was 1983 when we met at defence headquarters. The five generals and 20 colonels who comprised the computing cadre arrived in full dress uniforms, with medals, swords, and spurs on boots. This was the day that President Suharto was to be confirmed in the presidency for the third time. I shall never forget the tinkling of the medals and scrape of spurs as our customers made themselves comfortable. Mr Soedarpo made his introduction in Bahasa. Pandji stood and also spoke in the local language. I was aware that it was my turn.

'Good morning, gentlemen. It is my pleasure to conduct this annual review. I am sorry that I am still unable to speak in Bahasa. If I start to speak too quickly, do please stop me and ask me to, at least, slow down.'

At this point, Colonel Hardijono stood up.

'Come on, Chris, you must have learned some Bahasa?'

I looked at him, stumped. I could not even remember 'selamat datang' — good day. This was embarrassing. Suddenly, words came to me. I spoke them, to great effect and much laughter. I had invited our customers to join me in another drink — using the most crude of Javanese dialect. So much for Blok M, but it did break the ice that particular morning.

Mr Soedarpo had a reputation for falling asleep during long meetings or meetings with which he was bored. It was accepted, and we worked around it. But we had one long session where we experienced him at his fiercest. The Sperry 1100 equipment installed at the Ministry of Defence was coming to the end of its useful life and the army was insisting that Soedarpo again provide a back-up system if it replaced its installed system. We were discussing the purchase of two systems at the one time, which would have been a good order for Sperry. Soedarpo had negotiated an extension to the legislated value of imported equipment that might be allowed in this case, but the monies available were well below what would be acceptable to Sperry — the number was around US$2 million. Mr Soedarpo asked for a meeting in Singapore and brought Usmawi Saleh out of (computer business) retirement to the meeting, along with Pandji Choesin. We met in a suite at the new Pan Pacific Hotel on the reclaimed land at Marina Bay. Sperry was represented by vice president and regional general manager Gus Sichero; Don Ramble, the financial controller; Terry Thompson; and myself. We knew the figures every which way, and talked around them with Pandji and Usmawi in the lounge area of a suite, while Mr Soedarpo attended to *The Times* crossword. I watched Mr Soedarpo work carefully through the main crossword, something I never was able to achieve. He then turned to the back page to the small crossword, which he also completed.

Having carefully folded his newspaper, and consulted his watch — Usmawi, Pandji, Don, Terry, and I had been talking for about three hours — Mr Soedarpo announced he was leaving in 15 minutes and hoped that a resolution would be found in that time. He succinctly summarised the financial position and listed the discounts and final price that would be acceptable to him. At the end of the 15 minutes, he stood up and made to leave the suite, summoning Usmawi and Pandji to join him. I never saw Gus Sichero move so fast. He took Mr Soedarpo by the arm and led him into a bedroom. They emerged 10 minutes later and, rather like Neville Chamberlain before him, Gus was waving a piece of paper that he declared was a mutually beneficial solution to the meeting. Our Indonesian friends left the meeting after handshakes all round. Gus was exultant.

The Sperry people who were left had a coffee and relaxed for a moment. But Don Ramble could not contain himself.

'Well, Gus. What have you agreed with Mr Soedarpo?'

'We have sold the 1100/70, the middle configuration of the three, for US$1.92 million. I do not see what the problem was. Soedarpo is a reasonable man.'

Don was concerned.

'Gus, how many systems does he get for $1.92 million — one or two?'

'Merde', was Gus's explosive response. He hurled a chair at the wall — I do not think it broke — and swept papers and utensils from the coffee table at which we were sitting before collapsing in a heap on a chair. Don and I left the room. Gus had sold the two systems for a reasonable price for one. Don and I went after the Soedarpo delegation but they were unmovable. Mr Soedarpo had cajoled Gus into signing the price agreement they had agreed in the other room, and he was not going to negotiate any further. Gus did not stay regional vice president for long after that event. He just disappeared. I do not know if the Soedarpo mistake was a contributing factor.

The Soedarpo Corporation managed to survive the demise of President Suharto. I met Shanti in Melbourne during President Habibie's tenure when she was leading the Indonesian delegation at an ASEAN trade conference in 1998. We greeted one another with an embrace, much to the delight of Shanti's entourage and the consternation of other people waiting to meet her at the Indonesian Embassy display area. Shanti was later the Indonesian representative at the United Nations' Fourth World Conference on Women in Beijing 1995, where Hillary Clinton gave a famous speech. She was an influential lady. Paul Kimberley, who worked with Sperry in Australia, has subsequently become quite a good friend and through my introduction he has met with Shanti under the Megawati regime, where she was still exerting considerable influence in the IT sector.

More recently, Shanti told me that the family had moved Pandji into the role of CEO of the Indonesian Internet Association to give him exposure at a national level. He is currently the non-executive chairman of the Indonesian Chamber of Trade.

Malaysia

Malaysia is Singapore's nearest neighbour, but it is a world apart. Kuala Lumpur, known as KL, was an hour away by aeroplane, and Johor Bahru (JB) was the same time away by car across the causeway. The expatriate community in Singapore readily professed to island sickness, and the need to escape on a regular basis from the normality, discipline, and cleanliness of Singapore. Malaysia generally provided that escape. As Singapore green card work permits were sometimes difficult to obtain, many an expatriate visited JB on a monthly basis to be able to return to Singapore on a visitor's visa. JB also provided sex and casino gambling opportunities not available on the island. For a while during our stay, the currencies were in step, but the Singapore dollar spurted ahead, so trips were made to JB for petrol and to buy cheaper coin currencies which were worth more in the banks of Singapore.

When I arrived in Southeast Asia, Sperry had a permanent representative in Kuala Lumpur. I had met Richard Hawkins in the UK during my stint with Bass Charrington. He was dating the very classy receptionist at the Midlands regional office in Birmingham. At that time, Richard was working with the international division and had an expansive background that had included overseas humanitarian work. Richard is very tall and the ladies tell me he is good looking. He dresses very fashionably except when indulging in his passion: the restoration, racing, and showing of vintage sports cars. Richard was allocated full-time to support the sales and management activities of the Malaysian distributor. Richard was recently married to a tall, attractive Australian girl, Marion, who was the daughter of a New South Wales doctor. They lived fashionably in KL and had two boys. They led an active social life. In addition to his vintage cars, Richard exercised a passion for windsurfing.

Our distributor in Malaysia was Pernas Trading Sendirian Berhad Limited, the trading arm of the Malaysian Government. The Malaysian Government had implemented its Bumiputra philosophy, which favoured the indigenous Malay race, and we worked with a Malaysian manager and Malay management. The real bread and butter work was done by Chinese workers, who understood the system and appeared not to want to rebel against that status quo. Our competition for medium to large scale systems, which were our priority, was IBM and Burroughs. Richard had considerable success as sales director in KL and at one time was able to boast that he had won nine out of the 11 medium to large scale system orders that had been placed during his two year assignment. Richard was fastidious in his notetaking of dates and events, which he can still recite today, but was not willing to overtly display a technical interest or a need to be involved in the tedium of proposal writing. He relished my role in a pre-sales position and later technical operations because it let him allocate these responsibilities to me. Richard perceived himself as a salesman first and foremost. Richard had a very good rapport with the government-appointed executive director of Pernas, Tuan Syed Tamin. Syed was not computer trained but very receptive to being given a semi-technical description of what we were trying to achieve with the systems we were selling on his behalf. His interface with the management of the various government departments, through his membership and seniority in the ruling party, the United Malays National Organisation, opened the doors we needed to enter.

One story about Richard that I enjoy telling involves his contribution to the management of the 1982 South-East Asian Regional Computer Conference, which was held in Port Dickson, a seaside resort on the east coast of Malaysia. Richard had played a part on the local organising committee and it was his responsibility to introduce a senior IBM research fellow who was visiting from the US to give one of the keynote addresses. Richard stood up to introduce the speaker and read, in very great detail, the IBM employee's work history and background, which would substantiate what he was about to tell us of his vision for computing in the future. The speaker stood and moved towards the podium — but Richard was not finished:

'In anticipating our speaker's thoughts on the future I believe it appropriate to look back at where we have come from …

'I well remember when I joined the industry, the future was still very much hardware oriented and we were looking forward to disk technology that would allow us to consider substantial databases … and today when we consider the implications of end-user computing, as typified by Sperry's fourth generation language, Mapper, we are looking at enabling the end-user to …'

He rambled on in this vein, as those who knew him had started to giggle, and then laugh, as we watched the IBM man beginning to panic as his allotted 30 minutes were diminished, as Richard continued on and on. It was very funny.

It was at the 1982 South-East Asian Regional Computer Conference that I met Professor Colin Leakey of Cambridge University, who was presenting his computer model to determine the best mix of crops to be grown by Malaysian smallholders — this was also applicable to other Asian rural economies. Small isolated stands of rubber trees and bananas were becoming uneconomical, compared to the huge plantations that covered most of Malaysia, and some of these were being replaced by palm oil horticulture. Professor Leakey presented a most comprehensive model that included soil analysis and prevailing weather patterns. (Colin Leakey was the son of Professor Louis S. B. Leakey, famous for his archaeological and anthropological findings in the Olduvai Gorge in Tanzania. His academic protégées included Dian Fossey, whose work inspired the film *Gorillas in the Mist*, and Jane Goodall, who became famous for her studies of the behaviour of chimpanzees. A third disciple was Biruté Galdikas, who studied the orangutans in the Tanjung Puting National Park in Kalimantan.) I relished the thought of being able to help the economy through the development of Professor Leakey's work and assumed a personal mission to work with the Malaysian Department of Agriculture and Sperry to take this further. I also took copies of his presentation into the Department of Agriculture in Thailand. I am still amazed at the lack of interest for the project. I sustained a correspondence with Professor Leakey after I left Asia, but have not heard of the project in Malaysia since.

Richard's sales team (for it was he who led Pernas) consisted of six or so relatively inexperienced salespeople. Mohamed Haron was a small, dark man who was both lazy and political. On Friday he wore the Malay songkok, a black velvet hat, as a symbol of his Islamic faith. One of his accounts was United Malayan Banking Corporation (UMBC), which was owned by the governing political party, the United Malays National Organisation. UMBC was a Sperry 1100 customer, implementing a full online in-house banking operation. ATMs were to be the next challenge during 1982–1983.

The other salespeople were Chinese. Eddie Y. P. Low was probably my favourite. In his early 30s, bespectacled and looking as though he was going to put on a lot of weight, Eddie was desperate to learn, although his grasp of written English made it difficult for him to keep pace with his colleagues.

Figure 9.18: Two of the Pernas team at the distributor conference. On the left is K. C. Koh, Mohamed Haron in the centre, looking dapper with, on the right, Thomas Teo, the Sperry Singapore HR manager. The Pernas boss, Syad Tamin, did not attend the technical sessions.
Source: Author's collection.

Eddie was the salesman responsible for Banque Indosuez. Both the KL and Singapore branches of the bank had Sperry 90/30 computer systems. In both locations, the system was the wrong one to achieve the online banking activities the bank wished to implement. The original sale had been made in Paris for installations worldwide. The KL branch of the bank was larger than Singapore, and we believed we were in a good position to sell them a large Sperry 1100 system. The KL data processing manager was an IBM aficionado who was always looking for reasons to convert back to an IBM system, as used in the Paris headquarters. It was our most difficult customer situation.

As the trading arm of government, Pernas had access to other related business opportunities in town. Petroliam Nasional Berhad (PETRONAS), the national petroleum franchise, was a Sperry customer, with its computer centre at Menara Dayabumi. PETRONAS had a Sperry 1100/60 system installed. After Richard had left KL, PETRONAS was investigating how it might increase its competencies in the exploration area prior to releasing an invitation to bid to the general market. The invitation to bid had both an administrative and a scientific requirement. PETRONAS had franchised out the seismological exploration of Malaysia to reputable US and European petroleum companies, but had no facility to make its own value judgments about mineral opportunities. The petroleum companies provided their own seismic studies and analysis to PETRONAS, but it wished to have a more fundamental capacity. Mohd Sulaiman Yahya, manager of the computer services department, asked Sperry to investigate how we might jointly promote PETRONAS ambitions. He agreed to travel to the US with Sperry if we were able to make firm representations to meet his needs. At the time, Sperry published a catalogue of scientific application software for the 1100 series of equipment, and buried deep in that document I found a mention of a company called GeoQuest Systems of Houston, Texas. I contacted Sperry in Texas and developed a rapport (via telex) with Rosa Yang, manager, marketing support, worldwide scientific/energy marketing, who was confident that we would be able to provide a meaningful program of activities for PETRONAS's guests if they were willing to travel to the US.

Five PETRONAS people travelled. Sulaiman headed the team that otherwise consisted of three Chinese analysts and an Indian analyst. We all got on famously and the technicians proved their worth in discussions in Texas, evaluating mapping and contouring systems as recommended by Rosa Yang. It had been almost 20 years since I had last been in San Antonio and during a weekend excursion there I twice drove our car past the Alamo. In the 1960s, the Alamo was a building standing alone from the town. In the 1980s it was dwarfed and overwhelmed by modern buildings encroaching on this most famous of tourist entities. No new exhibits inside either, I noticed.

The PETRONAS team and myself met and spent three training days with GeoQuest Systems and were very well looked after by president Rex Ross and his team. GeoQuest showed us a specialised workstation that it had developed for the analysis of seismic records and was selling to the big players in the exploration market. The GeoQuest Interactive Exploration System used the very modern Intel 20286 processor, and incorporated an array processor and magnetic tape units capable of reading the 28 channel tapes used for seismic recording. The PETRONAS systems people, who had competencies in geology and geophysics, after a day and a half were able to drive the workstation and reduce the accumulated data into meaningful maps, and to assume the role of seismic interpreter. The software we were using was from Zycor Inc., whose president, Jim Downing, was present at the GeoQuest office for our briefing. Mohd Sulaiman slept, but the rest of the team became very animated at the opportunity being presented. We also met Peter Dennett, who owned a one-man computer consulting, software, and integration shop called Padsoft (named after his initials). Peter's interest was in (being paid for) the integration of the GeoQuest workstation into a Sperry environment for PETRONAS. The net result of the trip was a formal request from Sulaiman for inclusion in the planned invitation to bid on a full proposal and implementation plan for the introduction of the new hardware and software.

This was easier said than done, and I had several months of detailed discussion and risk analysis with Sperry before we were allowed to submit a detailed proposal. The proposal for a two-data-centre approach included the use of modern (for Malaysia) switching protocols and database synchronisation techniques. But I was confident in putting this forward after my work with Bass Charrington and Provident Management Services Limited. By this time, Sperry had at Pernas's request assigned a full-time customer services manager, Dr Bill Siple, who took over the project after my submission of the tender documents. Bill Siple, a slow to action American, took over the Pernas customer services function after a destructive power play by two longstanding Pernas employees, K. C. Koh and K. C. Low, both of whom missed out on the position in the end.

Three other opportunities stand out that became my responsibility after Richard had left KL to look after the Indian subcontinent for the company: the Department of Main Roads and Transport, Malaysian Airline System, and the Signals Directorate within the Department of Defence.

The Department of Main Roads and Transport requirement was looking to push the limit of point-of-sale technology for 1983–1984. The problem that the department was looking to resolve was the issue of driving licences. Face was important in Malaysia. Malaysians would lose face by failing a driving test, so they did not risk it. They hired a professional driving test–taker instead. Transport wanted to prevent this, as it was losing face, and it certainly did not help with the standard of driving, which seemed to be hazardous everywhere. With today's technologies, we are familiar with the inclusion of a photograph on a plastic card as a means of identity verification. In the mid-1980s, we did not have this facility, and instead researched the Sperry worldwide user and application database, and came up blank. We did some serious study on the use of coded descriptions of the person taking the driving test, as well as the incorporation of fingerprints into the licence, but did not achieve resolution in my time.

We put a great deal of effort into selling to Malaysian Airline System. Richard Hawkins and Wayne Bisbee had opened the path to senior Malaysian Airline System management, although IBM was the incumbent supplier, with whom it was happy. Terry Thompson and Ken Short Jr were experienced airline people. Terry and I met with Malaysian Airline System in several departments. We really tried. Going in our favour, we thought, was a contract we had won with Singapore Airlines, for which we had imported airline experts to look at the current range of boarding-pass readers for integration into standard Sperry and IBM software. Our crucial decision centred upon finding the person we believed might be our champion within Malaysian Airline System. We chose badly. We decided to ignore the financial director, Tun Daim Zainuddin, and concentrate upon a technical sale. Big mistake. Zainuddin became the Finance Minister in the Mahathir Mohamad Government during 1984–1991.

The Ministry of Defence was a Sperry 1100 customer. It used a Sperry 1100/60 for a variety of administrative applications — nothing very exciting. The ministry was constrained by the armed forces strategy to rotate its favoured (Malay) sons through the range of disciplines on a two year cycle. This meant our contact would take six months to understand his new job, and maybe 12 months doing the job before he removed himself from making any decision that might jeopardise the next appointment.

We were invited to meet Colonel Idris, the officer commanding the Signals Directorate, who had a very precise concept of what the role of the directorate was to the defence forces. He expected to provide all the communication facilities and foresaw the effect of data communications as a strategic key to future conflict. He wanted to ensure that this element of warfare stayed within both signals and intelligence — another communications-dependent facet of the military. Colonel Idris outlined his thoughts to Terry Thompson and me, and asked that Sperry produce a needs analysis, which we would then answer. It was an ideal situation for us. Terry recruited Ken Short Jr from the airlines group to help us with the definition. Ken was another Sperry ex–financial controller, who had a background in Vietnam and the military.

Ken, Terry and I met regularly with Colonel Idris and it became apparent that his budget for hardware and software and implementation was US$20 million. Terry asked me, as the technician, to be responsible for specifying products and services that would cost defence that US$20 million. Try as I might, that figure bought a lot of hardware, and we did not have that many software specialists or analysts that we could allocate to the project. We had an innovative approach to the provision of telecommunications switches, which was to use the Distributed Communications Processor 40 front end to an 1100 system as a remote switch within a countrywide network. We also looked at satellite and microwave technologies. In the end, the decision was to bundle as many Sperry products and services as we could possibly justify into a proposal and charge the budgeted US$20 million. Some money was to find its way back to Colonel Idris through the Pernas organisation. This was going to be difficult to achieve, as defence wanted to keep Pernas at arm's length on this project.

The timing became a problem. Gus Sichero was replaced by Tom Yam as regional vice president. Tom Yam, a Hong Kong Chinese with a long career in the Sperry international division, was initially very insecure in his new position. He was keen to close some big business, and the potential business of the Malaysian Defence Department was big. He sent for me very early in his new role. His questioning was very direct. Did I know the details of the deal with Colonel Idris? I assured him that I did. He cautioned me not to know. I was probably wrong in attempting to explain to our new vice president that I had to know. The way that Terry and I worked together was only effective if we had no secrets. Tom again cautioned me not to know. Terry Thompson was fired by Tom Yam. Terry tried to find suitable employment back in the US and did the rounds of former associates in the company, but was not successful.

9. ADVENTURES IN SOUTHEAST ASIA

I always enjoyed Malaysia. I did not have as much activity there as I might have liked, but with permanent Sperry representatives based in KL — Richard Hawkins and then Bill Siple — I was not needed.

Terry Thompson later returned to Singapore as director of distributor sales for the Burroughs Corporation, at the time the third-largest computer services company in the world. (Sperry was the second largest.) I heard through the grapevine that Terry was again pursuing the Malay Signal Directorate. In 1986, Michael Blumenthall, the CEO of Burroughs, initiated a successful takeover of Sperry. The merged company was named Unisys. Depending on which part of the world was being considered, it was most times the incumbent boss of the largest subsidiary who got the top job. Tom Yam was successful in retaining his position and became the Southeast Asia boss of Unisys. One of his first actions was to fire Terry Thompson a second time.

Terry did call me in 1988, when I was in New Zealand, to ask me to work with him again. This time it was to set up a US company's PC business in Singapore to cover the Asia-Pacific region. Terry was a shareholder in the company. I declined the offer. I'd already been there and done that, but I had certainly enjoyed his confidence and a freedom to pursue my own agenda to achieve and better the targets that Sperry had allocated over a four-year period. I do have a real regret to have lost contact with Terry. Even Ken Short Jr has lost contact with him. Terry and I had worked well together.

Party time: The Philippines

As with our other computer distributorships, the Uniphil Corporation in the Philippines was a developing business with a few prestigious accounts and mindful of the support it needed from us to support them in order to win success with new (hopefully large) customers. Carlos B. 'Bobby' Palacios and Sergio J. 'Serge' de la Fuente were the joint managing directors of Uniphil. I quickly learned that Filipino businessmen are keen to use their nicknames in business as well as privately. Bobby was the aggressive salesman, complemented by the quieter, dark and studious Serge. Bobby and Chito Beltran, Uniphil's sales manager, attended sales meetings with me. Serge would remain in the office, but he was ready to join us if our meeting extended into lunchtime or the early evening.

Family is important in the Philippines, as it was in most of the Southeast Asian countries, but this was the only Catholic state in which I worked. As soon as it was realised that I was English, I was told:

> 'We wish we had been a British colony, not Spanish and American. The British only ever took money away from their colonies — they did not impose their religion and customs on the indigenous peoples. The corruption here is as a direct result of our past.'

I thought it best to evaluate that sentiment before entering into an in-depth discussion.

Chito Beltran was the son of a friend of both Bobby and Serge. He looked and acted like a playboy. I did not feel that he contributed much to Uniphil business, a sentiment I shared with Terry Thompson. We kept our own counsel. Chito terrified me when he first picked me up from Manila Airport the first time I went there and we travelled into town. His driving posture and approach was that of a racing car driver, and he used the full range of gears as he nipped in and out of the traffic streams trying to gain advantage. He pointed out to me the telegraph poles that should have been carrying the data traffic from the airport to the Philippine Airlines computer centre in town. He said almost boastingly that a section of the copper wire would be stolen every night, but that the telecommunications authority was so used to this that it had a crew ready to make the necessary repairs each day. The drive into Manila took us through shanty towns constructed of corrugated iron, cardboard, and string. There was a strong odour and the place was seemingly teeming with children. My trips to the Philippines were obviously going to be a wild ride if Chito was to be my guide. A huge advantage was that everyone spoke English, with a melodic sing-song intonation that is unique and which I still find very beguiling.

Having spent some time with the Uniphil staff and visited a few customers, it was obvious that Uniphil was good with the hardware and very keen to learn more about the application software it expected us to have. Uniphil was looking for technology transfer and the very best deal it could get from Sperry. The days were long. We would spend hours in the office discussing how we might approach a particular customer and construct a deal. Deals were important. They had to be seen to be done, but the real manipulation was covert.

Figure 9.19: The Uniphil team at the Sperry distributor conference. From left to right: Chito Beltran, Bobby Palacios and Sergio de la Fuente.
Source: Author's collection.

When we were bidding a major online system to a bank, Bobby and Serge wanted the lowest possible cost for the system we had decided upon. I asked why.

> 'We have to pay a certain percentage as an incentive to purchase to the deciding company officer.'

I tried to put a different perspective on that statement:

> 'Why not charge more than the published list price so that the percentage is worth more to the deciding company officer? You also make more money.'

> 'Chris, you do not understand. Our customers are aware of and consult the US General Services Agreement, and will not pay more than the US Government.'

He wrote a table of numbers on the whiteboard.

> 'For Central Bank of the Philippines, we need to pay five per cent to the secretary of the evaluation committee — and he will tell us about all the other bids and what we need to do to win the business. We need to pay five per cent to the chairman of the committee. We need to pay five per cent to the head of the National Computer Board. We need to pay five per cent to Mrs Marcos's doctor. We need to pay eight per cent to Mrs Marcos's hairdresser.'

This was 28 per cent — the same number as the profit margin I needed to get the business approved.

Answering my query on the latter recipients, I was told that Mrs Marcos was not only the president's wife, she was also the Governor of Metropolitan Manila, which had a major shareholding in the bank.

Naïvely, I pursued the argument.

> 'I can just about understand that a gratuity be paid to the business recommenders — but why to Mrs Marcos's doctor and hairdresser?'
> 'Because they are the only people who can talk to her most days. The hairdresser she definitely sees every day.'

I talked to Bobby some more when we had another drink later that evening. The truth was that the full 28 per cent would end up in Mrs Marcos's hands, and she would be aware of all deals on and off the table. More than that, Bobby assured me that the bank appointees would already be paying a part of their salaries to keep their jobs.

Understanding some of the underlying realities made the Philippines easier to live in. I was coming back to Metro Manila late one evening from Ermita, a bar area, when the cab I was in was flagged down by a policeman. I was sitting next to the driver. The policeman asked me for my passport. I was not carrying it, or any other identity document. The policeman quickly had me out of the cab with my hands on the roof of the car, legs splayed out, when he advised me that he was going to arrest me for not carrying any proof of identity. The passenger window was open. I asked the driver for advice:

> 'What do I do?'
> 'Give him some money. That's what he wants.'

I did so, and was allowed to continue my journey.

When I discussed this experience with Bobby and Chito the next day, they laughed.

> 'That is an old scam, and quite common. The cab drivers know where to drive. They share any money with the policeman.'

Later that day, Chito showed me how graft was handled by the locals. He deliberately double parked on a double yellow line outside the office where we had our next meeting. Sure enough, when we finished the meeting and came out on to the street there was a policeman waiting for him. Money changed hands and no parking infringement was noted.

Whenever Terry or I were in Manila, Uniphil arranged a social event for us. Terry had his golf interest and usually carried his clubs to Manila. My task was to participate with Uniphil in the activities of the Philippine Computer Society. The society met fortnightly, however, I was asked to think in monthly terms, and I would quite often be called upon to make a presentation or participate in a panel discussion after a dinner in a good hotel. The society was another wonderful excuse for a party. Bobby and Serge were leading lights in the society and could manipulate activities to Uniphil's advantage. IBM was our main competitor in Manila, and I was primed to attack IBM at every opportunity. IBM's failure to win the Singapore National Computing Centre and its system replacement by Sperry at Telecom was well known, and questions from society members were a great opportunity to express a personal opinion with company authority. I was really surprised that IBM representatives never argued, but that could have been because they were local and non-confrontational, or perhaps just polite.

The Philippine Computer Society was a fun organisation. Every year it held a Miss Philippine Computer Society competition — a beauty contest with entrants from the real and the fringe elements of the computer industry — and every year the winner of Miss Philippine Computer Society was recruited by Uniphil as an account manager to one of its major customers. In any other environment this would have been seen as suspect, but not in Manila. It did occasionally cause a problem. At one crucial meeting with the Ministry of Defence in the Uniphil office, I was trying to make a point when I was completely stunned to be asked by a colonel if I was 'sleeping with Carmelita, the defence account manager?' How was this going to help me learn the defence thoughts about database structures? I looked at 'Millie', who was quite unconcerned. There were a number of very pretty girls in the office to flirt with.

One computer society event was more embarrassing. A one-day conference was arranged in Cebu, one of the Philippine islands, in September 1982. There were perhaps eight overseas speakers. The night before the conference we were at dinner and being entertained by the Governor of the Cebu province. His speech was both gushing and chauvinistic, which was unfortunate, as one of the speakers was a Hong Kong businesswoman, Ms Emma Li. Ms Li became increasingly angry as the speech developed:

> 'In welcoming you as guest speakers to Cebu, I would ask you to not to leave until you have all tasted the fruits of Cebu.'

I think we all understood the inference of his remark, but he made it worse:

> 'I want you to understand that the fruits of Cebu are our women.'

After dinner, the male speakers were gathered and taken out on the town by our computer society hosts. The first place we stopped was called the Lewd Bar. We were left in absolutely no doubt that we were each expected to select a companion from the gorgeous, scantily clad girls cavorting on the bar and stage. It was too much. The IBM representative was a young Swiss fellow. He and I determined that neither of us had any intention of a public indiscretion whilst representing our companies. We pretended that we were more interested in one another, in order to dissuade our hosts, and managed to get back to the hotel at a reasonable hour. We then spoiled it all by sitting talking and drinking until the small hours. Ms Li, the owner of a prestigious software house specialising in database software, was still angry the next day, and made sure that our hosts knew it. But it had no effect. The speakers were presented with a beautiful plaque to recognise our contributions to the conference. I cannot remember the conference at all, so much else was happening.

We did do some work and pursued some interesting business opportunities. Wayne Bisbee, Terry, and I invested a great deal of time in selling to Philippine Airlines. The airline world at the time was divided up between the users of IBM hardware and software and the Sperry solution based upon the Sperry 1100 systems with the USAS (Standard Airline System) software. Philippine Airlines was in the IBM camp for its passenger reservation system, so we concentrated on selling to Avelino Zapanta, who was the officer in charge of the Philippine Airlines international cargo division. 'Lino' was based at the airport in probably the only quiet area, surrounded by the melee that was the prevailing situation in the terminal. Cargo was perceived as a real growth area and to fulfil its potential needed to be viewed as a product in its own right, rather than being seen as an adjunct to passenger business. Wayne worked very hard to establish a cargo business plan for Philippine Airlines and other airlines in the region in more of a consultative role than as a pure salesman.

Banks were also potential customers for Sperry medium to large scale computers. The Philippines did not disappoint and had many banks for us to explore business relationships with. Lino Reglo, a vice president of the Republic Planters Bank, also became a friend through work and the computer society. I still wear a Coconut Planters Bank t-shirt, although I understand the bank was swept away after the downfall of the Marcos regime. We put a great deal of effort into the Central Bank of the Philippines' request for tender, but this was also suspended because of political changes at the highest level.

The Home Development Mutual Fund, locally known as Pag-IBIG, was the government housing authority. It was a Sperry 1100/61 user. Vic Raventar, the data processing manager, had a deep knowledge and interest in databases, and had implemented a system using the hierarchical database DMS 1100 software. He recognised the value of user-defined computing as represented by the Mapper 1100 relational database. Pag-IBIG was most helpful to us in defining the interface it wanted to see between DMS 1100 and Mapper. Pag-IBIG was a sophisticated user.

It was around 1983 that Uniphil prevailed upon us to place a permanent Sperry representative in Manila, in a similar management and sales role to that which Richard Hawkins had held in Kuala Lumpur. Ken Short Jr had been helping out in this position. Sumra Manning — slight and neat, with a thin blond moustache and a receding hairline — transferred from the Sperry Airlines Group, where Terry Thompson knew him. He moved his family from the US to Manila, where they lived in a guarded enclave. They seemed to settle in easily, but we learned that Mrs Manning was not happy and did not stay very long, my guess is less than one year. A permanent representative implied that Wayne Bisbee, Terry Thompson, and I had less reason to visit Manila, and we very much left Sumra to his own devices. We received the most positive reports from Bobby Palacios and Sergio de la Fuente as to Sumra's worth to them, and our sales prospects looked very good. Sumra became, to all intents and purposes, a Filipino.

Sumra took me out one afternoon to the most dreadful bar I have ever seen, worse even than the Lewd Bar in Cebu. The place was difficult to access. We went through a deserted cinema, across a fire-escape and through a controlled doorway, behind which young women were anxious to perform any deviant sexual act for 10 peso notes, rolled into a cylinder and stuck in the neck of a beer bottle — 10 peso was worth less than one

US cent. I found it disgusting, but my pal was quite at home. I would not stay long and tried to counsel Sumra when we had got back to the hygienic environment of my hotel. I told him he was in grave danger of going troppo. To his credit, he did not do so, partly because of the government changes that were imposed with the downfall of the Marcos regime. Sumra later transferred to Sperry International in London, where the family were keen to be reunited, and he found a niche situation again with the airline group.

Another story which requires a certain discretion concerns a consultancy we sought from another Sperry country, outside of our region. The Sperry 1100 systems were big, and we boasted ministry of defence installations in most countries. We learnt from the other subsidiary that a senior IT representative would be keen to visit Singapore to assist with a potential sale to the Singapore Department of Defence. We asked, via telex, if Jan Dickie (not his real name, for reasons that will soon become obvious) could extend his trip to include the Philippines, where we were also keen to sell the (fourth generation) Mapper software to the five defence elements — defence, army, navy, air force, and police. Jan agreed.

He had a good stopover in Singapore, where I met him for the first time, and we travelled to Manila. Jan told his prepared Sperry good news story twice on that first day, and on his first evening in Manila we were taken by Philippine Army representatives and Uniphil to a private function room in a high-class nightclub. The Filipinos were out for a riotous night. Jan was quieter. His reception from defence had been aggressive. It initially did not enjoy being lectured to, but the sessions had generally been positive. Jan was removed from the core of the party. I felt responsible and joined him. He had his nose pressed hard against the glass of the window of the function room overlooking the main club area. A young, bikini clad woman was working hard to gain any recognition or interest in her gyrations. Jan was spellbound: 'I have never seen anyone like that before.' I told him that, if he wished, we could leave the party and I would take him to the bar district, where we could get a lot closer to the girls. He was keen. We made our excuses and we took a taxi to Ermita, the infamous bar area.

One advantage of playing regular rugby matches around the Asia-Pacific, for various inter-port trophies, was that I knew Ermita quite well, as it was where the Manila Rugby Football Club entertained us right royally, especially on the night before a game. (Their team would stay sober and be early to bed, of course.) In Ermita, we visited at least six bars where young bar dancers were teasing the largely European audience in the hope of plying their (keen, but amateurish) ambitions. It is a sad place. Jan was entranced. He was not so naïve, however, as to not understand what was going on. He wanted to know if the girls were available, and, if so, he would really like to meet Beryl, a girl he had spoken to at bar number three. He asked me to go back to bar number three and bring the girl to the bar we were then at. I did so, paying the Mama-San the requisite 'bar fine', and formally introducing the two of them, pantomime fashion. Jan and the girl left together and I hightailed it back in to the party, which was just getting going.

The next morning, Jan was waiting for me to join him for breakfast. He had had a wonderful evening. He and Beryl had gone to a motel.

> 'She even took my shoes and socks off. She massaged my feet. I have never known anyone so gentle.'

I was not really interested, except for the necessity to be seen as an attendant host.

> 'How did you get back here to the hotel?'
> 'I took a cab back. In fact, I changed cabs twice.'

I enquired further.

> 'Why was that?'
> 'You have to realise, I am a one-star general in the intelligence service, and I dare not get caught in a compromising situation.'

Fair enough.

The next evening we were free to follow our own agenda. I asked Jan what he wanted to do.

> 'I'd really like to see Beryl again, but I cannot afford another motel charge. Would you mind fetching her back to your hotel room and I'll come and see her there?'

I did so and left them together for what seemed like a very few moments before Jan, replete with satisfaction, was back in the hotel bar, asking me to escort the girl from the hotel.

> 'Surely you can see her out?'

He again tried to explain:

> 'You have to realise, I am a one-star general in the intelligence service, and I dare not get caught in a compromising situation.'

The third evening, I had persuaded Jan that we might do a pub crawl in Manila. We were leaving the Mandarin Hotel when a girl approached him and asked: 'Do you want a good time?' 'Sure', says our intrepid one-star general, takes the girl by the arm, and marches her back into the hotel. I did not see Jan again. He left early next morning to fly back home. As a courtesy, I wrote to him at his office to thank him for the help he had afforded to us during his three days of talks with the Philippine Defence Forces.

Some six months later he wrote to me to tell me that he had been promoted and that:

> 'I have told my wife about what happened in Manila. We are getting divorced. What a wonderful three days. What is the chance that you might want another consultancy?'

We did not use Jan again, but he and I maintained a Christmas card relationship until his retirement.

Asia can be a seductive place for the unwary. It has also gone through my mind that this episode might have been a test for me, although I cannot think that anyone would be that bothered.

When the end of the Marcos regime occurred, as a US company we could only be interested observers. Foreign currency was a huge problem. US dollars were strictly controlled, and were the only currency acceptable to Sperry. Terry and I carried illicit amounts of dollars in and out of Manila as the only way of sustaining our business there. After work, in the evenings, the excitement would mount as people power swept the streets. I never felt myself to be in any danger in the midst of the crowds, but did accept I should probably not be there. Bobby and Serge were obviously constrained from being participants by their business interests. They were also a part of the Marcos way of doing things. Uniphil staff members provided me with two yellow 'Support Benigno Aquino' t-shirts following Mr Aquino's shooting at Manila International Airport. I took these back to my two lads in Singapore, but they would not wear them. Such was the pervasiveness of the Singapore Government that even expatriate school kids knew not to confront the political stability of the system in which they were living.

I was also put under additional pressure during this time by this sort of thing. One of the colonels I had met from the Army computer centre asked for me at the reception of the Sperry office in the Octagon in Singapore. He wanted US$50,000 that day. I was not able to contact either Bobby or Serge. All I could do was to talk to Don Ramble, the financial controller. It was a most difficult discussion, but Don made the money available to me against a personal IOU. It all worked out well and legitimately, but it was a risk at the time.

Taiwan

I always enjoyed visiting Taipei. Just looking out of the aeroplane windows at Taipei Airport, I was struck by the fact that the engineers attending the aircraft were dressed in quilted Chinese pyjama suits rather than the ubiquitous blue overalls of every other airport. It seemed to me that the security policemen were taller than elsewhere. The journey into Taipei was dramatic, with Chinese palaces comparing favourably against the consistent, predictable grey of the newer office buildings. The hotels were also of a high standard, certainly as good as those in Singapore.

Computer activity in Taiwan was reaching a peak in the early 1980s. Taiwan was about to manufacture, through the Acer Computer Company, its own PCs. The technical economy was on a high, with a large percentage of the world's shipbuilding undertaken in the country. There was as much building construction taking place in Taipei as in Singapore.

Mr C. C. Lee was my contact in Taiwan. He was a founder and vice president of EDP Taiwan Inc. Gilbert Mar was a formidable American who had returned home to set up EDP(T) and was the president of the company. Mr C. K Yang was vice president, and was responsible for the Datapoint equipment for which EDP(T) was also the distributor. EDP(T) did not have a large base of customers for Sperry equipment, although it could boast a most impressive large Sperry 1100 dual-processor system installed at Taipei Airport, which was running the UNIVAC Standard Airline System Flight and Departure Control software suite. EDP(T) also had two of the old Sperry 9000 systems installed.

Mr Lee was small, dapper, precise and very bald. He was always impeccably dressed in a well-cut suit and looked after me with a high degree of attention. Sometimes I would be embarrassed at the time it would take the two of us to have lunch. Mr Lee would personally select the live fish we were to eat, and he was fastidious at the table. At one restaurant he asked to see the chef, and the chef's wasabi roots. He grated several of the roots, mixing them with olive oil, before declaring which was the best to enhance the flavour of the sushi he had ordered. I seem to think that EDP(T) staff were always tolerant if we were late back in to the office for meetings. Mr Lee's English was not perfect and in the office we worked with Dick Lin, the director of marketing development, and later with James Wang, the marketing manager, who both had experience of working in the US and possessed a formidable grasp of English. Work in the Taipei office meant my taking a teaching role to explore opportunities. Taiwan was not noted for its software competencies, and the lack of viable software application programs again held us back. Sperry had a perceived problem in dealing with Taiwan: copyright of hardware and software. The EDP(T) office was a revelation. It was new, with the option of distinct piped music in each area. Mr Lee preferred the classics, but Gilbert Mar's office reverberated to hard rock.

The Datapoint side of the EDP(T) business was larger than the Sperry component. The Datapoint business included a large share of the credit union finance sector. Mr Lee was always interested to learn what we were doing for the two Banque Indosuez installations in Singapore and Kuala Lumpur, Bank Niaga, and P. T. Jasa Asurani in Jakarta, United Malayan Banking Corporation in Kuala Lumpur, and the Bank of Thailand in Bangkok as reference sites for the financial market in Taiwan.

Taiwan needed a Chinese character set for terminals that would be in everyday use by non-English-literate operators. The Summit Computer Company in Thailand had done a lot of work in converting Sperry terminals to work with the Thai character set, and I served as a conduit to Les Hales, who I had known as an operations specialist at British Petroleum in London during 1967. Les had joined Sperry International and was now based in Hong Kong, coordinating the non-English language requirements for the corporation.

9. ADVENTURES IN SOUTHEAST ASIA

Mr Lee was keen for the two of us to visit Japan to look for Japanese software that EDP(T) might acquire and convert for its local use. Sperry had been an early licenser of computer technology to Japan, and Nippon UNIVAC Kaisha (NUK) had a significant 30 per cent of the computer business in Japan, including a number of financial institutions. Through the Sperry International Visits Organisation, we were able to put together a program that would introduce Mr Lee and myself to half a dozen likely candidates. Our trip was to take about 10 days.

Our days were long and difficult. We were met at the NUK office or a customer office by about six company representatives, which would include one senior person and at least one interpreter. Mr Lee had been university educated in Tokyo, on a scholarship, and had some Japanese, but he did not sound fluent. As a courtesy to me, all discussions were translated into English and vice versa. It would only be at the end of the day, when farewells were taking place, that we would discover that the senior Japanese representative had a very good grasp of colloquial English. In the evening, Mr Lee and I joined the businessman's trek to the Ginza, where we would watch the nightly spectacle of the Tokyo office workers drinking themselves into oblivion. Mr Lee twice tried to talk us into a nightclub, but as foreigners we were not welcome. I suspect that he was trying to relive former student days. He was embarrassed that he was not able to entertain me to the extent he did in Taipei. He told me not to worry: 'When we get back to Taipei, I will take you to a Japanese cardshow evening.' We found basic software that we were keen to look at further, and took the Japanese character set specifications for Katakana implementation back to Taipei for further engineering and software examination. The software prices we were looking at were considerably higher than those Sperry was used to.

Back in Taipei we had a debrief session with Dick Lin and James Wong. Mr Lee and I had worked out the basics of a financial services package we could assemble. EDP(T) had the dominant supplier position in the credit unions through its sale of Datapoint systems. The strategic decision for EDP(T) was whether it should make a concerted effort to replace the established Datapoint systems with Sperry. Mr Lee asked Dick Lin to write a board paper.

Figure 9.20: Mr C. C. Lee at the Sperry distributor conference.
Source: Author's collection.

Mr Lee advised that he would take us to the promised Japanese cardshow the next evening. When Dick and James feigned an ignorance of what was planned, I asked Mr Lee to spell out, on the whiteboard, the word he had been using. 'C. U. L. T. …' Of course: 'cultural'. I still did not really know what to expect, and our evening did not start particularly well. We were at the restaurant by 6.30 pm but were not really wanted there until 8.30 pm. We sat in the bar and watched the restaurant come to life around us. Eventually we were shown into a large function room. One quarter of the room was dominated by a round table, with a lazy Susan in the centre, and seemingly very many chairs. The men sat equidistant from one another, with four empty seats between each of us. These were filled with 16 of the most beautiful and carefully coiffured ladies I had ever seen as a group. The lady on the near right of each gentleman was responsible for keeping his rice wine glass topped up. Beyond this functionary, the next lady was cracking sunflower seeds in her teeth and placing the nuts in a small bowl in front of me. To the left, the responsibilities were to keep the beer glass full and to feed the guest with food with a pair of very long chopsticks. The girls were permitted to drink the rice wine, but not the beer, and were not permitted to take any food. Conversation was encouraged within the group. The ladies introduced themselves — fortunately, they used anglicised names for my benefit. During the meal, eye contact and the raising of a wine glass towards one of the ladies was the excuse for her to join you in a drink, taken in a single swallow to the exclamation 'Kampai!'

I eventually realised that this was a game with consequences, and took Mr Lee's lead in slowing the toasts down, otherwise it might have been a short evening. As it was, the ladies circulated, and a new group of 16 joined us, then a third. Suffice to say that the food, the wine and the company were excellent. When the desserts and the coffee came to the table, all the girls came back to join us. They came back to entertain and from memory were very good. They performed by singing, playing instrument solos and then performing in groups. We also danced to the music. The final challenge was who from the four of us could remember the most girls' names. I quietly asked 'Jennifer' what each of the girls would have earned that evening — the figure was US$25. Thanks, Mr Lee. Even without the food and drink, EDP(T) had spent US$1,200. In closing the party, Mr Lee reminded us that 'these are good girls'. Well done, Mr Lee. It was a fun and memorable evening.

The distributor conference gave me the opportunity to reciprocate some of Mr Lee's generosity. He enjoyed eating at my home, with my family, and also in the most upmarket restaurant of the Singapore Cricket Club, for which I donned the business suit and tie he might not have realised I owned. Mr Lee was looking forward to retirement. He had grown-up children in San Francisco and was going to retire there. We exchanged Christmas cards for several years but have subsequently lost touch.

Taipei trips were not all wining and dining. EDP(T) was our smallest distributor in terms of the volume of annual business, but we did manage to sell a few major systems. Because of the language constraints, Terry and I were used less in a direct selling role than we were used to in the other distributors, but we both put in long hours of discussion and consultation back in the office.

Way back in 1973, Sperry Rand took over the Radio Corporation of America (RCA) computer services business. As well as gaining trained engineers and programmers, there was the expectation that we would eventually replace some of the RCA-built systems. RCA Taiwan was one such win, and acquired a Sperry 1100/61 system. The Taiwan Tobacco and Wine Monopoly Bureau took an 1100/61 using the same statistical software package as the Bank of Thailand. We were delighted to win the Civil Aviation Authority upgrade from 1110 hardware to an 1100/72 (two processor) system, also upgrading the USAS+FDC software set. EDP(T) did not haggle over Sperry prices. In my book that made for good business.

Taiwan became one of the Asian business tigers and I could understand how and why. EDP(T) was an early adopter of technology, ahead of its time in recognising that multi-vendor solutions were possible, and indeed preferable, in building the best computer solutions.

Thailand

It is a surprise that I come to Thailand, the distributor and country I most enjoyed visiting, as the last distributor country here. Logically, it comes last in the alphabetical order of distributor countries, but I have written my notes about later events before looking back to Thailand. Local policy allowed for a stopover in Bangkok for those travelling between Singapore and India in lieu of claiming the hardship allowance. A contributing factor was that flight arrivals and departures in and out of India travelling East–West were in the early morning around 3.00–4.00 am. So I was in Bangkok more often than the logical sequence of a seven week rotation of the six distributor countries, with a week doing expenses back in Singapore. Mind you, the two- or three-hour hassle travelling from Bangkok Airport into town was also a hardship, tolerated but never enjoyed.

Amorn Tavornmard was the managing director of Summit Computer Company, our distributor in Thailand. Amorn was small, with a florid round face. He struck me as a heavy drinker at the time and a most engaging personality. I found my way to the Silom Road office the first time on my own. I knocked on the door before entering into a very large, open-plan area. There was a small reception desk that was not manned. What impressed me was that as I went into the office everyone stood at their desks, clasped their hands in front of them and bowed in my direction. A

9. ADVENTURES IN SOUTHEAST ASIA

lady left her desk and I asked to see Mr Amorn. The office staff remained standing while the lady went to talk to another girl, who approached me and introduced herself as Nuttawee Ruchiwararat, Amorn's secretary. She guided me to Amorn's office and opened the door. Amorn bowed to me and asked me to sit down. We spoke for a few moments before he asked members of his staff to join us. We sat around Amorn's desk while I introduced myself, and many had the opportunity to tell me their roles with Summit. We talked for a few hours before four of us went for lunch in a small café on the ground floor of the Silom Building. We were joined by Somchai Srileearnop, who I took to be Amorn's deputy, and Surachai Siriluekopas, whose card showed him to be a marketing executive. Somchai was a conscientious supporter of Amorn's ambitions, and his English was excellent. Surachai was more hesitant.

After a quick lunch, we returned to the office and went into the boardroom, where there were as many as 20 people. We talked in that office until well after normal business hours, and everyone had an equal opportunity to have his say. I presumed that Amorn worked in a consensus management style, until I learned more about the Buddhism practised in Thailand. It was sometimes a real frustration to me that I could not talk to Amorn one-on-one in order for us to make a decision. Our meetings nearly always involved a group. The one exception to that rule — not one of which I was particularly proud — was that on subsequent visits I would carry a bottle of duty-free brandy into Bangkok at Amorn's insistence and leave it in the hotel, knowing that after lunch Amorn would want to come back to the hotel where we would drink the bottle. He would then call the office to be collected by his chauffeur. He would be fine the next day. I also learned, quickly, not to open the hotel room minibar after the brandy.

Amorn's people were totally loyal to him. He was a very well-respected boss. The team struck me as being very young. Somchai was the administration and financial manager who negotiated the selling price with us, always with a reasoned logic for stating the price he wanted. Patharin Kanjanawadee, bespectacled and slightly fuller in the face, was the salesman assigned to look after the Electricity Generating Authority of Thailand, EGAT. Surachai Siriluekopas, neat and tidy, was the salesman for the Bank of Thailand. Vichai Kraisingkom was the systems and programming manager, who had a narrow face and looked like an academic behind his rimless spectacles. Kosa Pongsupath looked the youngest of the management team, with his round face and longer hairstyle. He was a real worker, always first in the office and last to leave. Kosa was the Mapper programming expert in the team. Kosal Areekul was the elder statesman — he was possibly in his early 40s. Kosal managed the customer engineering team and the in-house computer bureau. I later met Mr C. K. Chung, who was the owner of Summit Computers, just one of the technical companies in the Summit group. He was an older Chinese businessman with limited English who exhibited affection for Amorn.

Figure 9.21: Summit Computer Company management at the 1984 Sperry distributor conference.
Source: Author's collection.

Thailand was not unlike India in that notifications of forthcoming government computer tenders were published in a calendarised list. The basic proforma response to hardware and software specifications from suppliers responding to the tender request was publicly displayed and was a secondary source of market intelligence as to the technical attributes of a competitor's equipment. But unlike India, in Thailand we sold the benefits of our proposals positively. In India, we concentrated on invalidating the competitor's stated facts.

Thai technicians understood both hardware and software. All computer acquisition proposals were scrutinised for approval by the National Computer Centre before a government order could be placed. Amorn had an ally in the National Computer Centre, Dr Vallobh Vimolvanich, who became a friend of mine.

The Summit Computer Company staff were all professional. Their presentations to me were always very competent. I was confident discussing any problem with them. The terminals around the office were showing mixed English and Thai character sets, which was good, as I knew that local language requirements were something we would need to confront at some time for Taiwan, China and maybe India some time. Mapper was an accepted tool by Summit, although some of the other distributors had not yet embraced it. Summit discussed its prospective customers in terms of application solutions rather than hardware specifications. Lack of application software was still a Sperry weakness, although we were circulating a thick three-ring binder as an index of available software. The directory was rather superficial, but it was a reasonable starting point for further research.

I became fond of Mrs Nongluck Vangsirirungruang, the deputy managing director of Summit Computer Company. Mrs Nongluck was an extremely smart lady in her late 30s who would join the group when we were finalising a proposal. Mrs Nongluck had worked in the US and was a very controlled person. I travelled with her in a Singapore taxi from Changi Airport into town one evening. The Chinese taxi driver asked her directly if she was a Thai. His next question was very Singaporean, and the most embarrassing I have ever heard. He accused her of being a hooker. 'That is the only reason you Thai women come to my country.' Mrs Nongluck was not overtly upset by the confrontation. She explained she was a computer businesswoman. Thankfully, that ended that conversation. When I was paying the taxi driver at our destination, Nongluck commented, 'I do not think he deserves a tip'. Neither did I. Most times, Singaporean taxi drivers' philosophies are forthright and interesting. This was the only time I might have wished that they just drive.

Summit already had a couple of good Sperry 1100 large system installations at the Bank of Thailand and EGAT and operated a successful service bureau business on its in-house 1100 system, which was also the immediate back-up, stand-by system for the bank and EGAT. Summit had also sold System 80s. Its first such was to the Prime Minister's office. Summit had to buy its own System 80 again as back-up to the system it had sold, and this was also used for service bureau tasks, which put pressure on the bureau manager in terms of the sale of two quite different systems capabilities and the need to cross-train the operations staff.

The Bank of Thailand was using a proprietary statistical software package from the UK. EGAT was using Mapper. Thailand was an early adopter of Mapper's user-defined software development tool. The EGAT CEO used Mapper every morning to conduct a survey of the volumes of water in the country's reservoirs, prior to making the decision about which generating plants to use that day. Summit had written the associated software with the CEO's input and it was seen as an essential tool. It was, however, putting constraints upon use of the hardware by other users when it was operating in Mapper mode. I knew some comparative figures (for an airline reservation system, standard airline booking):

Technology	Assembler language	Mapper
Number of instructions	30,000	300,000
Number of disk accesses	4½	12½

In other words, Mapper used a lot more resources than a system's native language. This was not something that we wanted to publicise. As ever, compromise was required.

During that first evening session it was decided that I should visit EGAT at Nonthaburi, a two-hour drive from Bangkok, to meet Mr Somkiet Phaloprakarn, director of the system planning department of EGAT. Amorn made it clear that he would not accompany me. The EGAT visit was something to look forward to on my next visit.

During my visit to Bangkok, Somchai explained the wai — the Thai greeting which consists of a slight bow, with palms pressed together in a prayer-like fashion — and the Buddhist philosophy of karma as he practised it: 'It is my responsibility not to disturb your karma. So I will smile and not raise my voice. I shall help if I can.' (Except when enveloped in steel, attempting to drive a car in a traffic jam in Bangkok. Then I shall sound my horn continuously. Your karma can take care of itself.) Back in Singapore Airport, I stopped off at The Times Bookshop and purchased my own copy of *Culture Shock! Thailand – and how to survive it*. There were other titles in the series and eventually I would own a set for the countries I was visiting regularly. Some are fun, especially *Culture Shock! Ireland*. I wish I had found it seven years earlier.

I went to EGAT my next trip. On the way there, Patharin explained that Amorn and Somkiet did not get on. 'Khun Somkiet is a most difficult man.' Mr Somkiet was indeed a difficult man. His business card showed that he had received his higher education at Oregon State University. My guess was that this had been 20 years earlier, as he looked to be in his early 40s, tall with iron-grey hair. Mr Somkiet was brusque and forthright:

> 'Your equipment works well enough, but it is very slow in the mornings. I want someone to come in and do a performance audit. You did one five years ago and that helped.'

9. ADVENTURES IN SOUTHEAST ASIA

The Nonthaburi Generating Plant was enormous; it covered a huge acreage. I was taken on a tour of the plant, by jeep, by deputy director Danai Manophars, a very gentle Thai. In his soft-speaking voice, he counselled me:

> 'Do not worry too much about Mr Somkiet. In time you will find that he is a kind man.'

That was some consolation. Back at the home office, Somchai expanded upon the feud between Amorn and Somkiet and the fact that Summit people, apart from programmers and the resident engineers, did not care to visit the site. EGAT was also behind in its payments to Summit. It is always easier to establish a rapport, any rapport, with a customer who is able to articulate his feelings. Somkiet told me why he was unhappy and demonstrated his frustrations by not paying Summit. I needed to fix the problem.

The next time I went to Nonthaburi, I went with Somchai, who explained the accounts payable problems to Somkiet, who certainly listened. We had also decided that I would conduct a site audit, but that Summit would charge EGAT for the job at Thai consulting rates rather than the excessive fees Sperry might have charged. Somkiet agreed to seek a budget approval for the audit. Talking to Somchai on the drive back to Bangkok, we also decided to ask Terry Thompson to visit Somkiet to emphasise our support commitments to EGAT.

On our return to the office, I was able to have a talk to Kosa Pongsupath and as many as a dozen other software people to discuss the Mapper constraints at EGAT. Kosa had attended all the sessions we had enjoyed at Summit. His opinions had been well respected by his peers when he contributed to the discussions. Kosa had written the Mapper application, written it quickly, but it so uniquely met an EGAT need it was in daily use and EGAT was not keen to have him optimise the code — if it ain't broke, why fix it? Kosa was enthusiastic and looking more like a student than the very experienced systems analyst that he was.

The Bank of Thailand was a contented customer. Director of systems engineering, Dr Vallobh Vimolvanich, was a personal friend of Amorn's, so my first and subsequent visits to the bank were primarily courtesy calls. Dr Vallobh was on the consent panel of the National Computer Centre, which authorised all computer acquisitions, and was very technically aware. The Sperry 1100 did not break down and had the capacity to handle the tasks assigned. We also had a good relationship with Mr Sumatarat Sitabut, who was the manager of the data centre. The Bank of Thailand was a prospect for the upgrade of the central processing unit of its system, which would also include the upgrade of some peripheral units to the latest technologies. I became a confidante of Dr Vallobh. I suggested he might like to accompany me as a referee on a trip to Manila when we were selling to the Central Bank of the Philippines. It was not a success. The Filipinos took offence at the thought of being advised by a Thai, something I had not reckoned with prior to the visit, and a salutary cultural lesson.

Summit was keen to win the Ministry of Agriculture account. We were hoping to build upon the installation success we had with the Prime Minister's Office, and were selling hard to provide a computer to the King's Office, as there was a commonality of interest in agricultural projects. We bid a Sperry 1100/61 to the ministry and were successful. We were aware that a project for the next year was the Ministry of Education. I was able to help with the pre-sales effort to the Ministry of Education because of the work that I had been doing with the Singapore Government and the Malaysian Department of Education, which had won us two university orders. I met with Dr Narong Boonme at the ministry in Bangkok and took him out to Nonthaburi on a site visit to EGAT.

Audrey came with me on one trip during school holidays — she was teaching at the Tanglin Primary School in Singapore. The Bangkok shops were good and the visit to Patpong was predictably fun. The bargirls were interested to talk to Audrey about her way of life, but not for long. They were working. We really enjoyed doing the tourist trip to the north of the country. Amorn's secretary, Nuttawee, had been distraught that she had been unable to get first class sleeper reservations on the overnight Bangkok to Chiang Mai train. We assured her that we would be fine with second class reservations and, in fact, that trip was a real highlight of that Asia stay. We befriended two Chiang Mai farmers returning home, who took responsibility for buying delicious food to share with us from the hawkers who passed through the train at every stop. Audrey and I bought the beer, and in the small hours the Thai whiskey. We pulled the bunks down in time to grab a few hours of sleep before arriving at Chiang Mai at about 8.00 am. It had been a super trip. In Chiang Mai we engaged a tourist guide, a very pleasant lady called Porntip, and enjoyed a wonderful few days in the country. I bought a carved teak bar that would later cause all sorts of customs and quarantine problems when it arrived in Singapore. It remains a treasured possession, although not in everyday use in Canberra.

On another occasion I took Audrey and our younger boy, Jason, into the office. We went out for lunch as a group, and later Amorn and I slipped away for our customary brandy session. Nuttawee took Jason in hand and showed him Bangkok while Audrey was taken out to the Jim Thompson Silk Shop by one of the other girls. We met up again for the evening at the Montien Hotel at the north end of Patpong. The Thais were always the most gracious of hosts.

Summit Computer Company was keen to see and sell the Sperry range of PCs. Sperry was late into the market with PCs, but embraced the new technology more readily than IBM had initially done. The trouble was getting hold of demonstration models for the distributors. There were three models of the Sperry PC that we rebadged after manufacture. The smallest and largest capability PCs were manufactured by Mitsubishi Systems, and the mid-range PC was manufactured by Acer of Taiwan. The prices were acceptable to Sperry. Somchai was a keen user of the Harvard Graphics package and he and Pandji from Soedarpo installed it on my home PC on the occasion of the 1984 Sperry distributor conference.

One interesting aspect of technical support occurred when the Sperry London Support Centre, which provided worldwide technical support, sent round a request to the regional offices for a three-month secondment of a Mapper expert. I discussed this with Amorn and Somchai. To my mind this was a wonderful opportunity to give Kosa exposure at the highest level, and we knew he would still be available for Summit work if needed. He was that sort of person. So I recommended Kosa, who undertook the secondment and was very successful. My only fear was that Sperry might want to seduce him permanently. It did, but he didn't accept. What was better was that Sperry paid commercial rates to Summit for Kosa's work, US$600 per day plus expenses. It also gave Sperry exposure to the skill base we were developing in Southeast Asia.

Somkiet received budget approval for an audit of the computer system at EGAT. I conducted the audit, which involved running software alongside everyday work called the System Instrumentation Package (SIP). SIP analysed the number of disk accesses the software wanted to make to the disk drive control unit, for example. If more requests were being made per second than the hardware could control, the net effect was that application software would appear to run slowly. With SIP, I could look at several aspects of the system at the same time — almost like an x-ray — to diagnose bottlenecks. Once these were known, they could be rectified. At some installations, SIP was a regularly used tool by operations management. At EGAT it was not. Khun Somkiet, I fear, regarded SIP as a tool for Sperry and Summit to induce him to spend more money. This was a shrewd observation and one I had anticipated. We did have a competitor at EGAT, Digital Equipment Corporation, who had a toehold with process control applications and was keen to develop an EGAT interest in scientific applications on its platforms. This was another occasion when a real Sperry applications catalogue would have been of considerable assistance. As it was, both Sperry and Digital coexisted at EGAT, each stimulated by potential competition.

Mr Amorn was a senior officer in the Thailand Computer Society and I was invited to speak at semi-technical functions a few times. The Thailand Computer Society's national conference in 1983 was great fun. Khun Amorn had arranged that I be the keynote speaker — with a general topic of 'futures' — at the conference, which was to be held in Pattaya, a seaside resort some three hours drive from Bangkok. Audrey was also invited by Summit to attend. I paid for Audrey's travel, but the hotel room was paid for by the computer society. Somchai picked us up at Don Muang Airport and drove us to Pattaya for the conference opening on the Wednesday evening. I was scheduled to speak on the Friday afternoon. Summit invited any of its staff who wanted to attend the Friday session to Pattaya. Perhaps 40 young people came in total. It was the first time Audrey had heard me address a technical conference.

That evening we hit the tourist strip. Most of the large open-air bars and restaurants had the most sumptuous floorshows and we looked into most of them as a group. We were waiting for the group to reassemble before moving on to the next bar, when I commented to Audrey that the ladies' shoes in the shoe shop window looked huge. Somchai picked up my comment, and he and Audrey had a huge laugh. Here I was, the man-of-the-world salesman, having spent the best part of a long evening in the transvestite capital of Thailand, in complete ignorance of that fact. I looked at the showgirls much more intently as we moved on. Later, well after midnight, we all moved to Kosa's family home, where we sat in the garden for a banquet. All the Summit people were staying at Kosa's, boys on the ground floor and the girls upstairs. It was assumed that Audrey and I would stay over with them, but we opted to walk back to the hotel. Somchai again kindly drove us back to Bangkok Airport.

Figure 9.22: Thailand's Princess Maha Chakri Sirindhorn, who attended the Summit programmer training courses.
Source: Author's collection.

The order for a System 80 system for the King's Office had caused great excitement for Summit. The King's daughter, the very much admired Princess Maha Chakri Sirindhorn, attended the programming course conducted by Summit personnel so that she might contribute to the planning and monitoring of the King's projects, for which the system was being designed.

I have the feeling that we did as well as we could have expected in Thailand. Visitors to our region naturally gravitated towards Bangkok as a part of their Asian experience and we tried not to make too many demands on Summit for its time and hospitality.

This has been a long chapter, but I believe it appropriate that I comment on doing business in the seven Asian countries I so much enjoyed.

10
As far south as we could go

The situation in Singapore was altered in 1988 by the Singapore Government's change in policy. It no longer needed technology transfer in support of its computer plans. This was now the responsibility of the National Computer Centre. Sperry was terrific and asked me to choose where I next wanted to live and work. Although we had never been to New Zealand, Audrey and I had a real respect for the majority of New Zealanders we had met in Singapore. New Zealand was our choice. Tom Yam, the Singapore vice president, encouraged me to approach Paul Travers, the vice president for Sperry Australasia, in order to explore that opportunity with Sperry.

I was interviewed over breakfast in Seoul by Paul Travers, white haircut with a fringe and tonsure (reminding me of a cleric of the Middle Ages), an aquiline proboscis, and a nose for business and people; sales director Dick Simpson, darkly aggressive and ambitious in a recognisable IBM mould; and regional financial controller Barry Hughes, squat and often talkative, despite a speech impediment. They were in Seoul for a negotiation round in the allocation of the sales quota for the 1986 fiscal year. Paul immediately advised that there would be a position in the region for me. He asked me to think about what I wanted to do and let him know. I called Paul a couple of weeks later and asked if I could go to New Zealand. His derogatory response was not the one I expected: 'You must be mad. No one wants to work in New Zealand.'

I now understand the relationship between the Aussies and the Kiwis and could have predicted such a comment from the Duntroon Military College–trained vice president who was, in all things, very proudly Australian.

Paul asked if I wanted to be the branch manager. I declined. I did not feel I had the financial background and I had seen the inordinate amount of time that Rom Slimak and Gus Sichero had spent on administrative, non-selling matters in Singapore. Paul recommended that I take a roving role with the title of marketing support manager, and that a general manager would be appointed on an interim basis while I learned the bigger job.

I flew to Wellington and Audrey flew back to the UK to settle our younger lad in the British Army and sell our property in Cheshire. The first problem was for me to discover the address of the office. I could not find the address in the directories I searched from the James Cook Hotel on the Terrace. The Terrace was obviously the place to be, as the Sperry office was apparently hidden at number 39. I was expected, but information about why I was there and what I was expected to be doing had not reached this far. The staff in the office believed I was the new branch manager and that my reticence to accept the role was false modesty. I met everyone in the boardroom to dispel these misconceptions, but I do not think that anyone believed me.

The branch secretary showed me into a sparsely furnished office that was devoid of any paperwork I might address. My first visitor was Geoff Brader, the financial controller. He was most apologetic: my car would not be available until the Friday. That was a nice surprise. My move had occurred so quickly and without any formal paperwork, I had not realised I was getting a company car. A company car was good news to John Smith — a rugby-playing friend from Singapore who was working in Wellington, via Jakarta — with whom I took up residence, in his flat overlooking the Wellington Harbour, two days after I arrived in New Zealand. The fact that the car was a station wagon was excellent news to John, who was a keen surfer with a great deal of equipment to transport.

Bill Everett, the technical support manager, had the Australian contacts and it was he who learned that Sydney-based customer engineering manager, Dennis Lavell, was coming to be branch manager. Dennis arrived about a month after I did. Dennis is a most acceptable person as a work colleague. Dennis had an extensive computer background. He had worked for the Varian Computer Company in Australia when it was acquired by Sperry in the 1970s and had progressed with the company since then. Dennis was not particularly pleased with the move, and succumbed to a business complaint I had seen before, a complaint whose recognition, as far as I am aware, has not been blessed with a name: he slowed down to half pace so that he could have work to do after normal working hours and thus be able to grumble about the number of hours he needed to spend in the office to get all his work done. Dennis initially also spent an inordinate amount of time on the telephone to his ex-colleagues in Australia and we were kept well advised of Australian politics. Dennis's family moved to Wellington but that did not improve his humour that much. He had chosen to rent a home in Khandallah, a district prone to fog, and a difficult drive into the city.

I returned to Singapore for a few days to help Audrey close that chapter of our lives, and we took the opportunity to visit Townsville, the Great Barrier Reef, and Sydney on our way to Wellington. I had to visit Sydney to be able to attend Sperry Australian headquarters and talk to the HR manager about establishing a salary. I agreed to be paid mid-point of the Hays' Grade 13, which was not really enough money. I regretted that Terry Thompson had not had the courage to move me to Grade 14 in Singapore, although I had asked him a couple of times. I suspect that Terry was at that level as a group financial controller in the US. The titles we adopted in Asia had no validity in the real world. I also had the chance to talk to Paul Travers again, and he was able to confirm Dennis Lavell's transfer. Paul suggested I should join in a sales meeting that was being conducted by Dick Simpson that morning.

Of the 20 or so people in the Northpoint, North Sydney, boardroom, Dick was the only person I knew. Impeccably dressed, he said that he would conduct a sales review by asking the Australian state managers to report on their first quarter performances. He prefaced his introduction of his managers by stating that he was unhappy about the level of success with the new UNIX platforms, and that each manager should address this and discuss his plans to remedy the poor performance of that sector of the sales plan. He called Peter Kalms, the New South Wales (NSW) manager, to the podium. As I would have expected, Peter was well prepared. He turned the top page of the flip chart to reveal a detailed matrix of numbers that compared the targets with actual results to date, with the expectation that the end of year results would exceed the targets. It was well done. I would have been pleased to present that set of figures.

I was just thinking that this was setting a high standard of presentation and content — the numbers for NSW were similar to those we had been achieving for the whole of Southeast Asia.

But Dick Simpson was not satisfied.

> 'Peter, where are your UNIX sales coming from? What have you done to train your staff for this market?'

Peter turned another page of his presentation and outlined the UNIX plan via bullet points. Dick continued to pressure him for the names of companies that Peter and his team had spoken to and their response to the sales pitch. Peter seemed a bit hesitant.

> 'Dick, I have to be honest. I do not think we are ready to mount a major campaign yet. We have no software and the in-house machine does not stay up long enough for us to commit to a demonstration.'

Dick asked if the other managers felt the same way. Cliff Patrick from the Melbourne office said he agreed with Peter. Walt Heuer from the Canberra office confirmed the story, as did others. Dick asked Scotty Wallbank, the customer support director, to comment. Scotty had no alternative but to say that the UNIX system was much better than the salespeople had suggested. Dick followed this up.

> 'I agree. We should be actively selling UNIX or we shall miss the opportunity.'

Peter Kalms responded:

> 'But Dick, I have explained the constraints we have in Sydney.'
> 'Peter, I have listened, but you have not heard. I have made the decision to double the UNIX sales target to ensure your enthusiasm for the product.'
> 'Dick, you cannot do that!'
> 'Peter, I just have — and that applies to all the state managers.'
> 'Dick, get fucked! That is neither fair nor logical.'
> 'Well, you can all get fucked. These are the new rules.'

Suddenly, the f-word was being hurled across the room accusatorially as everyone joined in the free-for-all. I sat there, stunned, bemused, confused, and suddenly aware that I was no longer working in the UK or Asia, where obviously business is conducted somewhat differently to that in Australia. I did not express my reaction: 'Have I made a terrible mistake?'

I did not participate in the meeting, which continued as if no real confrontation had taken place. The language remained colourful and the attitudes robust. Lunch was a convivial affair, and at the end of the day Paul Travers and others joined us for a drink in the pub below Northpoint. I did wonder how much interest Dick Simpson would have in New Zealand.

Once Audrey got to Wellington she found us a super house to live in, in Whitby to the north of town, overlooking the sea in the Pauatahanui Inlet on a street known locally as the Dress Circle, and I settled down to enjoy a new country.

Dennis Lavell joined us and we were beginning to find our feet. We had both been up to Auckland to meet Kim Bigby, the Auckland sales manager, and to look over his office in the suburb of Newmarket. Once again, Sperry was trying to remain incognito. There was no indication that we had a Sperry office in the directories. I had to call Wellington. We eventually found a very modern-looking three-storey office block with one problem: the architect had designed the skin of the building to be thick glass panes, which were stacked one upon the other, and the accumulative weight of the glass was prone to break the lowest pane with dramatic effect. It was, nonetheless, a nice office.

Back at our Wellington base, Bill Everett had assembled a competent customers services team around him. The team included Graeme Cameron, an older programmer who quietly got on with his assigned tasks and was an invaluable source of information about other computer professionals in Wellington. Graeme Denne was a tall, red-haired, independent spirit. He was the senior hardware troubleshooter and his temperament suited the basic customer engineering logic: 'It was working once and I need to get it working again.' It was commitment that sustained Sperry for all the years I worked with the corporation.

Carolyne Mitchell, our public relations manager, had a wonderful marketing project in hand. She had persuaded the company to be a major sponsor for the More–Sperry Business Woman of the Year and was working with the premier business magazine *More* as the other major sponsor. This was a New Zealand-wide accolade and a big event. It took a lot of her time and involved her in a lot of travelling to wherever regional candidates were being evaluated in anticipation of the final event in Auckland, which was televised and gained a lot of editorial. But it was too high a profile for the small Sperry New Zealand organisation and a huge drain on our finances. I believe it was obvious to everyone that it was not a supportable venture in the long term. When that decision was made, Carolyne left.

Carolyne was the start of a trend. Kim Bigby also left, as did both salesmen from the Wellington office. In late 1985 to early 1986 it was not easy to find suitable replacements and we took a long time to do so. In the interim, Bill Everett and I more or less took over the sales functions. Our two main accounts were the Wanganui Computer Centre and the Ministry of Defence.

Bill Everett had a really good relationship with Wanganui Computer Centre, which served three customers: the Police Force, the Justice Department, and the Ministry of Transport. The centre itself had a history. Wanganui is a two-hour drive from Wellington, and in many respects is a typical, large New Zealand country town, built around a main street containing the same retail outlets as every other town of comparable size. But Wanganui had the computer centre and the New Zealand Post Philatelic Bureau, which offered high level of technical employment in the town. The selection of Wanganui had been controversial and in November 1982 the centre had infamously been attacked by a suicide bomber who had caused considerable damage, blowing himself to bits and causing extensive damage to the front of the building.

However, due to the purpose design and construction of the building and its standby support services, the centre was not seriously prejudiced. (I was told that the installed Sperry 1100s 'did not miss a beat'.) When I first visited it, the centre was isolated and protected by a formidable fence and strict security systems. My first tour included being shown the visible scars from the bomber's attack; the impression of the bomber's spectacles was clearly discernible in the concrete surround. Bill Everett told me of his respect for Bill Whittock, the original centre director who had instilled a sense of discipline and a dedication in his staff. It was a good place to go. It was full of Sperry equipment and we could expect to make the New Zealand sales targets every other year from upgrades to the latest technologies. The trick would have been to get the Ministry of Defence to buy in the alternate years, but it did not work like that.

10. AS FAR SOUTH AS WE COULD GO

Figure 10.1: The broken front of the Wanganui Computer Centre in 1982 after the bombing.
Source: Author's collection.

Doug Hornsby was the Wanganui Computer Centre director. Doug was always well dressed, quietly spoken, and in control of what was going on. The politics were rife. It cannot have been easy supporting the needs of three contrasting organisations, and there were rumours that the Police and the Ministry of Transport enforcement force were to amalgamate, and that the David Lange Labour Government was looking to outsource the government's computing needs. Doug's office overlooked the security entrance to the centre and he knew what was going on.

The Ministry of Defence building in Porirua, a suburb of Wellington, was equally interesting. Porirua is built upon the earthquake fault line that devastated the original port of Wellington in 1848. The eight-storey building was protected against earthquake by being built in four quarters, with each quarter isolated from the other by huge rubber blocks, which were obvious inside the building. The main computer floor was designed to spread the units of equipment across the four segments in the hope that the chance of being able to continue business would be greater in the event of a quake.

We had one other Sperry 1100 computer customer: Capital Computer Company (CCL). Paul Kimberley, the director of marketing for Sperry in Australia, and who had been stand-in manager in New Zealand during 1983–1985, had sold to CCL. Paul was known as the 'Silver Fox' within Sperry circles, and was not totally trusted. He had sold two other computer bureaus in Australia, and had developed a most attractive proposal for CCL. Paul's deal, however, was a constant source of problems for those who followed him in Wellington.

CCL's expectations about the level of services and support from Sperry were much higher than we were able to deliver, and the relationship was a difficult one. Compounding these difficulties was the fact that our commitments to CCL were not recorded in a single document. Ross Davey, the managing director of CCL, was a constant source of stress. He summoned Dennis and me to his office to complain that we had not brought a single new client to CCL, remonstrating: 'I am not surprised, because I have not seen the appointment of a single Sperry salesman responsible for CCL business.' This was news to us. We told Ross that we knew nothing of any such arrangement. Ross responded, as he had done previously, and would do again, by reaching into his desk drawer to produce a letter signed by Paul Kimberley stating that Sperry would bring a specific monthly dollar amount of business to CCL. The letter stipulated that if CCL had not attained projected revenues on its own behalf, we would use the Sperry sales force to achieve that level of new business for CCL. At almost every turn we were confronted by a side letter committing us further, often beyond our capabilities. Ross was a huge man, a former Wellington provincial rugby representative with a wide circle of business contacts. We did our best to listen and understand, but it was not always easy, as we seemed to be constantly under the threat of litigation. Until we learned how to respond, as a single entity, to Ross Davey's theatrics, he held the upper hand in negotiations. It took both companies time, and lost opportunities, to come to a consensus in working together.

We also had smaller systems that were working well. The New Zealand Wool Board had a Sperry 90/30 system with a working solution for monitoring wool stocks and prices. The board's unique capability was to move a terminal into the wool trading auctions and to collect sales data in real time.

The Rhône-Poulenc New Zealand office in Naenae, the Wellington suburb beyond Lower Hutt, quietly got on with its support of the chemical manufacture and distribution business. I used to enjoy visiting the site for a monthly progress meeting and talking to finance manager Murray Georgel, and I always left believing in computers once again.

May & Baker in Auckland was still operating a Varian V77 computer system. Its system support came from the UK so our service to it was limited to keeping the hardware functional.

With all this going on, Dennis Lavell was under pressure to appoint an Auckland manager. The first I knew about it was a call from Tom Qureshi, who had just been appointed. Dennis was flying back from Auckland and had suggested I might be a good source of information for Tom. Tom sounded so excited that I was keen to help and emptied the Wellington library of marketing material to make sure that he had all he would ever need. Tom rang back the next day; the couriered material had arrived. Tom had a Middle Eastern background and was a UNIX man with a really positive attitude to that emerging standard. The guy was a real live wire and quickly enthused the Auckland office. He perplexed us in Wellington through his constant search of a deal for his UNIX prospects. The trouble was that the margins between the transfer price and the list selling price were really small. It was a new venture and, even with Tom's experience, we experienced as much trouble in getting Sperry UNIX capability recognised in the marketplace. Tom was an early adopter of the idea of joint projects in which both the customer and Sperry might benefit from any application software developed for the New Zealand market.

It was about this time that we had a visit from Paul Travers, who took Dennis, Bill Everett, and I out to dinner and presented us with the option of New Zealand becoming a Sperry subsidiary in its own right, or of formally acknowledging a link to Australia as a direct subsidiary. It would have been nice to be a distinct entity, but it did not make sense. We were approximately 25 persons, with an annual revenue of US$3 million or so. We could not afford to employ the specialist support staff we forecast we might need. Paul was offering support from Australia at the rate of US$600 per man day plus expenses, so we went with that.

I spent a lot of effort in recruiting two salesmen for Wellington. Gerald Fiddes had essentially interviewed me on two occasions and had requested a written confirmation, prior to contract, of the points we had discussed. I thought this a plus in terms of account management and pencilled him in as a candidate to look after the Wanganui Computer Centre. He seemed to have worked for most of the computer companies in Wellington and to have a good grasp of what we wanted to achieve for Sperry New Zealand. Gerald was a very neat and tidy man. (I did not read the signs that he was very structured in his approach but rather pedantic and would get on everyone's nerves at the Wanganui Computer Centre and they would eventually ask that we remove him from the account.) Mike Liapis was quite different; in appearance he was like a badly tied parcel. He needed a job and was seeking employment in Wellington to be near a young family from which he was removed, as he was then employed in Brisbane, Queensland. Mike came across as someone who was really keen to learn. I pencilled him in to look after our Department of Defence business.

Having salesmen to manage was the cause of some personal soul-searching. The Southeast Asia experience was one where I had, more often than not, been the only Sperry representative in the country. I had then carried a card that said I was a 'technician', and I had enjoyed taking the technical as well as sales decisions. When Dennis and I lost the sales team in Wellington, I had easily slipped into a self-sufficient mode of working. Now I had to get back to being a team player and leader.

Figure 10.2: I had managed to sell major systems for Sperry for 21 years before the opportunity arose for me to be senior enough to be included in the (almost mandatory) contract signing picture. Here, Murray Bond signs on behalf of Telecom. Neil McDougall and Dianne McDonald exhibit their relief that it is finalised.
Source: Author's collection.

Meanwhile, I had potential business to close. The Telecommunication Authority of Singapore had been implementing a system to help them track the underground (tail end) copper wires that comprise an essential part of networks (and still do today). I had discussed the system in Singapore with a representative of the Swedish Telecommunications Company, its Swedcom sales subsidiary, who had told me that he was also visiting New Zealand. The timing was perfect, and we were talking to Warwick Kay, the computer director of the Telecom Corporation of New Zealand, who was the correct level of executive. Swedcom was in the process of talking to Telecom and was amenable to our joining its sales effort. The Swedcom software ran on Sperry equipment in Farsta in Sweden, so it made sense for a joint approach. Warwick Kay instigated a business case analysis based upon the Swedcom figure of an effective 40 per cent increase in revenue potential from the copper wires which would be rediscovered through the street-based database. The database would be created from in-house historical data and actual discovery during day-to-day operations. Better still, Telecom recruited Murray Bond from the Department of Defence to head the business case project. Murray had two independent contract consultants working with him, Neil McDougall and Dianne McDonald. As it happened, I had met them both through the New Zealand Computer Society. Murray made the business case and we signed the appropriate contracts. The application software was to come from Swedcom, so the Sperry support obligations were principally in the training area.

Telecom appointed a most amiable, rotund project manager, Eddie Palmer, to oversee the system installation and implementation. Eddie was not daunted by the size and importance of the overall system to be installed in Palmerston North, a two-hour drive north of Wellington. Eddie reported to the Telecom area data processing manager. They worked well together with the project staff in a strong union environment. The union did not wish to be too conscious of the rule book, and the project moved forward. Sperry appointed a project manager from the Sydney office, Col Cunningham, who fitted into Palmerston North and was seen to be doing a great job. Engineering support was provided by the Wanganui Centre staff as required until the system became operational.

Eddie Palmer instituted a Thursday-night sports evening for the project and I was in Palmerston most Thursdays, taking on all comers at darts, dominoes, bar bowls, ten-pin bowling, or any other activity. We played a few games of cricket, including one against the Sperry Wellington office. The resultant team spirit was excellent and project matters were progressing well, but the dark clouds of 'rationalisation' were hanging over us. The Lange Government was one of the first in the world to attempt to disengage government from the day-to-day operation of state-owned enterprises. The New Zealand Post Office was broken up into New Zealand Post and Telecom New Zealand. Our project was eventually a victim. Before it died, the hardware was moved into the Telecom New Zealand data centre in the Wellington CBD.

One challenge I was keen to take up followed Sperry's announcement of an initiative to promote a presence in artificial intelligence. A significant grant was to be awarded to 20 universities selected worldwide, and the grant package would include the award of the (Texas Instruments rebadged) Explorer LISP-based processor, which was very fast, and had huge memory. The specialised software to translate the expert's thought processes into manageable algorithms was provided by IntelliCorp through its Knowledge Engineering Environment. Why not have some New Zealand participation in the scheme, I thought. I went to see Professor Stan Smith, head of the computer and systems engineering department of Victoria University of Wellington. Professor Smith was an American mathematician, and he was keen to make an application for a grant. He introduced me to Peter André, a senior lecturer in the department. Peter was a wonderful character, well respected and very recognisable about the campus as he had decided that he was comfortable in shorts and did not need to wear shoes. Peter would sit cross-legged on his seat in front of a computer terminal as we put together the grant application. It was a good application. Peter won the confidence of the head of the engineering school and our project would be to try and build a representation of the thought processes of an engineer consulting on the efficiency of a continuous production process — we had in mind the Mitsubishi assembly plant in Porirua.

10. AS FAR SOUTH AS WE COULD GO

Figure 10.3: The contract signing with Victoria University, Wellington. Professor Stan Smith, Dennis Lavell, and I attended.
Source: Author's collection.

I was really pleased when Victoria University became the recipient of a grant. We used the occasion of the contract signature to invite Paul Travers to be a signatory. Paul came and was a delightful guest. Professor Smith arranged that the Vice Chancellor of the university would be their signatory and we met in the Vice Chancellor's office for the photo opportunity. Professor Stan Smith, Dennis Lavell, and myself attended. We enjoyed a sherry during our informal meeting and completed our business. As we walked through the university grounds, Paul commented: 'Sherry is a most civilised drink. I wonder why we do not drink it more often.' Paul stayed for lunch that day and we did drink some more sherry. Most civilised, we agreed.

The Australian National University in Canberra was also successful with its grant application. Graeme Denne installed the Texas Instruments box and the software at Victoria University, and kept the system operational, despite the fact that spares took several more months to arrive. Not only had spares been an oversight, the company also failed in putting a monitoring liaison system in place to follow-up and coordinate the three-monthly reports on progress that the award recipients were contractually obliged to submit. That became rather a burden to the two Australasian offices, but we did attempt to keep interest going in the

Wellington activity. Peter André had two PhD students working with the equipment, but they lost the support of their expert. This was a limitation of artificial intelligence — it is a people limitation, as the expert has to have the time and the inclination to explain his thought processes for their translation into a repetitive process, which is tedious and time-consuming. The university liked the equipment and made good use of it for postgraduate studies, although not strictly for the purpose intended. Professor Smith, whose speciality was the predictive management of telecommunications networks, persevered with the two assigned students, developing a model of his own expertise and the two students were awarded their doctoral degrees.

Another piece of business I wanted was from Air New Zealand. I felt quite confident that I knew enough about the UNIVAC Standard Airline System to be able to prompt an interest from Air New Zealand. In the first two years I was in New Zealand, I must have made four appointments to see John Englefield, the computer centre director, and spent several hours waiting to see him. He would eventually appear, looking and behaving totally stressed, to ask me to forgive him, and for me to speak to Alex McFarlane, the network manager who seemed to be Mr Englefield's deputy. John Englefield had a terrible reputation for agreeing to see supplier representatives but never being available, and was always anxious to buy the latest and greatest from IBM. I really did want to speak to Mr Englefield about an initiative in which Peter Williams — an engineer based in Christchurch who was used to fending for himself and had been encouraged to look for business when he was not busy in his customer engineering role — was making progress in his endeavours to get into the maintenance division of the airline.

The Air New Zealand maintenance division in Christchurch was progressive, and was expanding its portfolio to offer services to other airlines and aircraft operators, including the military. Peter Williams had unearthed a Mapper-appropriate application. At about this time, Sperry announced a PC-based Mapper 5 hardware and software system that dramatically reduced the price of a small Mapper package. When Air New Zealand maintains an engine, it breaks it down into its constituent parts for inspection and certification before rebuilding the engine. It was Peter's proposal that each part be assigned a barcode and that the physical movement of each part as it progressed through the engineering workshop be recorded in a Mapper database. This meant we had to design a barcode reader interface, but it was an ideal application. The Air New Zealand engineers understood the value of knowing where engine parts were at any time and were not about to attempt too much, although it made sense to compile the cost of new spare parts when they were required as well as the time spent working on each part as it moved through the maintenance shop. Peter had done a great job with the airline. I spent time with him putting a formal proposal together and then worked with the engineering manager on the business case before we got approval.

When the Air New Zealand engineering director raised the issue of head office support for a computer system that was not wearing an IBM badge, I convinced him that Mapper was a tool, not a system. I knew we were potentially avoiding a major issue, but it seemed expedient at the time. One of the reasons I had wanted to talk to John Englefield was to tell him about the maintenance division's interest in Mapper. The division was looking ahead and could see the application of a similar system to monitor staff placements. The scheduling of planned and preventive maintenance for the airline and its external clients was also being discussed. I had advised the airline's marketing group of what we were planning, and it sent an analyst to help with the system documentation, which might be used in the future as a marketing document, subject to Air New Zealand allowing us to sell its application to other interested users.

In early 1986, we had heard rumours that the Burroughs Corporation was talking to Sperry about a possible takeover or merger. We did not pay much attention to the rumours. My knowledge of Burroughs was sparse. We knew that it had provided systems to two government computer centres in Wellington, and we were enviously watching the progress of a new building carrying a huge Burroughs banner opposite our office on the Terrace.

The merger took place in late 1986. The merger was initiated by the dominant player, depending upon the market presence of the companies in their own parts of the world, so, in New Zealand, the 360-strong Burroughs Corporation was easily able to absorb the 20 Sperry people it chose to keep. Dennis Lavell was pleased and relieved to go back to Sydney.

The target date for the effective merger to take place in New Zealand was 1 January 1987. I had an interview with Brian Clarke, the Burroughs New Zealand general manager, in October 1986. Brian was an impressive man in his early 40s, tall, dark, and wearing a neat, clipped beard.

Brian presented the merger to me as the opportunity to join what had been designated Burroughs's top country team that year. He was very confident. He told me that I would be left with responsibility for the Sperry business and business plan until 1 January 1989, and he asked me to give him and the new company a two-year trial period. I made that commitment to him with a handshake.

Brian Clarke was the only Burroughs manager to approach us. That worried me. I thought it appropriate to meet someone else. I rang Burroughs, and eventually spoke to Dave Arlidge, the manager of government business. Dave and I met a couple of times, had lunch, including a couple of beers, and wondered which of us would hold that appointment after 1 January.

From 1 January we were a combined company. Those of us left moved from the Terrace into the shabby old Burroughs office on Thorndon Quay, pending completion of the new Burroughs office. It was obvious why the company had decided to move. The Burroughs people were of a kind. While they were a mix of ages, with different backgrounds and education, they exhibited a common committed discipline and a practiced response. I was reminded of the rows of terracotta soldiers that stood in rows as a part of the Chinese funeral celebration, all different, but essentially indistinguishable.

I had another short interview with Brian Clarke, who instructed me to convert all of the Sperry 1100 mainframes to Burroughs A Series systems, and to lose the smaller Sperry systems, without making it obvious that we were trying to get rid of them, and to report on these objectives to Bruce Christianson, the Burroughs sales director. My initial reaction was one of horror. Trying to be pragmatic, I asked Brian to consider the amount of development effort that had been put into their systems, particularly by the Wanganui Computer Centre and the Ministry of Defence. I told him that it was most unlikely that either customer would even begin to consider a change. I reminded Brian that the newly merged entity had written to its combined user lists to state that all product lines would be fully supported for a further five years. Brian suggested that how I went about my new tasks was up to me and that Christianson was there to help. It was not the time for a debate. My concern also extended down to the smaller users. I knew the effort that had gone into the implementation of viable systems for them. It was a black day for me.

The Burroughs style was different. Its people were not as worldly-wise as my Sperry colleagues. If my new colleagues had travelled, their overseas experience had been of their own volition, a traditional rite of passage undertaken by most Kiwis. They were a considerably larger group of people than I had experienced so far, and, it seemed, involved less mixing of disciplines, even in a bid situation. In the Burroughs case, the bid manager would formally seek written input from the appropriate company disciplines. I had been used to small group discussion and consensus. On reflection, the largest Sperry division I had worked for had been the first one, with perhaps 50 people in the UNIVAC division of Remington Rand. Every subsequent move had taken me into a small group dedicated to opening a new market where we had needed to be generalists rather than specialists.

We worked for a few months without a new name for the merged entity. Every employee was invited to submit names, with a fairly substantial prize for the winner. Brian Clarke handled the announcement of the new name imaginatively, until the moment of the unveiling. Everyone in the company was presented with a bottle of champagne and a written invitation to watch the television at 6.00 am the next morning for the formal announcement. On the television, Brian announced the name of the company as UNI-sys, or was it uni-SYS? Brian emphasised both start and end of the name in his presentation. My guess was that he had not heard how to pronounce the new name and was working from hardcopy. It was not a name that slipped easily off his tongue. The underlying theme was unified systems, or universal systems. Audrey and I drank the champagne early in the morning before we drove into Wellington to work. By the time I got in to the office I already had a facsimile from Unisys in the UK, the footer of which carried the new company logo and an explanation: 'UNISYS–UNIVAC is still your supplier.' This did not go down at all well with my new colleagues. I thought it quite funny.

My place in the new Unisys had been made apparent on the day we moved into the new office. Burroughs bureaucracy pervaded the new office. Senior managers had enclosed offices and were given black desktops. Everyone else was seated in a low cubicle in the open-plan area. Junior managers were allocated a black workbench, workers were allocated a plain white worksurface. Of course, my workstation place was white.

I was made to feel less welcome than I had anticipated: I was not initially signed on to the in-house computing system, and was not allocated a terminal, although I did have an allocated (white) workspace. My car, which was due for renewal, was not renewed, and I was not allocated a place in the company car park — in fact, the car park attendant took it upon himself not to allow my older car into the company car park at all (as I was not on his list, even as a casual user). I was expressly forbidden to meet a visiting former Sperry colleague, Alfred Tong, at Wellington Airport. Alfred had won a regional marketing appointment in the merged company. He had been a real friend to me when I arrived in Singapore, but I was told that it was not policy to meet people at the airport. The company paid expenses to travellers. I argued that Alfred was a friend as well as a former colleague, but Christianson formally forbade me from meeting him. To add to a feeling of isolation, I was denied the acknowledgment of a salesman of the year trip to South America for the Telecom New Zealand order and other 1986 business, because it had not been on the Burroughs list of prospects. Another excuse was that, although the value of the contract would have qualified me as a Burroughs salesman, it would not have qualified me as a Burroughs sales manager. I had both roles in the Sperry sale. The value of the contract, however, was used to allow two former Burroughs salesmen who had not achieved their targets to make up their numbers.

I was aware that Bill Everett was fighting Unisys for monies that it had agreed were owed. The company even took possession of the original Sperry car from Bill's home. It was a ridiculous situation — the administration manager of the merged company had been a colleague of Bill's when they were both younger engineers with Burroughs. To top it off, the new human resources department asked me to repay the monies that Sperry had spent moving me from Singapore to Wellington. Its argument was that the Burroughs Corporation did not pay such expenses and in discussing the move I had told Brian Clarke that I had instigated it. The numbers would have passed through the Sperry books two years previously, but HR had dug them out.

Brian Clarke was an innovator. The New Zealand organisation was selected by Unisys to explore the potential for organisational development, which we called the 'flattening of the organisational pyramid'. Today we describe it as empowering staff to make decisions based upon their understanding and knowledge of company principles. An organisational change manager was appointed, and he and Brian met every one of the company employees, in small groups of up to eight people, and would present the theory and practice of the changes they wanted to introduce. The session I attended was a virtuosic performance by Brian. He ran the session at the pace he wanted and gained complete acceptance from the participants. I know that he also won over the Wanganui Computer Centre engineers, who had been far removed from management philosophy at Wanganui, when they attended their sessions with the new boss. Brian set and published the rules for the process. The small group would meet at 8.00 am and not be interrupted for any reason until noon. Brian won kudos from the entire organisation when he refused entry to one of his directors who wanted to join the group, having missed the 8.00 am start.

Bruce Christianson took it upon himself to talk to me once a month. This was, at times, quite enjoyable. I was having some fun at his expense. Bruce and I would discuss a raft of issues without seeming to ever reach a conclusion. On the first such occasion, he was interested to learn who had authorised my introduction to a defence artificial intelligence visitor a few weeks earlier. I told him that no one had authorised this. He stated that he was astonished. On another occasion, we discussed at length the technical merits of the Sperry 1100 36-bit word architecture and multi-program real-time operating system versus the Burroughs A Series 60-bit word single-program operating system, from a salesman's perspective. Another time, we argued the merits of Mapper against the Burroughs Linc fourth generation software development tool. One day, we even discussed the merits of the Sperry personnel policy that had seen me change my role from sales, to technical, to administrative, and then back to sales on a two-year cycle. He admitted that the former Burroughs people found it difficult to place me: 'Are you a technician or a salesman?' He seemed totally content with his 40 years with Burroughs in Wellington, starting with the basic accounting machines and developing his portfolio to include the biggest hardware systems. We discussed Burroughs's paper-driven, bureaucratic approach and compared it with Sperry's more initiative-driven attitude. What I did not realise until much later was that Bruce was in the process of counselling me to look for another job, as Unisys was going to fire me when my two-year agreement with Brian Clarke was up. I did not fit its mould, so I did not deserve to be employed. At the time, I thought that Bruce might actually be interested to learn about the way Sperry had been used to doing things.

It was a surprise to be called in to the office and be given a written dismissal notice. I was to leave in six weeks time, on 30 September, the second-year anniversary of my commitment to Brian Clarke. The man who saw me expressed disappointment, but his demeanour was not one of contrition. As hard as I had tried, I did not fit the New Zealand Unisys pattern. I sought legal advice regarding whether six weeks notice was appropriate after 23 years of service. My solicitor said that it was not in accordance with New Zealand practice and wrote to Unisys, who replied that it considered my tenure to have started when I had come to New Zealand four years previously.

Richard Hawkins, with whom I had worked so closely in Malaysia and India, had left Singapore before me and returned to Sperry Australia, and had recently contacted me. He had not stayed with the new Unisys Australia and was working with Société Internationale de Télécommunications Aéronautiques (SITA), the airline's private network operator and outsourcer (before the service was defined as such), who was a major user of Sperry systems. Richard asked if I had an interest in joining SITA back in Singapore as he had done. I asked Audrey if we wanted to go back to Singapore. We did not. But she did add that I was more interesting a person when I was travelling, and I had hardly spent any time out of Wellington since the merger. In Singapore, I had been used to being out of the country for 200 days a year. One reason for our move to New Zealand was so that we might spend more time in support of one another, as our two boys had opted to go back to the UK rather than stay in Singapore and do national service. I read into Audrey's comments the implication that I might seek a job with travel opportunities.

11

Working with the airlines in the Australasia-Pacific region

With my tenure at the new Unisys on shaky ground, I asked former colleagues if they knew of a job opportunity for someone with my skill set. I certainly wanted to stay in the Asia-Pacific area. New Zealand, as a relatively small country, did not present any immediate opportunities other than working with a computer consultancy or setting up on my own, and I was not keen on the latter. Richard Hawkins had left Unisys in Hong Kong and joined the Société Internationale de Télécommunications Aéronautiques (SITA). He had already spoken to SITA on my behalf and advised me to call Ms Irene Legay in SITA's Hong Kong office.

The SITA opportunity was attractive. I knew the organisation and had overseen its Sperry installations in Bangkok and Jakarta. I knew SITA to be technically aggressive. It used Sperry second-level communication processors, without mainframes, for its communications network, and I had recently liaised with SITA when the New Zealand Defence Department had contemplated a similar application.

After the end of World War II, international telephone lines had been hard to obtain, so the airlines decided it would be to their advantage to pool resources. SITA was set up to control those resources and provide additional services. In the 1980s, as SITA approached its 40th anniversary, director general Claude Lalanne had instructed McKinsey & Company, as consultants, to investigate the strategies that would keep SITA viable for the next 40 years. McKinsey had recommended that SITA set up a sales and marketing operation — a group of 32 people — to optimise its potential. Until now, the airlines, who were also SITA shareholders, had been creating demand and SITA was providing services on an ad hoc basis. This had been working, and SITA was a 3,000-person-strong company with a turnover of about US$300 million from a diverse product portfolio.

SITA was essentially a communication network company. Its network drawing, which was updated on a semi-annual basis, was an icon in the industry and a prized possession of every airline communications manager who could read it (and understand the acronyms employed). The basis of the network are the 18 message and data distribution computer centres, shown in blue, to which every airline in the world was connected. Older versions of the drawing were distributed to hang in airlines' boardroom and reception areas.

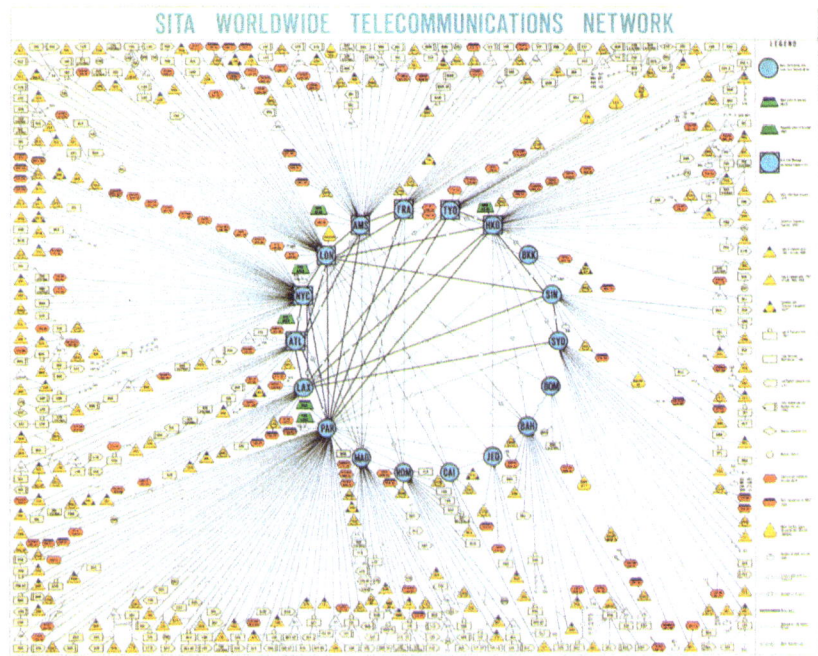

Figure 11.1: The SITA network circa 1990.
Source: Author's collection.

11. WORKING WITH THE AIRLINES IN THE AUSTRALASIA-PACIFIC REGION

Richard had won a job as a regional airlines manager/account manager looking after the SITA business with Singapore Airlines. He also looked after Indian Airlines — which Richard and I knew from our Sperry India assignment — and Ansett airlines of Australia. SITA was seeking additional people to complete the new group, and Richard had recommended me, anticipating that my employment would again be in Singapore. The timing was perfect for me.

I met Irene Legay, the SITA Asia-Pacific administration manager, in the Rockman's Regency hotel in Melbourne. Irene was a very small Vietnamese lady. She was an excellent interviewer. I can remember talking a lot without her asking too many questions. A long-term SITA employee, at the time based in Hong Kong, she was not particularly pleased with the self-aggrandising approach of the first batch of marketeers who had been inducted into SITA. She illustrated her concern with a business card which featured the name of Richard Hawkins printed in a larger font than the name of SITA. Irene was keen to know about my desire to work in Singapore. I sensed apprehension in her question and guessed that the cost of living in Singapore might be a concern. I told her that I would be equally keen to stay in New Zealand, if feasible, or elsewhere. It did not have to be Singapore. She asked if I would be prepared to base myself in Sydney if I was assigned to look after Qantas Airways, Australian Airlines, and Air New Zealand, as account manager. I told her that would be acceptable.

Ms Legay agreed to endorse my application and said she would arrange for me to meet Bernard Leroy, the regional vice president, in either Sydney or Hong Kong. She explained that she and the vice president were still in Hong Kong awaiting a move to the new regional headquarters in Singapore. I was pleased with the interview. Irene said that she would confirm the next appointment with Mr Leroy by telephone, and that I should then call Dave Barker, the New Zealand manager in Auckland, who would arrange the aeroplane tickets. She was as good as her word. I attended a Hong Kong interview which was, I felt, a formality, and agreed with Bernard Henri Leroy — a grey sort of man for whom English was not easy — that I would start in Sydney on 1 December 1988.

I was surprised to be asked to start on this date, knowing that Australians and New Zealanders take their summer holiday during December and January. It is midsummer, schoolchildren are on their long vacation, and an employee taking the public holidays as well as regular leave could have a really long holiday. But the offer allowed some flexibility in that I could do three weeks work, and then have a couple of weeks off before starting again. Stand-by tickets were supplied by Dave Barker, the implications of which I understood, and I was delighted to have been upgraded to first class on the Wellington–Hong Kong return leg with Air New Zealand.

Mr Leroy confirmed that SITA had never had a designated sales and marketing function, but had a very strong technical and operational infrastructure. The Sydney switching and operational centre was at Kent Street in Sydney, opposite the back entrance to the Sydney Town Hall. I was welcomed to the company by Ms Jan Hyman, the Australia country manager; the three Australian-based airlines were her major customers. SITA listed the annual expenditure of each airline customer and nominal shareholdings in the not-for-profit cooperative were allocated annually based upon the next year's anticipated expenditure. In terms of ranking, Qantas was SITA's number 16 customer in the world, Ansett Australia was 32, and Air New Zealand was 25. Jan explained the air-travel ticketing situation. The airlines were shareholders of SITA and on written request, with reasonable notice, their SITA country manager would provide tickets to staff travelling on business free of charge. More often than not, the decision as to whether we were travelling on a particular flight was left to the last moment, but generally the seat would be provided in first or business class. If you were particularly lucky, you might get to travel in the jump-seat just behind the pilot. I was to learn over time that most SITA staff were aeroplane nuts and really did enjoy the chance to travel in the pilot's cabin.

I was allocated a desk in the open plan office and given an electronic message, sent through SITAtex, the SITA messaging system, that advised that I had been allocated the code 'SW' — 'S' indicating that I was a member of the sales department, and 'W' that I was the 23rd person appointed in a sales role ('W' being the 23rd letter in the alphabet). As I was based in Sydney (SYD) and was based in the SITA office (XS), I became instantly recognisable in airline parlance as SYDSWXS. This was a firmly established system that allowed any airline user to correspond via SITAtex or teletype message with a position holder in any airline in any city — so long as you knew the codes. These were published by the International Air Transport Association (XE). It was a system that worked and was used extensively by every airline.

I asked for a copy of the latest bills for the three airlines for whom I was now responsible, and was greatly surprised to learn that copies were not sent to the regional offices. The Australian office of SITA did not have a copy of the SITA products and price list. Was there such a document? Jan believed there was but she had never seen it. So how did we advise the airline of what we could do for them and how did we price it?

I was advised to speak to the local network specialist, Alfie Ma, a Hong Kong–born Australian citizen who gave me a very good idea of the network capabilities and data processing services we were able to offer. Pricing, however, was not his concern. Paris would advise on this. SITA had two data processing centres. One was in Atlanta, Georgia, which specialised in passenger reservation systems, using mainly the UNIVAC Standard Airline System as the base product. The other centre in London specialised in cargo reservation and flight operations systems using software from the IBM stable. This was an interesting mix. For so many years IBM had been the competition against whom I was selling.

The network products were mainly for the sending of messages — known as Type B traffic — and real-time transaction-based short messages sent from reservation terminals in the airline sales offices to the airline's reservation system — Type A traffic. Both were charged on a monthly connection fee plus a charge calculated from the number of characters sent in both directions. A rate was struck between SITA and the airline community reflecting the location of both ends. As a not-for-profit organisation, SITA expected to charge near to actual costs for all services. The connection cost in Sydney was, therefore, less than the connection cost in Vanuatu, as more airlines would be expected to use the Sydney SITA facility. Logically, the airline costs would be less in Sydney than on an island in the Pacific. Alfie was able to give me a great deal of information and provide me with operational manuals that described the various services in detail. I had to think hard about Alfie's statement that Type A traffic from a terminal into a reservation system was not secure, and might be discarded. This bothered me. I initially thought that Type B (teletype) messaging could be discarded. To illustrate the airline practice, Alfie took me to a local travel agent where we watched the operator set up a travel enquiry on the screen to meet a customer's wishes and hit the send button. When the operator did not get a response within three seconds, she hit the send button again and again.

'Obviously', said Alfie, 'the operator only wants one reply, despite the fact that she has sent the message three times. So we discard the two repeated requests. But if an airline manager has taken the trouble to type out a formal message from his desk and send it, he needs to know that we will take the greatest care to deliver it intact.'

That made sense. I had also learned a vital fact: an airline reservation clerk expected a reply within three seconds. This was, in fact, the recognised industry standard response time and a measure of the airline's competence to handle reservation traffic. Alfie was also able to tell me the names of the communications staff of my three airlines and give me some background about their particular networks.

Jan Hyman had a really good relationship with Telecom Australia, and SITA purchased services from Telecom Australia which were shared by all the airline users. It didn't create difficulties when rival airlines such as Ansett and Australian Airlines shared facilities. Most airlines actually owned their own networks in their home countries, in order to gain every advantage over their competitors. This was also the case in Australia and New Zealand, and SITA only carried traffic to and from the airline reservation system from overseas. So we only had significant Type A traffic with the airlines that had an international interest, such as Qantas and Air New Zealand.

I exchanged Type B SITAtex messages with Richard Hawkins in Singapore, who confirmed that my airlines were a part of the medium airlines group headed by Harpel Bamrah in the Paris office. He also advised me that Harp wanted message headers sent in a particular format — for example, QF/cargo reservations/request for price variation ('QF' is the airline code; 'cargo reservations' is the product of interest; and 'request for price variation' is the subject). Harp looked after some 30 airlines and used a SITAtex sorting facility to store messages by these headers. SITA people sent a huge number of SITAtex messages, which was a free service for us that really did work. There were times when one could achieve, before the implementation of the internet, the same chat room facilities we now take for granted. SITAtex even offered the facility of searching for keywords in headers. The SITA products in 1988 looked to be excellent and relevant.

Alfie also explained that SITA was a company incorporated in Brussels, Belgium, and headquartered in Paris. Most staff were expected to have a competence in French to deal with head office. There was also a tradition that head office and SITA regional managers were recruited from Air France.

I sent messages to the communications managers — who were code 'XC' — to ask for an appointment to introduce myself and offer my service. AKLXCTE found its way to Alex McFarlane at Air New Zealand, who I already knew; MELXCTN went to Barry Devenish at Australian Airlines; and SYDXCQF found its way to John Kearney, the Qantas communications manager.

I also sent a message to and telephoned Ian Riddell, the chief information officer of Qantas. Ian suggested I meet with him. He immediately presented me with what he perceived as a SITA specific problem.

> 'As you know, we provide free air travel to SITA staff on business-related trips on request, and we usually agree that you can travel first class when we have the space. I have just been given the figures for this year so far. We have provided to SITA the equivalent air travel for two full jumbos travelling first class around the world. It is too much! How many seats are Garuda Airlines providing? I cannot expect you to make a decision now, but I shall appreciate it if you can reduce the number of seats you take, because they are not really free. As the CIO I am charged a nominal fee for every SITA trip. By the way, welcome to SITA, it is good to have someone in your position to discuss these sorts of issues with. It will be helpful to have SITA's response before Christmas.'

I discussed this with Jan Hyman before taking it to Harp Bamrah in Paris. Jan had kept good records of the number of seats that she had authorised as the SITA Australia manager. These numbers did not match Ian Riddell's numbers. It then became obvious. Because Qantas gave such good seats, the astute members of SITA staff were choosing Qantas but were not necessarily flying in or out of Sydney or Melbourne. People were requesting, for example, Qantas seats between Los Angeles and London from the Los Angeles SITA manager, who was putting in the request that was approved by Qantas headquarters, but Jan was not being advised. It seemed obvious that we should try and quench this uncontrollable outflow of Qantas generosity by restricting the use of tickets for travel legs that started or finished in Australia for business that had a direct Qantas purpose. This was the recommendation that I made to Harp Bamrah when I reported the problem. Jan also made that recommendation to Mr Leroy. It had been fortuitous that Jan and I had been able to work this out sensibly so early in our relationship. Our suggested guidelines were implemented across the company.

SITA internal communications had not been so effective. Jan Hyman did not want a Sydney-based salesman and told me as much. I suspected that she could see herself losing control of the country for which she held the appointment as manager. However, Jan warmed to the idea when I was able to discuss the airline background I had acquired though my Sperry career. I had already had considerable success selling the same software and hardware that was the basis of the SITA service, and she was not going to have to hand-hold me.

By the end of January I had made my visits to see the three airlines. I thought that Qantas communications manager John Kearney may have been listening to Jan Hyman: 'We do not need a salesman. I will contact you to tell you when we need a service.' Basic sales school had taught me that the best sales opportunity would come from answering the strongest objection. After we had spoken for about an hour, John and I agreed that he would assist me, as a mentor, for my future activity within the airline. John advised me that he was a SITA director, as the top 25 spending shareholders were invited to take a place on the SITA board. John was the representative of the other airlines in the region as chairman of the SITA Pacific user group. I learned that John's predecessor both at Qantas and as SITA board member, Bill Swingler, who had taken the position of CEO of the Australian Federal Airports Corporation, would be asking me if a non-airline might be permitted to use the SITA network. John Kearney had not needed any prompt from Jan Hyman to be anti-salesman. He is very technical and knows what he wants.

John walked me around his section. He looked to be in his mid-40s, his hair in a fringe above a somewhat florid complexion, a nose beginning to show the ravages of a passion for fine wines, and a matching moustache. His team consisted of mostly older engineers, and all were keen to discuss their interests and the Qantas use of SITA services. I also learned that John and his team were consulting on network matters to Sabre, the American Airlines computer reservation system, and its entry into the Australian market. Qantas operated its own Australian network, leasing communications lines from Telecom Australia with built-in redundant paths to ensure that terminal access to the reservation information was always available for the reservation clerk. Qantas was an IBM user, and its reservation software was a British Airways derivative of the IBM original. Qantas used the SITA network overseas. Qantas also used the SITA Aircom Service to be able to send and receive messages to inflight aeroplanes. The application services used by Qantas included the SITA Bagtrac (lost baggage recovery), and Bahamas (hotel reservation interface) systems.

John Kearney also spoke to me in his capacity as the region's SITA representative. He requested a course on 'Reading the SITA invoice' for the airlines, to be held in Australia. When I got back to the office, Jan told me that the SITA invoices were a common complaint. She did not get copies, but understood they were complicated. I had learned a lot in a single meeting from a company not wanting a salesman, and had acquired a mentor. I had also been subjected to two Qantas meetings where the opening remarks from the customer were initially aggressive but were more rational after a few moments. I initially wondered if this was something that was taught as a Qantas style, but this was not the case. Perhaps it was the fact that SITA had not employed salespeople before, or perhaps the technicians who travelled the world for the company prior to the changes were indeed aggressive. There was no doubt that SITA services were perceived as being expensive. SITA provided services in places where the airlines did not want to run their own facility, which was difficult, hence the expense. John Kearney's explanation was, as ever, pertinent: 'SITA hubris needs a good kick in the arse.'

I had no more success in seeing John Englefield at Air New Zealand as a SITA representative than I had done as a Sperry person. As Mr Englefield's stand-in, Alex McFarlane was pleased to see a SITA salesperson and expressed Air New Zealand's satisfaction with the service that it received from SITA, singling out the high level of support provided by Dave Barker and his team. Alex introduced me to Greg Ball, the network development manager, and the pair confirmed that as an international carrier it also used the Bagtrac and Bahamas services, and was looking at Aircom and SITA Cargo as additional services. I also learned that the Air New Zealand staff knew, as ex-colleagues from Auckland, three senior SITA people in the Singapore office with whom they were in regular contact.

I met up with Barry Devenish, the Australian Airlines communications manager (data), in Melbourne. Australian Airlines operated a domestic airline and Barry was not a big user of SITA services, although he was spending approximately US$100K per year on each of Type A, Type B, and Aircom services. Australian Airlines paid its subscription to Bagtrac and Bahamas, but did not have much cause to use them. Barry did not get many visits from SITA. He also had a share in the Overseas Fixed Tariff System, another airline network-only arrangement, not dissimilar to SITA itself. What was of immediate interest was the fact that Barry's boss as computer manager was Bill Chatham, with whom I had worked in the London UNIVAC office in 1965. Bill had been recruited from Rediffusion Television to join Erle Milburn when Erle set up UNIVAC Australia in 1967–1968. Bill was keen to know how my career had taken me to Melbourne. That was not our only point of contact, as Richard Hawkins had been the Sperry salesman who had sold a great deal of equipment to Bill Chatham. It was as if the intervening 20 years had never happened, which gave me an entrance to the management of Australian Airlines. Bill reported to chief financial officer Gary Toomey (who would eventually become the CEO of Air New Zealand and Ansett Australia). Gary Toomey's boss, with whom he was close, was James Strong, who was charismatic and instantly recognisable. James always wore a bow tie and was lampooned by the political cartoonists about this. He would eventually become the CEO of Dominion Breweries in New Zealand, and then CEO of Qantas. He took Gary Toomey with him to both Dominion Breweries and Qantas. James Strong later moved to be a very successful chairman of Woolworths in Australia, but Gary Toomey has taken a low profile since his retrenchment following the demise of Ansett Australia and the New Zealand Government acquisition of 80 per cent of Air New Zealand. The airline business cycles its managers amongst itself.

I felt I was in control of my role with SITA when, after three or four months, I was invited back to Hong Kong to attend a three-day SITA induction course. There I met and palled-up with Dale Griffiths, who was employed at about the same time as me, and who filled the last place in the medium airlines group based in Singapore. Dale was an ex-manager of an airport in the Middle East, from where he had been recruited by Harp Bamrah. Dale's assigned airlines included Pakistan Airlines and Air Bangladeshi. If I remember correctly, both Dale and I were awarded 100 per cent in the quiz that concluded the training. Dale was as small as me, bespectacled and with a typically American confident approach. He generally wore a jacket and tie, but gave the appearance of being on constant lookout for mischief, a man after my own heart.

I first met Harp Bamrah when director general Claude Lalanne convened a meeting of the sales and marketing group in London. The invitations were issued by the sales director, Carl Chaffee, another Paris-based American and a newcomer to SITA. We were asked to prepare a 10-minute presentation to introduce ourselves and our airlines of interest at the start of the conference. That first real introduction to a SITA meeting was a surprise. Carl Chaffee introduced Mr Lalanne, who welcomed us to the company and to the conference. The next item on the agenda was for the attendees who constituted the new marketing group to stand up as individuals and say who we were and state our SITA objectives. At 32 lots of 10 minutes, this was going to be around five to six hours of presentations — it was going to be a long day. Carl said that he did not want to dictate the order in which people would speak, but he did ask for Harp Bamrah to start the proceedings and for me to follow, before the others of the medium airlines group. Harp got up and gave a reasoned, seemingly unscripted account of himself and the ambitions of the team. I followed, and my presentation, which featured a series of 32 mm slides with a fishing theme, was well received. Mr Lalanne obviously enjoyed Harp's presentation and showed an interest in hearing me. But he stayed for only a couple more of the introductions. I was amazed when it became apparent that I was the only person who had actually prepared material. No one else had made an effort, and it became almost a procession of one liners: 'My name is Joe Bloggs. I am based in New York and I look after American Airlines and United Airlines.' We were finished well before lunch. This was very disappointing.

Carl Chaffee came up to me at the conclusion of the session and apologised for putting me on at the front. He said he was grateful that I had prepared material. He had guessed that Mr Lalanne would not stop long, and that my peers would not have prepared anything. Carl commented that discipline was not a strong point of the sales and marketing group.

Note had been made that I had included Southern Cross Distribution Systems in the list of names of airline accounts for which I was taking responsibility. Some of my new colleagues were angry that a Computerised Reservation System (CRS) had been assigned to me as a prospective customer. That afternoon we discussed, in full, the implications of the rise of the CRS in the industry and debated SITA's response. The CRSs were, by definition, not airlines, although they were owned by airlines. Should we provide a service?

CRSs had evolved from an extension to the American Airlines travel agent reservation system. American Airlines could book passengers on its flights, in and out of the hub-and-spoke regional airports to which they fly in the US. Those passengers would have then needed to go to another airline to get to another hub. American Airlines decided to keep other airlines' schedules as a part of its information system, and the next step was to charge a (US$6) fee to the airline upon whose flights American had made the booking. To improve the operation, the other airlines sent their latest flight availabilities to American Airlines, who was authorised to book their flights and decrement the inventory of available seats on their behalf. This system developed to the extent that the charismatic CEO of American Airlines announced that the CRS was making more money than the parent airline. The floodgates opened and other CRS arrangements proliferated. The travel agents needed access to a CRS to be able to offer a complete booking service to their travelling customers. Initially, there were two CRSs of interest in Australia. Qantas supported the use of the American Airlines system, Sabre, calling its offering Fantasia. Ansett Airlines and Australian Airlines (purportedly sworn rivals) supported the use of the European-based CRS known as Galileo and set up a joint marketing and distribution company called Southern Cross Distribution Systems (SCDS). These two major rival CRS organisations were operating in Australia — the only country in the world where this situation existed at the time.

11. WORKING WITH THE AIRLINES IN THE AUSTRALASIA-PACIFIC REGION

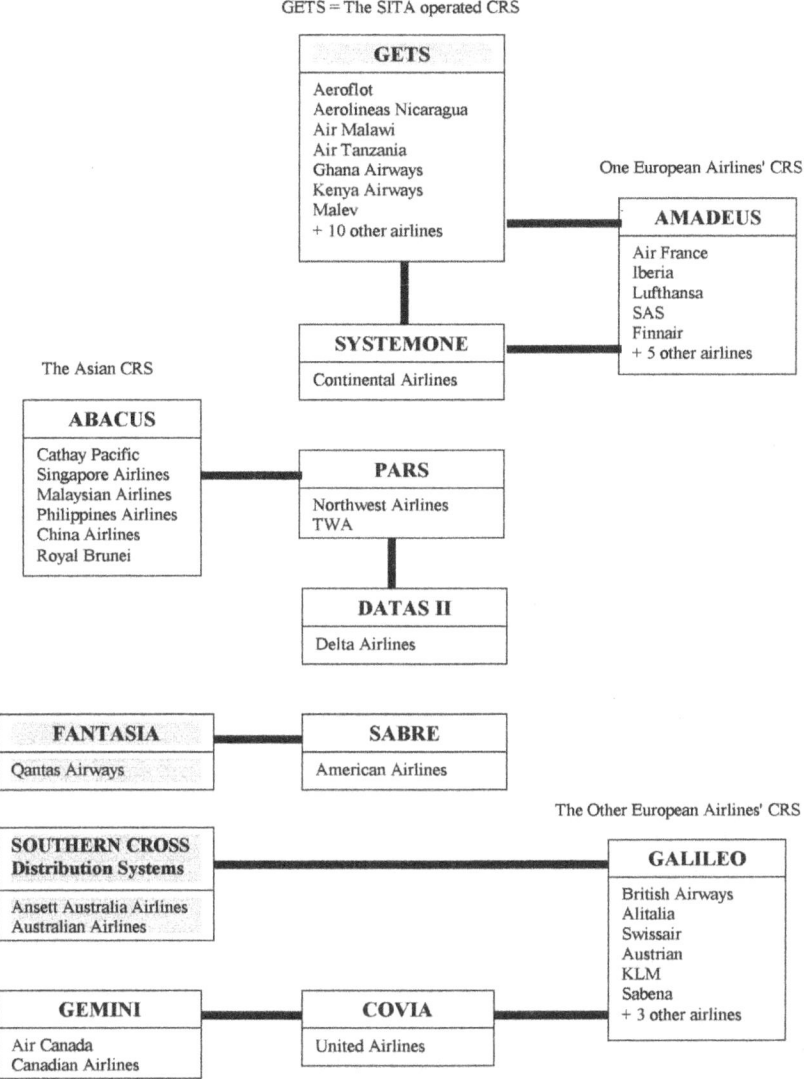

Figure 11.2: CRSs in mid-1989. Air New Zealand (one of my SITA accounts) has yet to make its CRS decision.
Source: Author's collection.

One of the SITA speakers at the meeting was the reservations specialist of the SITA Atlanta data centre. The subject was raised: should SITA have its own CRS? Towards the end of 1990, SITA had made that decision and Dave Bradford was appointed general manager of the Gabriel Enhanced Transaction System (GETS) Marketing Company. The SITA passenger reservation system was used by some 100 of the smaller airlines, although the world's largest airline, Aeroflot, did have an interface to Gabriel. (Gabriel was also the SITA derivation of the Sperry USAS*RES system that Sperry had sold to Aeroflot in the 1960s from London, and which Ian Meeker had left the real-time sales team to manage. I knew USAS*RES quite well from my previous work with Aer Lingus and Indian Airlines.) Another ongoing challenge was the extension of SITA membership to customers other than the airline shareholders, such as the CRS and aeroplane manufacturers who had a need to communicate with their customers, the airlines.

These were certainly challenges that were discussed in public, but the answers to them would be decided in private. SITA was very much a French company and its management was thought to be autocratic. Being based in Sydney, as an adjunct to an operational centre, I was very much isolated from the Paris headquarters. This was to change, but not until the next year: 1990.

Late in 1989, Harp Bamrah called a meeting of his medium airlines group in Singapore. This gave me the chance to meet my peers again, along with the technical specialists based in Singapore whose support was available to me.

My Sperry pal of 20 years acquaintance, Richard Hawkins, was enjoying being back in Singapore and had moved two of his vintage cars there — or was it three? He had required special dispensation to import the cars, as Singapore legislation only allowed cars of less than 10 years of age on public roads (with the exception of taxis). Richard was developing his value-added hobby and entrepreneurial skills through his regular cyclic travel opportunities. His business cycle was pragmatic. He took suitcases full of fake watches from Singapore to India, when he visited Air India. There he traded the watches for brass antique manufactured items in the street markets of New Delhi and Bombay — clocks, theodolites, and other surveying and scientific instruments. These he transported to Melbourne when he was due to call in on Ansett Airlines. In Melbourne he sold the antique artefacts to wholesale dealers and purchased vintage car parts with the proceeds, which he shipped back to Singapore for his own use and that of his aficionado friends. His SITA colleagues soon learned not to respond to Richard's requests to carry parcels for him, especially car parts. The airlines were providing free travel to us all as SITA representatives and did not appreciate having to carry large items and excess baggage free of charge. I once carried front and rear Triumph bumper bars from Melbourne to Sydney and had to hide them in the SITA office, waiting for Richard to take them to Singapore, unless I was to travel there first. Despite this obligation, it was good to be working with Richard again.

Harp Bamrah would typically call the medium airline group together every quarter to discuss progress, enable some specialist training, and for team building. We were all doing well, the group's targets were being exceeded, and the concept of a sales-orientated operation was becoming accepted by our customers and also, importantly, by the company. Harp ran his meetings as a report from each of the team with subsequent discussion. As always, the restrictions of relying upon the generosity of the member airlines for aeroplane seats was a hot topic. We analysed the three key words that might prompt the flight manager to allocate a stand-by seat to us, rather than someone else in the stand-by queue. These three words were 'regional' — implying a need to travel; 'airline' — confirming we were in the airline business; and 'manager' — giving us a status. Harp said he did not mind what we had printed on our business cards, and he was happy if we called ourselves regional airline managers if we felt that would assist. Harp also agreed to seek a budget for paid-for travel. Dale Griffith seemed to have particular problems getting to Bangladesh when he needed. During my Sperry travels in Asia, I had always enjoyed travelling Garuda, the Indonesian airline, and did so by choice with SITA. Jan Hyman never had trouble getting me on to Garuda, who took me to Singapore and to Paris in first class whenever I asked.

Although SITA was incorporated in Brussels, Belgium, headquarters were in Paris, and we would often be called upon to go to Paris for a meeting — sometimes a meeting that only lasted an hour. I argued with Harp Bamrah and Carl Chaffee that I had the furthest distance to travel and that a 60-hour return trip to attend a one-hour meeting did not make sense. It was an interesting discussion. The SITA not-for-profit (but certainly not for loss either) mentality was obvious in argument from head office: 'Travel does not cost SITA anything and you are being cared for — in first class — as well as you could ever expect. Please do not raise obstacles.'

I became very conscious of the unspoken corollary: 'Your time has no value to us. We almost prefer for you to be travelling than selling.' This realisation became a real concern for me in my relationship with SITA management and I discussed it many times with various colleagues. It was a prevalent attitude of SITA management.

So why did I stay with SITA? My realisation was that SITA had the most comprehensive single-industry portfolio imaginable. IBM could not match it. The products were of value to our potential customers and were fun to sell. The fact that our customers were our shareholders, and often our competitors, was an additional challenge. Added to this, working not-for-profit was a new experience. As a single business presence in Australia and New Zealand, I was master of my own destiny. The choice of whether to travel, and the extent of travel, was more or less mine. The money was good. I was paid a premium as an expatriate employed in Australia from New Zealand. As salespeople, we were not paid a commission, which was different, but I could live with it. My immediate management and peer colleagues were experienced computer professionals whose company and encouragement I appreciated. New business was immediate. Additionally, my wife and I were enjoying Sydney. We were renting a four-level apartment in Neutral Bay, with a harbour view, and I was able and keen to walk to and from the office, in the CBD, across the Harbour Bridge. Audrey worked in the city as a project manager for NSW Volunteering. The SITA portfolio was also expanding. Flight planning and crew scheduling were obvious additions to the services we would be offering. The sale of SITA Cargo to Air New Zealand was to be significant, as its success opened the doors to other opportunities. Greg Ball, the network development manager, a young New Zealand Olympic sailor, was allocated to look at the use of SITA Aircom. I expected to win that business, and did.

Southern Cross Distribution Systems (SCDS), also known as Southern Cross Galileo, was the CRS assigned to me. It bought network connections and started to install the SITA network for its travel agent customers and would eventually have more travel agent connections than any of SITA's customer airlines. As SCDS was not initially a SITA member, we contrived to effect a process whereby the early travel agent connections were made in the name of United Airlines.

Richard Hawkins was finding it difficult to schedule regular visits to Melbourne to see Ansett Australia. I had also discussed this as a problem with Joe Girbau, the Ansett communications manager. I had met Joe when

11. WORKING WITH THE AIRLINES IN THE AUSTRALASIA-PACIFIC REGION

Gunter Stephan called a joint meeting with Ansett and Australian Airlines to discuss their mutual interest in the Aircom service, to which they both subscribed. I had an informal agreement with Joe that if he believed he needed help quickly and was unable to contact Richard, he should call me. Richard and I spoke to Harp Bamrah and Ansett Australia and Ansett New Zealand business was allocated to my care.

Australian Airlines and Ansett Australia, the protagonists in the Australian Government two airline policy, had two tall office blocks almost next door to one another on Franklin Street in Melbourne. Both were maintained to very high standards. Not so the small annex to the Ansett office, whose actual address was Swanston Street and which overlooked the original Melbourne public baths. Joe Girbau had a corner office above the tram lines which was approached through an open-plan office with tightly packed desks on which Joe's engineers would be working on terminals and other items of communications equipment. The assault course leading to Joe's office was complemented by nests of cables in the spaces between the desks.

Joe and his team had all been at Ansett for a decade at least. Joe would always include his technical lieutenants in discussions. This was a good team. Joe was insistent on talking the issues out and making sure that his team was working towards the same stated goals. Initially, I worried about the amount of time this always took, but it was not just Joe. The Ansett organisation itself was fragmented. Joe wanted his efforts focused. We talked about the ramifications of the use of CRS right through, from the initial sales call to the check-in and post-flight analysis. Joe's network obligations were going to be quite different under the various scenarios we discussed.

When I was in Auckland, I called on Ansett New Zealand in Grafton Road. It had an enormous problem with the SITA service we were providing. The SITA network was closed down from the Paris headquarters once a week for necessary software upgrades. This was done at 2.00 am in Paris on a Tuesday morning, the time of minimum disruption to European and US airlines, but which caused maximum disruption to Ansett New Zealand. At this time, it was expecting the down-line load of the latest passenger manifests from the CRS for a mid-morning flight from New Zealand to Australia, and it was a peak time for New Zealand domestic flights. This was eventually resolved through a service level agreement I was to negotiate between SITA and the airline.

After perhaps nine months with SITA, I was asked to go to Paris to speak to the boss. Mr Lalanne acknowledged the increase in business from Australia and New Zealand and said that he was considering creating a new SITA region to be based in Sydney.

> 'Do you think you should be the new region vice president?'

This was unexpected. I realised that Mr Lalanne did not want to give me too much thinking time.

> 'Mr Lalanne, I am very flattered that you should even think of me for the role. I do wonder if I am the correct person, as I do not have an airline operational background. That seems to me to be a prerequisite.'

I was warming to the theme.

> 'Another prerequisite seems to be an Air France background.'

Mr Lalanne, smiled, offered a Gallic shrug of the shoulders with open hands, stuck out his lower lip, and commented:

> 'I see you are a pragmatist. I thank you for that. I will keep you advised of our plans.'

I talked over the interchange with Harp Bamrah. He had not known of the planned change of status of the Sydney office, but did not expect it to affect our personal relationship. He and I went out for dinner that evening to put the world to rights after a few beers with colleagues in the bar under the office. It was all very civilised.

The appointment of Jean-Paul Schittenhelm as vice president and general manager of the new Australasia and Pacific region of SITA did not come as a great surprise. Jean-Paul was tall and tanned, with a somewhat foppish wave of hair that fell over his eyes, but always well dressed in suits that fitted. I thought him a typically flamboyant Frenchman. His English was heavily accented but he was confident in his use of the language. He was a proud triple-bypass heart operation survivor, which apparently had not slowed him down at all. He looked very fit. I had seen Jean-Paul around Jan Hyman's office on a few occasions and knew that he was the ex–Air France regional director who had been based in Sydney for perhaps 10 years. Jean-Paul's approach to Alfie Ma and me was a quiet one. The three of us met over lunch, and Jean-Paul stated that he had been working towards the development of the new region, and that he was keen to remove those staff he perceived to be regional staff from the Australian Operations Centre, where Alfie and I were currently guests. He then disappeared for a couple of months.

Jean-Paul was very excited when he reappeared in the Kent Street office. He had found the new regional office premises. We were to take over the offices of Banque National de Paris in Pitt Street. It was contracting and moving to George Street. We also took over the bank's furniture, which included a great deal of wood panelling in most of the offices, along with matching boardroom suite and individual office suites. It was obviously second hand, with awful pink carpeting, but it suited Jean-Paul. It all looked expensive and suited his persona.

We planned a formal opening for the Sydney-based SITA region for February 1990 and I was given a free hand to organise the opening function. I had not known it was possible until I approached them, but we were able to hire the north wing of the Sydney Opera House. It was a magnificent venue overlooking the harbour, and we partied through early evening and dusk. We were able to use this event to announce that SITA had negotiated two highly significant deals with the Australian Government: a formal not-for-profit recognition for the SITA regional office, and the creation of SITA as a New South Wales Government research and development grant–aided organisation. Senior federal and state politicians were on hand to announce these developments.

We had perhaps 200 guests at the opening party — mostly Qantas representatives and their spouses, but we also had SITA regional managers on hand to talk to the press. The notable absentee was Mr Leroy, the Hong Kong vice president. Our new region had been carved from his area of previous responsibility. The opening party was deemed to have been very successful. In some minds the location and expense may have endorsed a charge of SITA arrogance. It was reported to me that Messrs Ian Gay and Julian Hercus, senior Qantas directors, had asked John Kearney at the end of the function, 'OK, Kearney. What do these bastards want and how much is it going to cost us?' We eventually won Ian Gay over as a supporter, but it took a few months.

ALSO INNOVATORS

At the event, both Jean-Paul and Ian Gay delighted in telling a particular story about Ian travelling first class on a Qantas flight. The flight steward asked the gentleman seated in front of Ian if he was a Mr Gay? He was. Ian leant forward and told his fellow passenger, 'I'm a Gay as well'. The steward could not help himself: 'Whoopty doo! Are we going to have a great flight!'

One person I had been pleased to be able to invite to the February 1990 opening of the SITA Australasia-Pacific region at the Opera House was Peter Butler. Peter had been the Sydney-based Sperry airlines manager for the Asia-Pacific region during my time in Singapore. He came to Singapore just the once, although he impressed with his keenness and knowledge — he had also impressed Jan Hyman as the only one of the supplier hardware people who understood airline protocols. Peter Butler was now the chief information officer of TNT and I was keen to sign him up as a SITA member. We had a meaningful discussion at the party and I kept in touch subsequently. His problem with SITA was that he saw the mainstream airlines as competitors and he was a committed private network fan.

Figure 11.3: The north wing of the Sydney Opera House. What a great place for a party.
Source: Author's collection.

11. WORKING WITH THE AIRLINES IN THE AUSTRALASIA-PACIFIC REGION

Figure 11.4: Four photographs from the Opera House function.

Clockwise from top left: Mr Lalanne's address; Jean-Paul Schittenhelm, with Maurice Irwin of United Airlines and Mike Ayres the SITA Sydney centre manager; no one wanted to go home; Dave Barker, SITA New Zealand, Venkat Swami, SITA Fiji, and David Craig, SITA Sydney network manager.

Source: Author's collection. Photography by Brian Moffatt.

The new region was launched in February 1990, which was a bad year for the world with the First Gulf War. The war had a really dramatic effect on the airlines. People stopped travelling. The days of big airline profits were gone. But this created many new opportunities for SITA. There were SITA offices everywhere operated by airlines and SITA employed the technicians that understood the business. I was able to talk to Greg Ball of Air New Zealand and suggest to him that the next time a terminal broke down in Los Angeles he ask SITA to fix it rather than send an Air New Zealand engineer from Auckland, carrying a spare terminal on the first-class seat beside him across the Pacific and back. The timing was perfect. It was not only Air New Zealand, of course. The same argument in some form applied to all airlines. SITA established a for-profit subsidiary called Information and Telecommunications Services (ITS), set up worldwide for just this opportunity. The competition to ITS was commercially tough, as a large number of the airline terminals in use were produced by Memorex-Telex and Westinghouse, who had their own support infrastructures. ITS was a reseller of computer hardware and software.

I had not thought too much about ITS up until this point in time, although rumour had it that ITS was the mechanism used by SITA management to pay itself big wages. Our shareholders, the airlines, did not want SITA staff paid more than their airline equivalents — the fees that senior SITA managers took from ITS were not declared to the airline shareholders. It was with knowing glances that the news of Jean-Paul's and Beth Jackson's appointments to the ITS Australia board was greeted by the more experienced of the office staff.

I developed a report for each of the airlines of my interest; for example, 'SITA: A vendor profile from an Ansett Australia airlines perspective'. We had so many services, effectively covering all (or most of) the airline's operational areas that very few people knew the full scope of where we were helping. In the report, I described each SITA service and reviewed the degree of participation by the airline along with my personal expectation of its future interest. I found it a most useful sales tool and regularly updated my set of personal objectives with the airline. I also circulated this document to interested SITA operational staff.

One morning Jean-Paul came in to my office.

> 'I think that marketing [Alfie Ma and myself] need an assistant to help you with proposals and when you have visitors to the office.'

I replied:

> 'I had not thought of that, Jean-Paul. I do not think we really need anyone. Having a PC on the desk has meant that we do our own typing these days. I do not think we could keep anyone busy enough. Besides which, Alfie and I spend a couple of days every week travelling. What did you have in mind?'

He looked me in the eye knowingly.

> 'I think it would be good to have a young woman about the place. She could make tea. I shall be happy for you to make the selection. She might be blonde and have big tits.'

Yuk. I did not say anything to him. It would not have been worth it.

11. WORKING WITH THE AIRLINES IN THE AUSTRALASIA-PACIFIC REGION

I had half forgotten the suggestion until one day when the girl on the reception desk rang through to say that Nancy Leon was in reception and was hoping to speak to me. Nancy Leon was a beautifully presented American who was married to a Frenchman. I let her talk. She had just completed her MBA on the effect of CRSs upon the travel agent. I asked her if she had a background that included Jean-Paul Schittenhelm. Nancy had worked for him for several years as a marketing consultant when he had been a Sydney-based Air France director. This was too good to be true. I invited Nancy to take her coat off and sit and talk. She did. I had to have a quiet chuckle. Nancy was perceptive and asked what she had said or done to amuse me.

> 'Nancy, I will always be totally honest in a business context. I can see that Jean-Paul is keen that we employ you. I also note that you are a blonde, but not quite the shape Jean-Paul anticipated.'

Nancy was terrific. She was not offended by what I had said. She also laughed when I described to her the attributes Jean-Paul had asked me to look for in a marketing assistant. I also told her that she was far too qualified to be a marketing assistant.

Jean-Paul had finessed a decision from me, and I had learned more about his approach. Nancy joined us and took the office between Alfie and myself. Nancy's office soon underwent a major expensive overhaul to her specific instructions to make it more to her liking. She was immediately an effective member of the regional team. I asked her to take over for me as the marketing representative for the weekly Key Performance Indicators (KPI) session convened by Jean-Paul that looked at his perception of the management aspects of the region, except for 'sales', the responsibility for which stayed in Paris. After about two months in the job, Nancy announced that she was off to Paris for her induction course. That made sense as well.

I had a telephone call at home the day that Nancy got to Paris. It was Harp Bamrah.

> 'Who is this Nancy Leon woman? She has walked into my office to announce that she is the new sales manager for the region. I have told her that she is not. Representing SITA at a sales level requires a particular approach and skill level that she has not demonstrated to me. I would not have called except she has also seen Claude Lalanne. He has asked me to find out what is going on.'

I said nothing to Jean-Paul. Nancy got back a week later and was most apologetic. She said that Jean-Paul had briefed her to see Messrs Bamrah and Lalanne and discuss with them the role he wanted for her in the region. I realised that in Jean-Paul we had a man working his own ambitious agenda, an agenda he was not necessarily going to discuss with his colleagues. Another common feature of his style to date was that he had employed two very attractive women, Beth Jackson and Nancy, both of whom were blonde and formidable in a business sense.

Nancy was an American with a passion for skiing. She had met her French husband Pierre when they were both ski instructors in Switzerland. Nancy's French was excellent. The mother of two boys, she and Pierre bought a million dollar mansion on the seafront at Balmoral, where they moved when Nancy joined us. Pierre's business was the importation of European ski clothing into Australia, although rumour had it that Nancy's family had provided the capital to buy the mansion. Nancy took over in a sales role looking after the Pacific airlines. She was a high-maintenance traveller and could not leave the office without burdening herself with a heavy load of sales documentation and the gifts for the airlines she thought appropriate.

Jean-Paul was married. His wife was Sonia Brookes, a very visible Sydney personality who fronted a local pop group and was the focal point of their videos. Sonia also appeared regularly as a model and cover girl for the fashion magazines, as well as being an artist and author. She was a most striking woman who was exhibited by Jean-Paul whenever he had the opportunity. Sonia accompanied us on an Overseas Fixed Tariff System meeting in Hong Kong. I got to the airport in good time to put my name on the stand-by list to be met by Jean-Paul and Sonia who already had their first-class boarding cards and were promenading the Qantas check-in area in order to be seen by as many people as possible.

Figure 11.5: Sonia Brookes, model, pop singer, painter, author, and wife of Jean-Paul.
Source: Author's collection.

Jean-Paul and Nancy having declared their hand, we needed to find an additional responsibility for Nancy. She was not computer literate but was an enthusiastic user of SITAtex and SITAfax. Nancy learned to effectively demonstrate these products and we had a constant stream of people associated with the airlines, or needing to communicate with them, coming in to the office to see her. One drawback was the requirement for our users to join SITA. Joining was expensive. However, if an airline was prepared to host the third party user, and that user was prepared to have a SITA address using that airline's code, we could add them to the network. We were early pathfinders with this approach, although we knew that plans were being drawn up to extend pseudo-membership to airline-related companies. This was a line that Richard Dorey, the regional small airlines manager, had been promoting for some time with the smaller airlines.

Jean-Paul now produced another rabbit out of the hat. He had employed John Englefield from Air New Zealand. John moved to Sydney with his wife, daughter, and son, and it was a different John Englefield that arrived, now free from under whatever weight was holding him down at Air New Zealand. John had become quite gregarious and took one of the empty offices on the sales side of the building to share space with Alfie, Nancy, and me. John's appointment was not specific, but he had been hired to be the eventual project manager of the Common Use Terminal Equipment (CUTE) 2 implementation at the new Sydney International Airport. John knew CUTE, as Air New Zealand had flown in and out of Honolulu and Los Angeles airports where early CUTE were installed. The airline wanting to use those airports had to use the check-in system provided by the airport, which was CUTE. The same regime would apply at the new Sydney International Airport. We had adopted a two-pronged approach to the Sydney CUTE project during the sales phase. I was selling to Bill Swingler, the (ex-Qantas) Federal Airports Corporation CEO, and Nigel Dickson was working with the steering committee representing the 36 potential users of the check-in system. Qantas was the airline that would be the most affected by the introduction of CUTE, as it logically carried at least 50 per cent of all passengers through the airport.

Suddenly, SCDS was one of SITA's biggest users. The figure below shows a cartoon I used at one of Harp's sales meetings. My sales target for the year had been something like 250 new network connections. SCDS alone had ordered over 2,000.

SCDS was owned by Ansett Airlines and Australia Airlines, who were rivals for the domestic market. Qantas was supporting the American Airlines Sabre CRS through its CRS Fantasia. I never gave up trying to sell Fantasia the SITA network. In my opinion it was an inevitability. Qantas was an airline operator, not a network operator. However, there was to be one significant decision before that could happen. The four largest regional airlines — Qantas, Australian Airlines, Ansett Australia, and Air New Zealand — initiated a joint-operations company that was to be known as Travel Industries Automated Systems (TIAS).

11. WORKING WITH THE AIRLINES IN THE AUSTRALASIA-PACIFIC REGION

Figure 11.6: 'Thank you, SCDS. More connections than we expected.'
Source: Author's collection.

The four airlines managed the operations company, with the general managers of SCDS and Fantasia reporting to the TIAS board. Marketing was to remain competitive. One reason for the establishment of TIAS was that, despite Australia being the only country in the world with two CRS systems, the CRS owned by the Asian airlines had opened up its doors and was appealing to Asian travel agents to join their network. CRSs increasingly became the modus operandi of every airline. The CRSs were able to offer full booking facilities for the airlines in that CRS, which in turn had connectivity to the other CRS systems around the world. It became a matter of expediency that airlines use their CRS to the full, and eventually the airline's reservation system accessed the CRS database rather than its own database. The implications were that the airlines became obliged to keep their records on the CRS database as accurate as possible while the CRS had the requirement to tell the airlines about bookings it had made on the passenger's behalf. The CRS also had to provide a full passenger name record (PNR) to the airline to enable it to achieve passenger check-in and flight departure control. The CRSs also catered for hotel and car hire. CRSs were very big business, and the IBM-hosted hardware systems installed at Sabre and Galileo were amongst the biggest computer systems in the world. The development of new CRS software caused a worldwide crisis in the availability of programmers who could program in IBM in the interactive programming language of TPF (Transaction Processing Facility) and PL1 (Programming Language 1).

The CRSs charged US$6 per PNR and a percentage fee for the booking of hotels and car hire. As a PNR was created for every segment of a passenger's flight, flights from Melbourne to Canberra, and Canberra to Sydney, for example, would contain two PNRs, and the CRS would thus charge a $US12 booking fee. Eventually, both SCDS and Fantasia would develop the portfolio to include other events and local tours as extensions of service opportunity. CRSs were a subject in which I became proficient, and I was able to find my way around the airlines to advise them on the impact of CRSs upon their own operations. With the advent of CRSs, every airline was under pressure to make a decision as to whether to be in or out of CRS. If it agreed, it would join the grouping of choice as a partner or participant. As a partner, it might share in the CRS profits. As a participant, it would pay the US$6 per PNR to the CRS. If it was not a participant, the CRS did not acknowledge that the airline existed and could not make flight bookings on its behalf. Effectively the airline becomes a partner of one CRS and participant in all.

The increasing use of CRSs was not readily understood by all departments in the airlines. From the ever increasing SITA invoice, they were aware that they were spending more on international traffic, but the implications of CRSs, which was a marketing decision, were not being discussed with the network departments. Marketing was riding high with increasing sales, but the network departments were being hit with ever increasing bills — for monies they had not budgeted.

As CRSs became the mechanism adopted by airlines, it required quite sophisticated background accounting procedures. The local travel agent makes a computerised booking, prints the tickets (in the days before e-ticketing), and collects the traveller's money. The money is sent to the bank settlement plan, where the payment for the air travel is paid to the carrying airline/s. Regardless of the number of airlines, each will need to pay the relevant CRS for the booking — nominally US$6 per flight sector. Should the travel agent also have booked a hotel, a similar network has been established by the CRS. The marketing interface between the CRS and the travel agent is the local marketing company, who will have negotiated the fees for making the CRS available and online to the travel agent. In the below diagram, the CRS is shown to be Galileo, and the local marketing company is Southern Cross Distribution Systems, whose distribution (communications) network is provided by SITA.

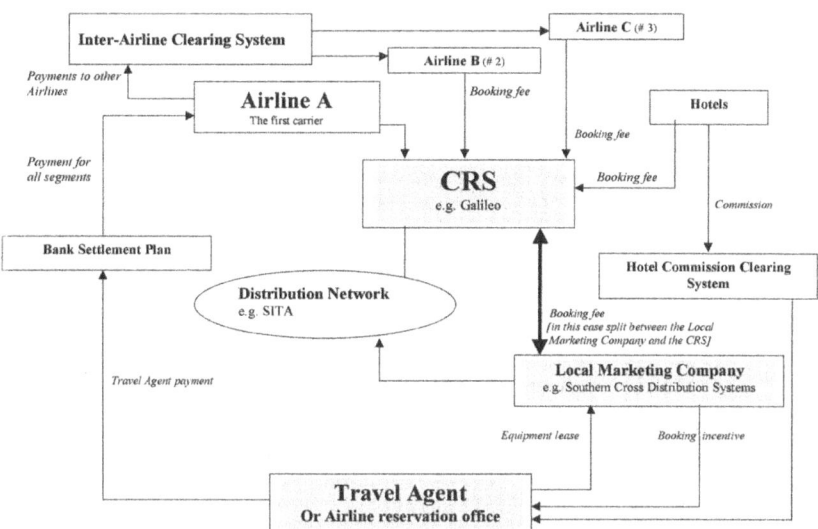

Figure 11.7: A representation of the money and service flows in an airline computerised reservation system (CRS).
Source: Author's reconstruction from figures derived circa 1990.

Such was SITA's commitment to the airline business that services such as the bank settlement plan, the inter-airline clearing system, and the hotel commission clearing system were being continually updated. The ambition of the local marketing company was to be able to expand its product range to encompass every event and attraction associated with a destination and charge the appropriate booking fee.

Harvey World Travel became a SITA member. One of its directors, Doug Norton, a travel agent in his own right, was a great believer in Harvey World Travel taking advantage of the network that was being developed by SITA on behalf of SCDS which would eventually encompass all the Harvey World Travel agents. If the network was there, why should Harvey World Travel not use it for its own purposes? Doug Norton was an individual, not only in his thinking but also in his country tweed style of dressing, most often in a beige raincoat and a tweed pork-pie hat, which he would doff in the presence of a lady. Under the hat was a bald head and a sharp intellect. We never knew when he would appear in the office or at events. I liked him. I am not so sure that the management of Harvey World Travel or SITA liked him, as he was a great boat-rocker. His ideas sounded unreal and impractical, but he had thought out most of the objections that would be raised. He tormented the life out of SCDS to provide services. SCDS loss was SITA's gain, and Harvey World Travel paid its fees and became a member. It never did get much use from the network, but it was not from want of Doug Norton's trying.

The Federal Airports Corporation (FAC) also joined SITA. Its CEO, Bill Swingler, had used SITA when he was the computing boss at Qantas. His vision was not dissimilar to Doug Norton's. His customers were the airlines and he needed a secure network to talk to them. He was also planning the new Sydney International Airport and was already committed to implementing CUTE. There was no other way to accommodate the 36 international airlines who were effectively seeking their own check-in lines. Bill is a big man who gives the impression that it will take a lot to deter him from his set course. He asked me to work with a diverse FAC team to optimise use of the SITA infrastructure. Mr Swingler eventually became frustrated by the length of time this team took to report back to him and took SITAtex connections to help prove his point.

Mr Swingler telephoned to ask me to join him for a meeting of the Gourmet 13 Club, which he described as an industry luncheon club. I asked if I could bring Jean-Paul, and he and I took a taxi to the international airport at Mascot where we met up with club members in the restaurant upstairs. We paid our contributing $50 each and enjoyed a five-course menu served with paired drinks. The other guests were mainly the general managers of the airports controlled by the FAC. It was a most convivial occasion. Jean-Paul became increasingly uncomfortable as the party became boisterous and the pronunciation of his name became totally English, and was eventually abbreviated to 'Jean'. He stood to remonstrate 'My name should be pronounced as "Jon Pol". My family name, I know, is difficult. You will not remember it. You will think: what is his name? You will say "shit" and "hell", because you will not remember. But you are half way there: "Schittenhelm". My family name comes from the Alsace in France.' I had heard that explanation many times before, but it was too late. He was 'Jean' until we left the party, worse for wear, in the late afternoon.

Bill Swingler telephoned the next day to ask if I wanted to join the Gourmet 13 Club as a regular member, as it had a spare membership. I suggested that he invite Jean-Paul. Bill replied that membership invitation had been discussed after Jean-Paul and I had left the restaurant and that 'that was not an option'. I declined the offer. The luncheon had not been gourmet — it had been gluttony.

Jetset Travel is based in Melbourne, with a distinctive black-glass office on St Kilda Road overlooking Albert Park. At this time, Jetset was jointly owned by the Melbourne Leibler family and Air New Zealand. I called David Clarke, the Jetset CEO, to see if he might have any interest in using the SITA network for his increasing number of franchisees. David Clarke had a reputation of being a hard man, but I found him agreeable enough. David Clarke's ambitions were personified by the name of the database that was being constructed by Jetset: 'Globedom' did not leave much to the imagination.

Another non-airline member of SITA was the New Zealand Meteorological Service — Te Ratonga Tirorangi. Its New Zealand office delivered weather information to Pacific airlines and had an interest in providing weather details to the SITA London data centre in support of the flight planning, weather and Notice to Airmen (NOTAM) services (alerts to pilots of potential hazards). Using the SITA infrastructure was decidedly cheaper than its office leasing private circuits from Telecom New Zealand. It was also of interest to me that Ric Godenho, a colleague from my brief flirtation with Unisys New Zealand, had been appointed manager of sales and marketing to the office. With a SITA connection he now had access to, and could sell, Southern Hemisphere weather details to the South American market.

Compass Airlines arose from the controversial 1989 airline pilots' strike in Australia. Bryan Grey, who was ex-Ansett, was putting the new airline together from his Victorian farm using his four sons and a daughter and his own media profile to promote the new enterprise. He was looking for an initial A$50 million to float the new airline. Here was the chance to get SITA in on the ground floor. Compass was logically a prospect of Richard Dorey of the small airlines group, based in Singapore. Richard gave me a free hand to work with Compass, as he was already grossly overworked and had no real interest in visiting Australia. I spoke to Bryan Grey on a regular basis, but was too late to influence his thinking for a reservation system. He had signed up with the Sabre CRS and it would use one of its connections to the Eagle Farm, Brisbane Reservation Centre that Compass was implementing with the assistance of the Queensland Government.

I am sure that this narrative will have given the reader a hint as to the pervasive nature of the SITA network in the airlines' operational infrastructure. Compass duly took a few SITA connections — not many, but we were pleased to win them as a customer. The youngest son, Andrew Grey, was appointed administration director. He and I worked well together and SITA was on a number of occasions able to provide connections that Compass had not previously considered — such as to its caterers and Bagtrac, the baggage recovery service. I travelled Compass when I visited Andrew Grey in Brisbane. It was a good airline, with the friendly staff it used as a brand image. Bryan was beaten, however, by the deep price cutting conducted by Ansett and Australian Airlines. The A$50 million float was not big enough to fight that level of aggression from the established airlines. It was a pity. I had become a Compass shareholder at the float, so I was as keen as anyone to help it to succeed. I did not get financially involved when Compass II was mooted by another Australian entrepreneur.

Gunter Stephan and I became involved in the initial planning for two other start-up airlines in Australia. If Compass could get up, we were confident that Transcontinental Airlines of Australia would also fly. Managing director Alex King had been a chief pilot with Ansett, and operations manager Dennis Cahill also had an Ansett background. These were senior technicians setting up a new airline, based near the Tullamarine Airport in Melbourne, and we took a wide-brush approach with them regarding reservations and flight operations. We constructed a matrix of discounts from standard charges — the more SITA services they took the greater the level of discounting. Transcontinental ordered a new fleet of aeroplanes from Boeing, but never achieved the level of financial backing to get off the ground. We also talked with AAA Airlines, which was based in Kings Cross, Sydney. AAA was just playing — although it cited an impressive list of airline executives behind the venture.

Harp Bamrah's group were active on many fronts. We met quarterly, most often in Paris, where we were joined by an attractive Frenchman, Patrice Durand, who spent a lot of time in New York and always had good tales to tell of his adventures. Another newcomer was the young, tall and sophisticated Arshad Siddiqi, who moved to Karachi to look after the group's airlines in the Middle East.

During one meeting in Paris, Harp invited us to visit him at home at Auvers-sur-Oise, an area of inspiration for some of the most famous of the paintings of Vincent van Gogh, and we visited the gravesites of Vincent and his brother, Theo, at the nearby township of Méry. Harp's wife, Laraine, an English girl, was very gracious and we had lunch in their large farm-style kitchen. Auvers is a delightful village, perhaps 90 minutes from Paris. It suited Harp, who was at ease showing us around. We ended up by the canal in Auvers and were sitting, talking and enjoying a wine when we heard a splash. Richard Hawkins, ever the showman, had stripped down to his underpants and was swimming across the canal. During a sumptuous meal that evening in the village inn, Harp asked me to keep an eye on Richard. He was acutely conscious that Richard's swim had been through water of a doubtful quality.

Jean-Paul's region was increasingly successful. Revenues were going up because of CRS, the uptake of travel agent connections through SCDS, our success in selling data processing products, and our membership uptake from travel-related service providers.

Figure 11.8: The red carpet treatment we all received at the SITA sales and marketing meeting in Singapore. Richard Hawkins is at the far left and Arshad Siddiqi from the Pakistan office is at the far right.
Source: Author's collection.

In mid-1992, SITA made an organisational 180 degree turn. Regional vice presidents were given responsibility for meeting SITA's sales targets. For three-and-a-half years, I had been reporting to Harp Bamrah in Paris. Initially, Jan Hyman, as Australia country manager, and then for two years Jean-Paul Schittenhelm as regional vice president, had an administrative responsibility to support my selling efforts. This was a huge change. It was a time of soul-searching. Richard Hawkins left SITA and returned to Sperry in Sydney. Harp Bamrah moved to London to work more closely with Carl Chaffee.

I had to think about the enigma that was Schittenhelm. He was the first boss for whom I could have no respect. His agendas were personal. He had amazed me at the end of a one month SITA-sponsored exhibition of his wife's paintings in the Ramada Renaissance Hotel. We were attending the cocktail party when Jean-Paul instructed me to 'buy a few paintings for the office'. He said he would approve the cost via an expense report, which could be submitted to him. I told him I could not. I shall never know the circumstances that induced a colleague to buy several of the paintings that were displayed on the sales area walls. Jean-Paul understood marketing and public relations, but not the implications of some of his public pronouncements. SCDS was installing more and more new network connections than any other SITA region and our unit costs were low. It was an in-house key performance indicator that should have stayed in-house. But Jean-Paul announced to our user conference that each new installation was costing US$25. The fact that our users were paying a minimum of US$280 per month for that facility meant nothing to him, and I was left to explain what looked like a discrepancy in our not-for-profit status. Jean-Paul was skilled at saying the wrong thing when he strayed into technical areas — and what we were doing was always technical.

When my second two-year contract with SITA was due for renewal on 30 November 1992, Jean-Paul did not renew it. I had been expensive because I was paid as an expatriate New Zealander, and I had probably served my usefulness in the region. I had no regrets. It had been great fun. I had been my own master, working at my own pace, with a really super portfolio of products and very well paid.

After the early 1990s, the internet caused the ultimate downfall of the SITA network. Networks became ubiquitous and online services were available to everyone, without a requirement to pay membership fees for network privileges.

12
The ups and downs of a contractor

Jean-Paul kept me on at SITA for a couple of months after my contract ran out. I believe he was expecting head office to agree to him employing a pricing manager, and that I would stay to do that job. There was very little chance of either of those ambitions coming to fruition.

During the spring of 1992, whilst still at SITA, I had met two representatives of British Telecommunications (BT). They were on a 'fishing expedition' and were seeking information on SITA pricing philosophies. I was happy talking to them. Ben Fursman was a typical — potentially high-flying — young, energetic salesman, from whom I was able to extract market intelligence of interest to SITA. BT had just won a huge contract to provide and operate the communications network for the New South Wales (NSW) Government. It was reputedly worth A$1.5 billion over 10 years, and was a contract that SITA should have known about and bid on. Ben was accompanied by a neat sales support engineer with a closely trimmed beard and the title of systems development manager, Ron Perry, who looked a bit older and was well practiced in telling the BT story. I later learned that Ron often had to be restrained from repeating the same story, such was his enthusiasm for his art. Ron was a communications consultant with an overtly academic approach. The two of them seemed somewhat overwhelmed by the SITA price book — some 200 pages of tabular pricing to provide a network connection between just about any two locations in the world. They asked if BT might use the SITA network for the NSW Government project.

I thought of the lads when I knew I should be looking for another job. I had spoken to Audrey and we were quite keen to look at another overseas posting. We did not want to go back to Singapore, but we were keen to pursue the chance of living and working in Thailand or Vietnam. I rang Ben Fursman and had a positive conversation with him. Ben suggested I call John Poston, the sales director for BT Asia-Pacific.

I met John Poston during a week's break with Audrey in Singapore, with the excuse that we were attending the Singapore Cricket Club annual February seven-a-side rugby festival. John had not been in Singapore that long and was suffering badly from the heat, and his face was reminiscent of a brilliant, shiny, and uncomfortable lobster. I was able to recommend the doctor who looked after a large number of the expatriate cricket club members who I knew had helped others with a similar problem. Mr Poston told me he would look out for something suitable for me and I left a CV with him. I had a second meeting with him five days later and we discussed terms of possible employment.

The unexpected BT follow-up, 10 days later, occurred through a telephone call from Adrian Coote, the sales director of BT Australasia (BTA). I went into BTA's George Street office to meet Adrian and took him to the Rugby Club for lunch. He told me that John Poston had suggested I be offered an interim contract in Sydney while BT got to know me and determine a future role in the company. Adrian was a charming Englishman, bespectacled, smart in a double-breasted suit, and oozing confidence. I immediately really liked the guy. Adrian talked to me at great length about opportunities in BTA and the potential for additional business as a result of the NSW Government contract. He told me that several complete departments from BT in the UK, each with a particular skill set, had been offered secondments in Sydney to implement this business; 250 people were in the process of moving from the UK on two-year contracts. It sounded exciting, and Adrian said he had the ear of John Poston with a view to obtaining the overseas posting I was seeking. I signed a contract with Adrian on 23 March and started the next day.

Was it a mistake? The next Monday when I attended the BTA office on George Street, Adrian handed me two packs of business cards that read 'Chris Yardley, BTA Regional Airline Manager', and 'Chris Yardley, BTA Account Manager, TIAS'.

12. THE UPS AND DOWNS OF A CONTRACTOR

Bugger! The bastards had taken me on to sell against SITA (along with every other network company in the country) for the Travel Industries Automated Systems (TIAS) business. I could see it made sense to BTA, as it knew I had an intimate knowledge of the TIAS deal with SITA — as I was the architect of the deal — and I understood the TIAS deal with Qantas which provided the network for 2,000 of the 4,000 travel agents of its interest.

I asked to be excused. I did not want this. I had always been conscious of salesmen who flitted from one company to another, promoting brand X products one day and brand Y the next. I always found it difficult to respect this style of salesman. I left the office and went into Darling Harbour to sort my mind out.

I did not want this. But I wanted a job. BT had looked like a good fit to get me back into Asia. Adrian Coote was obviously a good guy, and I was impressed to be given business cards on the morning I arrived. The contract was only for six months and if it did not work out I could always go elsewhere.

I returned to George Street and went straight into writing mode to win the TIAS business. This was the first time I had seen the TIAS request for tender. It was huge and reflected the background of Bruce Prior, the TIAS network manager, who had spent many years with SITA in London before his three years at TIAS. Bruce was a friend. I wondered if our friendship would survive the bid and the selling process.

BTA had requested the tender specification, but no one had looked at it with any serious intent. The response to the tender request was due on 7 April. I had two weeks to write a proposal worth … I was not sure of the exact amount, but SITA had been charging over $5 million per year to provide service to half of the TIAS customers, so we were looking at about $10 million per year — $50 million over the five-year contract period.

Confronted by the tender request, I sought to discover, quickly, how BTA worked, and who might be able to offer assistance. The name on everyone's lips was Charlie Rizzo, the ex-Telecom Australia senior manager who had been the BTA bid manager and salesman to the NSW Government. Of Mediterranean appearance and in his 50s, Charlie told me not to expect any help from him or his project team — they were too busy working on his own project — or Wally Cook, the BTA commercial sales manager: 'The man is a clown and well named. He is a wally!' Nor could I expect any help from Lakshman, the Sri Lankan–educated customer services manager. Lakshman and Wally Cook had been brought to BTA by Adrian Coote as yes men. On the positive side, Charlie was complimentary about Adrian Coote, who 'really understands communications and his way around BT head office in London. He is very ambitious.' Charlie described Ron Perry as 'a thinking, constructive systems designer, but subject to the whims of Wally Cook. He has too much to do and too many new salespeople to support.' Charlie eventually suggested I contact Peter Elsey, the systems development manager in BT Singapore, whose ambition was to sell large projects: 'Peter is intelligent, keen and helpful.' He also recommended I seek the good will of Peter Hutton, the BTA managing director, initially on secondment from BT London. His advice was to be positive with BTA when it came to pricing. The world's telecommunications companies were in the process of changing from nationalised monopolies into aggressive free-market sales companies. Costing was well understood, but pricing was not. This had been a meaningful discussion and I was lucky to have had it. Charlie was so busy within the NSW Government he was very seldom in the home office.

We were still communicating via telex — although in early 1993 we were hearing about the internet — so my first telex was to Peter in Singapore. He responded the next day to tell me that BT did have some experience in the handling of airline-related business, and gave me the names of British Airways and United Airlines as solid users of BT services. That was a start. As ever, the questions from TIAS were related to the airline communications protocols P1024B (IBM 5-bit Baudot code) and P1024C (the 8-bit Sperry–UNIVAC protocol). Any technical information that Peter might send was going to be the meat of any proposal.

On that first day I also telephoned TIAS to let it know that I was looking forward to being involved with it again, and planned to squeeze into the next two weeks the introduction of BTA players to the TIAS team. I arranged separate meetings with the TIAS managers to gain as much exposure as possible for BTA people, particularly Peter Hutton and Adrian Coote. As well as wanting TIAS to get to know BTA, I was in constant in-house meetings with various interested parties in BTA who knew nothing about the airline or travel agent business, but believed they needed to.

After three hectic days in the office, I spent the weekend at home, reading the tender request. The requirements were formidable. It was a wishlist. I started to write the BTA bid on the Tuesday. I sought assistance from

12. THE UPS AND DOWNS OF A CONTRACTOR

Wally Cook in finding the boiler-plate technical data and information to give substance to what we would be claiming as competencies in the submission. As ever, he referred me to Ron Perry. I also needed to design and find a printer for the (inevitable) three-ring binder that would hold the proposal. I would have expected BTA to have suppliers organised, but it did not.

How were we going to price a managed network for TIAS? John Poston's acumen in recommending that I be employed by BTA now became apparent. BTA did not have a clue. I knew what SITA was charging. I had derived the SITA algorithm with Bruce Prior four years previously. That agreement had been significant for SITA, as it was its first major contract without a character count and charge for each character passing through the network. Bruce and I had agreed upon a monthly connection fee of A$80 per travel agent, with an inbuilt discount structure.

Number of travel agent connections	Monthly charge (AU$)
1–500	80.00
501–1,000	77.50
1,001–1,500	75.00
1,501–2,500	72.50

Note: The scale of charges agreed by SITA and SCDS — the more travel agents connected to the network, the cheaper the connection fee.

We had not gone any further than this, as TIAS was only buying the Southern Cross Distribution Systems (Galileo) network connections from SITA, with a target of 2,000 travel agent connections.

The Galileo agent paid TIAS the $80 fee, plus the appropriate Telecom Australia fee for the use of the Telecom Australia network to get data to and from the TIAS network. This kept the TIAS pricing simple. It did have a small margin with the higher number of connections. TIAS made its money from the airlines as a part of the booking fee for every airline sector. When I looked at BTA pricing, I found that the BTA pricing algorithms were simpler and were related to the network transmission protocols used, with hefty connection charges. I spoke to the financial people at BTA and, as Charlie Rizzo had warned, they were looking to me to tell them what we might charge — they would then apply costing to determine if there was a profit to be made. There is that word: 'profit'. The SITA ethos was not-for-profit. How could I justify any price that was comparable to the SITA price to BTA, who were in business to make a profit? I had long discussions with Adrian Coote and the financial people, all of which were inconclusive. As the bid date hastened nearer, Adrian asked me to state the per agent fee that would win BTA the business. I recommended A$65 per month. The financial department went away to weave its magic with that number. It was acceptable to them, provided I obtain sign-offs for the technical and engineering aspects of the proposal. We submitted our bid, on time, on 7 April. Bruce Prior told me that BTA was the surprise bidder. TIAS had expected SITA to bid, of course, and Bruce was looking forward to seeing its price. He expected bids from Telecom Australia, Optus, Telecom New Zealand, IBM Global Services, and Electronic Data Systems. He also pondered an approach from another airline-related consortium that was probably headed by the Amadeus CRS.

The following week, Adrian Coote sat me down in his office to ask what other projects I would be working on with BTA. I had not given it much thought, and he surprised me by giving me another tender request, this time from Air New Zealand. Tom Ryan, the Air New Zealand CIO, had written to BT in London asking for a proposal for a complete outsourcing of the airline's computer centre and network, worldwide. That was interesting, and was a sign of the times. I wondered if SITA knew Mr Ryan was making such enquiries. Expecting to pursue this opportunity, I learned that BT had a sales division, Syncordia Global Services, devoted to outsource business. I spoke to Tom Ryan and arranged to go to Auckland to talk to him. At the same time, I would call on the Air New Zealand TIAS representative and the TIAS managers in New Zealand.

I spent a lot of time with Irene Woods, the BTA financial manager. She was most concerned about the bid price we had submitted to TIAS. I did not blame her, as I had struggled to justify anything that was comparable to SITA's not-for-profit pricing to BTA. As I was to learn, the NSW Government contract had been predicated upon similar thinking: 'What price will win the business?' In the case of the NSW Government, working with the finance minister, the bid was an unsubstantiated offer to provide the same services as the existing suppliers at a discount of 30 per cent. The NSW Government had made a politically motivated decision to outsource services. The big problem that Charlie Rizzo was facing was antagonism from those government departments who had not been consulted about the telecommunications outsource contract. They were obstructing Rizzo's team as they attempted to determine what it was BTA had been contracted to deliver. Another obstacle was that most departments had numerous contracts with their suppliers, with no obvious and significant cut-off dates that BTA might target to provide the alternative service. BTA, therefore, had no firm project plan to achieve the core network for government. Yet, when I went through my suggested TIAS pricing with Peter Hutton, Adrian Coote, Wally Cook, and Irene Woods, they told me not to worry too much about pricing, because the NSW Government X.25 network, which was being paid for by the NSW Government, would be available for use by TIAS and they presumed that travel agencies would be congregated in the same urban and rural locations as government offices. Supposition upon supposition. I had my doubts, and so did Wally Cook. Irene recommended that we submit a supplementary proposal requesting that the pricing be regarded as negotiable. She did not win this battle.

I had a sales plan to follow. I needed to make contact with the airline directors of TIAS to introduce BTA as a potential provider. Paul Perrottet at Australian Airlines and Geoff Dixon at Ansett Australia Airlines both claimed to have no interest in the technical aspects of the network, so long as a move to BTA would not prejudice any marketing initiatives TIAS might adopt. We tried to assuage any doubts they might have, but my own doubts were growing. After the meeting with Geoff Dixon in Melbourne, Wally Cook told me that Mr Dixon (the same Geoff Dixon who was to enjoy success for several years as the CEO of Qantas) was ineffective.

We answered two sets of fairly basic questions from Bryan Wishart and Bruce Prior of TIAS, which led us to believe that they were trying to understand our bid. TIAS asked for a formal presentation of our proposal. I thought it would be a good idea to ask someone from head office to make a video. Adrian Coote was optimistic, and recommended I talk to the office of Alfred T. Mockett, managing director of the business communications group. I called Mr Mockett's office and was surprised when his secretary put me straight through. After a briefing, he was enthusiastic to participate. All he required from me was a script. He would arrange the studio recording and getting the video to Sydney. It was an excellent video, which I had the chance to view the day before we were to use it. He had followed my script exactly. In the video, Mr Mockett introduced himself, welcomed the TIAS management team and our presentation team by name. In my script, I had written:

> 'BTA anticipates a lively question and answer session, and knows that TIAS will not hesitate to ask the hardest of questions. We thank you for your interest and please be assured that I am personally involved in our bid and look forward to meeting you on the earliest occasion I can get to Sydney.'

I delayed this wrap-up until the conclusion of the presentation. It worked perfectly. Richie Hall was delighted.

When we met for the first time, an outside consultant was assisting TIAS with the request for tender. Virgil Iliescu, a very precise engineer, was driving the request for tender and analysing supplier responses. The presentation itself went well enough. We managed to answer the queries thrown at us. TIAS also presented a written questionnaire of 23 specific areas of interest, which was predictable and a bit dull, until Adrian Coote unexpectedly jumped in.

> 'It seems to me that we are agreeing that we might be able to do business on a technical level. Your questions do not test us technically, but you do not know BT and our competences. I propose we initiate a two-level ongoing dialogue. One morning a week, for as long as necessary, we shall attend TIAS to introduce our management team and their objectives, and Lakshman will arrange for a technical discussion for your technicians every Friday afternoon. We'll buy them a beer afterwards. How does that sound? We will call it a "quality cell". In return, TIAS will make the time, through a business needs workshop, to ensure BTA technicians know every facet of the TIAS aspirations.'

To my mind this was a perfect proposal. Ron Perry told me Adrian had done the same when BTA presented to the NSW Government, and it had certainly helped.

We had 23 questions to answer to the appropriate BTA people. Question 23 asked BTA to examine its bid price, and to detail its components to see if the price might be honed. We amended our sales plan as a result of the current situation as we saw it, and, while maintaining supervision of our response, I took responsibility to address the technical matters with Bryan Wishart. He was an unknown influence. Mr Mockett's video was shown around BTA. It was a hit in-house. I wrote to Mr Mockett to explain that the video had been well received. He replied, committing to visit TIAS when he got to Sydney and asking I keep him updated.

12. THE UPS AND DOWNS OF A CONTRACTOR

The next week TIAS extended its tender and asked leading questions about the pricing of circuits at 4,800/9,600 bits per second, twice the speeds it had originally requested. It also required that we sign a non-disclosure agreement, implying that it had other issues it wished to discuss. We were also asked if we could extend our services into the Pacific, including the Cook Islands. These were positives from a sales perspective, and we were encouraged.

In early June, Adrian Coote announced that he was leaving BT. I tried to minimise any effect on TIAS negotiations, but it was difficult. He had created a good impression. Another effect of Adrian's departure was that Ron Perry and I lost any support we might have anticipated from Lakshman, who should have been orchestrating the 'quality cell' process with TIAS.

On 7 June, Ron Perry and I began to conduct the 'quality cell' and 'business needs workshops', which introduced us to another, specialist level of TIAS management. Later that same week, we conducted a significant demonstration for Bruce Prior and three service desk employees from the network control centre that BTA was constructing for the NSW Government. Bruce Prior requested that he be able to visit with some colleagues to discuss their Pacific service ambitions. I was asked to write a technical paper discussing the migration of the Fantasia and Galileo networks. With the invaluable help of Peter Elsey, Ron Perry and I were able to sustain enough material to visit TIAS on a daily basis during June and July.

On 10 August, Richie Hall took me into his office at Bondi Junction to tell me that his technical review team had recommended the BTA bid, and that a decision was anticipated from the TIAS board meeting of 12 August. The technical team had access to pricing algorithms, so I was most encouraged. Not so BTA, who went into panic mode. I was obliged to explain the TIAS financials in detail to many accountants.

On tenterhooks, I called Bryan Wishart the afternoon of 12 August. No decision yet. The Air New Zealand director had not been able to fly out of Auckland that morning due to fog. The next board meeting was scheduled in three weeks time, on 2 September. The response from that later meeting was negative. Richard Hall would tell me no more, but did invite me to visit him after the weekend.

On 6 September I visited TIAS to meet with Richard Hall, who told me that the TIAS board had decided to continue to use SITA to provide its total network. Richard was at great pains to remind me that TIAS was owned by the three airlines — Qantas, Ansett Airlines, and Air New Zealand — who also owned SITA. Qantas provided the regional director on the SITA board. He was at pains to thank BTA for providing stiff competition during the decision process, and rubbed salt into the wounds by saying: 'You did good a job too, Chris, representing BTA to convince the airlines to revoke their previous decisions.'

The decision was a blow. I had several other bits and pieces of potential business to pursue, such as Air New Zealand outsourcing; the Queensland Government travel network; Cardinal Network of Christchurch, New Zealand; and the Harvey World Travel network, with Doug Norton still rocking the boat. BTA instructed me to report to Kevin Draper, who had been recently recruited from London. I assumed a new role as travel and transport manager, and wrote a comprehensive market analysis of the sector for him.

I met with Kevin and he complimented me on the work I was doing, but two days later BTA told me it would not be renewing my contract. My six-month contract had run for six months and three days. It had been a classic win or lose situation. Had we won the TIAS business, I would have been paid a huge commission and been a star for a while. But would BTA have ever been able to handle the 4,000 connection network transfer? Would BTA have been able to provide the satellite network control centre from its regional centre? I have grave doubts to this day.

BTA was not able to fulfil its obligations to the NSW Government, and arbitration of the failed contract went to court, with both sides seeking A$1.5 billion recompense from the other.

13

Not a multinational this time

Getting the heave-ho from BT was not what I would have chosen for myself, had a choice been available. I had no contingency plans in place. A brief holiday would be an unexpected pleasure.

I received an invitation to attend the opening of the Adacel Telecommunication Services office in Melbourne, which was to take place on 16 February 1994, and drove over 1,000 kilometres to Melbourne, stopping off in Canberra on the way. Adacel Telecommunication Services was founded in 1987 by Danny Rowley, an ADA programmer;[1] Silvio Salom, who knew C programming; and Dave Smith. All considered themselves electronic engineers (EL), so they put together the name thusly: ADA + C + EL. At the time, the group were working at the Civil Aviation Authority in Canberra on software maintenance of Thomson-CSF radar systems. Adacel was created with the assistance of Thomson-CSF, who took a 30 per cent share in the new company.

The smart, modern building that was the Adacel head office was in the middle of a parade of retail establishments, with a hairdresser on one side and a Jetset franchise on the other. The shops along Bay Street in Brighton conveyed an air of success. There were a number of restaurants, banks and estate agents among the premises. Adacel Telecommunication Services (ATS) shared the huge ground-floor space with a subsidiary, Adacel Multimedia Limited. The first floor of the building contained the

---

1 The ADA programming language was named after a daughter of Lord Byron, Lady Ada Lovelace, who was a respected mathematician of her day.

reception area and Adacel Pty Ltd proper — system developers, software writers, and technical expertise. It was a young company, and its people were mostly very young.

As many as 80 people attended the party and my impression was that the event had been successful. At the conclusion of the event, a group of about 20 retired to Mitzi's, a nearby hotel, where we drank several beers before crossing the road for an Indian meal and a late evening.

The next evening, I had the opportunity to talk to Silvio Salom, one of the founders of Adacel. He is the most disarming man I have ever met. He was just 34 years of age and already operating his own software development business with a staff of approximately 150. I was impressed with his unassuming attitude and direct questions. I told him of my conviction that there is no money in travel. I had witnessed first-hand the decimation of airline profits that occurred in 1990 as a result of the Gulf War and the worldwide drop in tourism. At SITA, we saw a 30 per cent annual attrition rate of travel agents.

We sat at a small round table in his office that was deep in papers, although somewhat less deep than Silvio's desk, where his PC screen sailed the sea of papers. Silvio was born in Belgrade. He wore his hair in a wild afro style, but that was the only wild thing about him. He asked about my SITA experiences, particularly my selling of the Aircom satellite communications service to Qantas and Air New Zealand, and we discussed the terrestrial network system I had developed for Ansett Australia and Australian Airlines. Silvio explained the Adacel vision to provide air traffic control systems to the world's airlines, following the principles understood by the acronym FANS — Future Air Navigation System.

Silvio's argument was that the pilot knew where he was flying. He had registered a flight plan before take-off and was monitoring his progress along the route. The on-board computer knew where the plane was through the global positioning system, with communications provisions being provided through satellite. But the radar-controlled air traffic control systems that were in use did not know where the plane was unless they were specifically monitoring its position via radar, during its approach to an airport, for example. Silvio illustrated the point by examining the actions of an air traffic controller in Sydney waiting for a regular Ansett flight from Melbourne at 10.00 am in the morning.

13. NOT A MULTINATIONAL THIS TIME

This flight usually appeared at a set time, but the controller was lost if it did not show up when expected. There might be many reasons for a delay — fog, mechanical problems, late arrival of an incoming flight, etc. — but it would take a radio call from the controller to the pilot to establish the actual location of that flight. Adacel had been working with the Civil Aviation Authority in Canberra towards the best use of radar technology, with a positive eye towards FANS. Adacel was about to enter a joint venture with American Airlines and the US Federal Airports Administration, to be called Airspace Management Systems. Adacel was to provide the CEO of this venture, who would be based at Adacel head office in Melbourne. Was I interested?

I definitely was interested. Silvio asked that I consider joining the company, subject to satisfactory interviews with David Smith, the Adacel technical director, and Jeff Barrow, the joint managing director (along with Silvio) of Adacel Communications Pty Ltd, who I had met the evening before at the ATS opening. The next day I was able to meet David Smith, a cuddly teddy bear of a man whose office was certainly more disciplined than Silvio's. David did not want to commit to anything with me, but I did feel that he would not veto my employment if that was what Silvio wanted. Silvio confirmed the job offer following my meeting with Jeff Barrow and I eventually attended the Adacel office, having travelled via the overnight train from Sydney two nights before.

My first day was not auspicious. Silvio Salom was not in the office, nor was he expected for a few weeks. Jeff Barrow was not in the office, but was expected. When Jeff arrived he took me into Eddie Pacula's office. I had done some consulting work on travel and transport for Eddie Pacula — a very big man with an aggressive moustache and an attitude to match — at Ron Perry's instigation at the end of 1993, and it was Eddie who had invited me to the ATS opening. When Jeff declared to Eddie that I had been appointed a CEO in the group, Eddie was apoplectic. He left for a long session with Jeff to express his concern at my appointment to a role higher that his. Jeff subsequently asked that I attend to ATS matters in support of Eddie.

The ATS 'promise' was summarised in a spreadsheet that Eddie Pacula had used to sell his idea to Adacel. To my mind it illustrated a business disease I recognised as rampant spreadsheet syndrome. It is all too easy to forecast small increments in business that become magnified out of reality when compounded. Eddie's forecast for ATS was a profit of $20 million in the first year of operation. The business plan was not realistic. Eddie would not listen to or answer any questions. I think he anticipated that he could browbeat me into agreeing with his projections and was initially keen to have help in confirming the business plan. It was fanciful. I kept my head as low as possible. My perception was that I was only helping out with ATS as a favour until I had the chance to meet again with Silvio.

When I presented my version of a business plan to the Adacel Communications board it was met with muted aggression. The prevailing attitude was expressed by Jeff Barrow: 'I have never, ever, seen a business plan that showed a loss of $400,000 in the first year and took three years to get into a profitable situation. That is not a business plan.' After the meeting, I was forever branded as not understanding business planning. I had found that ATS was a crusade, with staff but very little substance. ATS might achieve one new customer every three months, but because we could not implement any quicker would never be in a position to introduce 10 new customers a month, which Eddie had convinced Adacel was achievable.

Jeff Barrow asked that I provide a revenue model for him to better understand our objectives. Silvio reacted promptly to the revenue forecast I had put forward, suggesting that the ATS team accept pay cuts in order to help financially.

Adacel was pursuing several diverse paths of software development, including air traffic control and simulation of air traffic control functions, the cornerstone upon which the company had been founded. The HMAS Watson in Sydney was a significant customer, with Adacel supplying and maintaining seaboard simulation systems. The machine language translation team, which had as many as 10 linguists at any time, although working on generic principles, was concentrating on the translation of Indonesian Bahasa to English. The team leader was Helen Lam, and the project had the name of 'Memtah'. Helen had a real passion for language, but was uncomfortable with the business realities of working for Adacel. The basis of the work the team was doing was an extension of the software developed as a part of her Master's thesis. The work was supported by a $5 million grant, over five years, from the Australian Ministry of Defence.

13. NOT A MULTINATIONAL THIS TIME

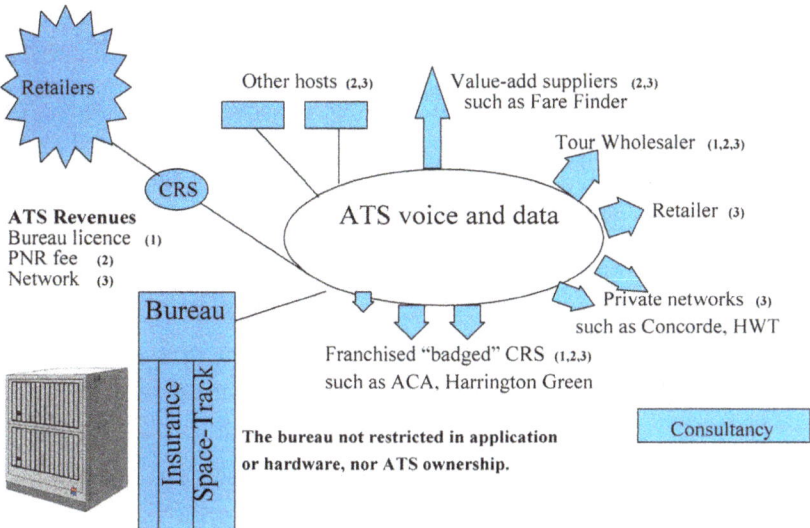

Figure 13.1: The ATS revenue model.
Source: Author's collection.

Adacel Communications Pty Ltd was a general reseller of hardware and software, a mechanism through which the parent company would be able to buy any hardware or software at a discount.

Adacel Multimedia was a group of very young technicians working in emerging technology. In 1994, it had developed a self-service information kiosk for the Government of Victoria, and Brian Hennessy, the young Canadian team leader, was a favourite of the local television news program. Brian had retained a 30 per cent shareholding of the multimedia company after it was acquired by Adacel Pty Ltd. The multimedia team appeared to work all day, every day, and certainly seemed to be enjoying what they were doing. They also became involved in one-off projects to build a revenue base. One team member was a gifted penman with a penchant for cartoons, who went by the nom de plume of 'Grob', and kept us all amused through his interpretation of our world.

Adacel should have been a vibrant environment, but it fell short. Most things seemed to be done in a penny-pinching fashion. Silvio's mother's discarded kitchen table in the managing director's office was symptomatic. Apart from the ATS computer room, the ground floor was squalid in comparison with the client offices we visited when representing the company. The main Adacel offices on the first floor of the building were open plan, which was being confounded by readily moveable partitions as team leaders of the various projects staked their territorial claims. It was a rabbit warren where it was easy to hide or get lost according to temperament. The work ethic, however, was huge. Weekends did not exist and Silvio was always in attendance. Any technician could involve Silvio in the solution of a technical problem and he would be lost as a manager while he reverted to his favoured role as a technical problem solver and software engineer.

I was disappointed that the different groups did not really mix in a business sense. The company tried to tie the organisation together with an in-house magazine, *Adacel Antics*, and the groups did some socialising in Mitzi's Bar, particularly on a Friday evening, but the average staff member was not a drinker. The young technicians had not yet acquired social graces.

Eddie Pacula was a potent force and would not take 'no' for an answer. In the past, he had bullied potential customers, including some who had previously been his friends, into signing contracts with little thought for implementation. When Eddie called out James Strong, the charismatic CEO of Qantas Airlines, demanding that ATS should be allowed — encouraged even — to carry all the airline communications in Australia, the argument was documented by the Australian Broadcasting Corporation and featured in a 10-minute section of an emerging technology television program. The confrontation was also played out within the pages of the Australian travel press. Eddie cajoled Ian McMahon, the editor of *Travel Week Australia*, to visit us to see the ATS offices and listen to the ATS sales message. Mr McMahon gave Eddie full page treatment, describing him as 'Pugnacious Pacula' in the headline.

After a few months in the job, I was finally told I had been employed by Adacel to rein in Eddie Pacula and the grand disaster. Eddie was under tremendous pressure, was not a well man and left Adacel to concentrate on his consulting interest, his company called Chesscab Consulting.

13. NOT A MULTINATIONAL THIS TIME

Figure 13.2: Eddie Pacula as a particular butt of Grob's brand of humour. This sequence is an indication of affection for the boss, Silvio Salom.
Source: *Adacel Antics*. Cartoon by Grob.

Figure 13.3: Silvio was not seen as a spendthrift.
Source: *Adacel Antics*. Cartoon by Grob.

ATS spent considerable time and effort trying to increase its presence in the networks and business of Harvey World Travel and the Abacus CRS. My pal Doug Norton was no longer the data processing director of Harvey World Travel, which was now firmly controlled by Paul Fleming and Paul Kieran. Harvey World Travel had not stipulated which of the two major CRS systems, Sabre or Galileo, the franchisee should choose. ATS proposed and facilitated discussions whereby Abacus would become the Harvey World Travel CRS of choice. We provided circuits to Harvey World Travel for its head office functions, although it did not earn us significant revenues. Ian Norris, the general manager of Abacus, was keen to take advantage of any cost savings we could provide to reduce travel agent costs and encourage the uncommitted travel agent to affiliate with Abacus. We also hoped to win business for the ATS Space-Track bureau from Abacus tour wholesalers.

But we were being thwarted with everything we attempted in the travel and tourism world by ATS's inability to interface with TIAS and the main airlines' booking systems via the TIAS network. ATS had several meetings with TIAS, who was adamant that ATS would never bring anything to the table that TIAS would not eventually control as a result of its own strategies.

This point was being discussed with the Adacel board when Jeff Barrow snarled: 'Sue the bastards.' It was not often that Jeff would be available to discuss matters. We followed his advice. I met with Jeff's company lawyer. He advised that matters concerning the Trade Practices Act would require that a specialist approach be taken. I took it upon myself to take the matter to Minter Ellison Morris Fletcher Lawyers — now MinterEllison — and prepared documents for a young partner, Glenys Fraser. Ms Fraser said that we might have a case under the Act sections 46 and 47, citing a TIAS abuse of market power. Ms Fraser also recommended that we open discussion with the Trade Practices Commission (later to become the Australian Consumer and Competition Commission (ACCC)), based in Canberra. We met with and received a receptive hearing from two of its lawyers. Glenys Fraser earned her money for the calm wisdom contained in her summing up at the conclusion of the meeting. We committed to write a paper for the Trade Practices Commission (TPC), outlining our concerns. Harvey World Travel was a keen supporter of the ATS initiative with the TPC, and it acted as a middleman between TIAS and ATS as it sought the best deal it could effect. It was Paul Kieran who realised that the TIAS pressures and negativity towards ATS was because it saw us as a competitor in realising a 'landbase' tourist database covering events, functions, and specialist tours available in Australia and New Zealand. Mr Kieran attempted to arbitrate a meeting between ATS and TIAS and, late in the day, John Lilley of TIAS suggested a way that connections might be made between the ATS and TIAS networks. It was a stalling tactic.

13. NOT A MULTINATIONAL THIS TIME

The TPC invited ATS and TIAS to a meeting in Canberra. Richard Hall, the TIAS managing director, was not happy to have been called in to explain that TIAS was not monopolistic or using market power to thwart a competitor. The meeting did not come to a decision.

The competitive strategy of TIAS had been easy to read. To confuse the argument, it denied the existence of ATS in any public forum, and referred to ATS as British Telecom (at the time ATS was a reseller of BTA services), while accusing BT of sour grapes at not winning TIAS business and suggesting that BT was subsidising network costs to gain entry to the market. TIAS would delay any activity to facilitate ATS and used its national marketing company (NMC) to stall activity and would confuse ATS customers and the TPC by referring all questions to the NMC — buying time to catch up with the ATS network functionality, while suggesting that TIAS was changing to a more user-friendly organisation — and even rebidding prior to ATS prospects' decisions to cause further delay.

Richard Hall and his lawyer did not attempt to refute anything we said with much vigour or determination. They resorted to stating that everything they did conformed to the industry code of practice. This seemed to be the opening that the TPC was looking for, and it asked TIAS to send a copy of the code to itself and to ATS.

The TPC took a positive step towards resolving the matter in our favour when it called all interested parties to meet in Sydney on 1 September 1995 at a TPC conference to be convened by Assistant Commissioner Alan Lewis. Would this be too late to save ATS? We helped compile the list of interested parties and when the date arrived, we sat around a very large table that would seat perhaps 40 people. The room was equipped to allow further people to sit behind their principals at the table. We knew most of the participants, and lined up as TIAS versus ATS. Supporters sat lined up against one another on opposite sides of the table. TIAS supporters included Southern Cross Galileo NMC, Fantasia NMC, Qantas, Ansett Airlines, and Australian Airlines. Adacel supporters included Abacus NMC, Harvey World Travel, Concorde Travel, and Jetset Travel. Journalists sat on the crossbenches.

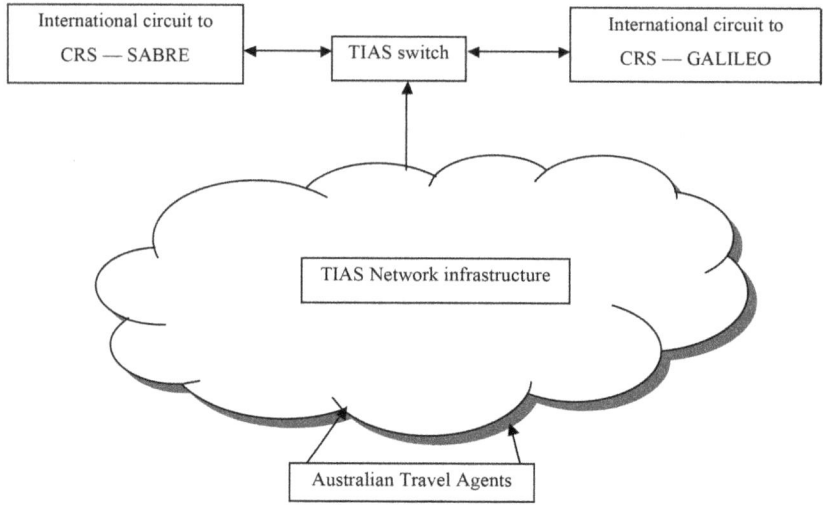

Figure 13.4: Mr Hall's drawing of the TIAS network.
Source: Author's recollection.

Mr Lewis outlined his understanding of the code of practice and asked Richard Hall to explain the problems in allowing Adacel network users to access the TIAS network to gain access to the two CRSs, Galileo and Sabre. Mr Hall attempted to describe the network in words, but was asked by the deputy commissioner to use the whiteboard. Mr Hall drew it simply.

Mr Hall's argument was that TIAS had been formed at a time when CRSs had cost the airlines up to $70 million to establish, that the TIAS marketing company had further invested, and that it was not in its interests to allow other network providers to use its infrastructure. This produced a lot of head nodding from the TIAS side of the table.

An Adacel colleague, Harold Horsfall, took up the cudgels for Adacel, arguing that ATS's activity was complementary to TIAS, and that we would be automating a different client base to TIAS. We would potentially bring more business to the CRS.

Richie Hall looked dumbfounded, and asked how that could happen. I stood up from the table and changed his drawing:

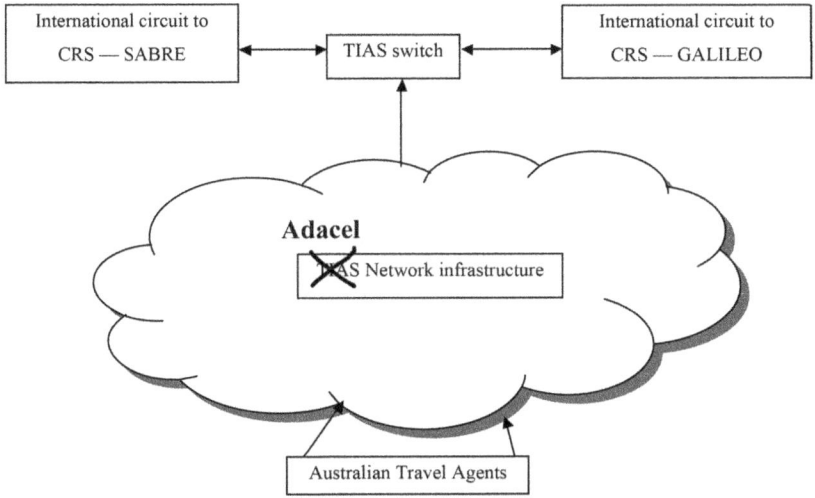

Figure 13.5: The revised drawing.
Source: Author's recollection.

I argued that the Adacel network was no different technically to the TIAS network — they were interchangeable. That statement opened a floodgate of comment from the attendees and in no time it was the lunch recess.

We convened again after lunch and I was amazed to see that the amended diagram was still in view of every participant. If I had been a TIAS representative, I would have removed the diagram. The afternoon session was not long. Mr Lewis summed up, recommending that the code of practice be looked at to state that the Australian customer of TIAS should have a choice of networks to carry them as far as the TIAS communications network. This was potentially a huge victory. It was a Pyrrhic victory, however, as ATS was struggling to keep afloat. We did, however, propose alternate wording for the code to the newly established ACCC, which it accepted.

Shortly after this, a new person appeared at Adacel. Shane McEwan had recently left the employ of a major business consultancy and now spent time with Silvio and the general managers of the various business units. Shane examined the telecommunications side of the business intensively and asked us to update the sales plan as best and as honestly as we could. We subsequently learnt that Shane and Silvio had presented our sales plan to two potential purchasers of ATS — but it did not share that information or any feedback with us, which was disappointing. ATS was clearly not going to be a contributor to Adacel's long-term plans.

We also spent time investigating whether we could combine our expertise with that of BCS-Focus, a Melbourne-based company that was also pursuing travel reservation computer business and was in the same situation as ATS — it had no money. BCS-Focus had an accountant with money to invest, but he was concerned that it looked vulnerable as a stand-alone business and that an association, however tenuous, with Adacel might make sense. We also spoke with BT about a closer relationship, but this was never going to work. It had more problems than it could cope with.

There was business to be had. I did not heed my own advice — that there is no money in travel — when starting negotiations with Kiwi Airlines, a start-up New Zealand airline. While there was real potential for ATS to provide the infrastructure for its administrative services, they were children playing in a tough adult's world. Ewan Wilson has written the brief history of his airline in the book called *Dogfight: The Inside Story of the Kiwi Airlines Collapse*. There is no doubt that Kiwi Airlines spotted a niche market but the established airlines — Air New Zealand and Qantas — were not about to relinquish any of their market power. Kiwi Airlines was excluded from using established systems such as TIAS. In the end, Air New Zealand added a new no-frills subsidiary, Freedom Air, to its flight portfolio in order to kill off Kiwi Airlines as competition.

Jeff Barrow had been making waves with his plans to take over the world, but limply collapsed into bankruptcy, owing Ericsson telephones some $14 million. The money to operate ATS had long dried up, so this came as little surprise, but one or two of Barrow's managers did talk to us to seek a joint venture approach to anything that looked at all promising — a case of too many entrepreneurs, too many egos, and not enough practitioners.

Meanwhile, a management consultant had completed an overall Adacel business plan, excluding the communications company and ATS, as Adacel moved towards going public. A new manager appeared on the scene and pared Adacel expenses in anticipation of the float. By mid-1996, I had quietly left Adacel and ATS to its own devices. In truth, I was pleased to be released from Pacula's legacy, which I had done my best to put right.

13. NOT A MULTINATIONAL THIS TIME

I was, however, keen to see the Adacel initial public offering (IPO). IPOs were popular at this time of the dot-com revolution. The Adacel IPO was unique in that its main assets were its intellectual property. I met Helen Lam one morning after the issue of the IPO. She was distraught and in tears. Her machine language translation group's intellectual property value had been placed at $6 million. It was Helen's contention that the intellectual property was hers alone, as Adacel had not developed the software that she had brought to the company. There was a similar feeling amongst other employees I spoke to, but the IPO was well received by the investing public. The float valued the Adacel intellectual property at $14 million and made Silvio Salom, David Smith and Ian Russell into instant paper millionaires. The IPO stated that Adacel directors' emoluments would be related to the share price — no gain in share value meant no payment. What a lovely concept. It did not last long.

During the time of the IPO, I was in no rush to seek other employment. I was enjoying getting my stamp collection and reading up to date. But by the time that 1997 came around, I was keen to get back to work. Finding the right job was not easy. I was approaching 60 years of age and could boast of a stellar career — until I had hit Adacel, which had a terrible reputation in Melbourne; it was not a company of good reputation with any Melbourne recruitment company. I was beginning to worry about age being a barrier to future employment when I was called back into the Adacel environment by Ian Russell.

BTA was giving Adacel and ATS grief. Adacel was a reseller of BTA services, and BTA was claiming it was owed monies for services that had not been supplied. The situation had got as far as the exchange of solicitors' letters by the time that Ian Russell called. We agreed on a daily consulting rate for me to come back to Bay Street and sort out the BTA accounts. It did not take long. Adacel owed BTA nothing, although its claim was for several hundreds of thousands of dollars. I was convinced, at the time, that any rebuttal from Adacel would get BTA off its back. Such was the case. The dot-com businesses were beginning to grow up.

I did not enjoy this consultancy. I found Ian Russell arrogant in not wanting to understand the background or the arguments put forward to BTA as a rebuttal of its claims. I went so far as to describe him to Silvio Salom as a dilettante. Silvio asked me for patience and not to leap to a quick decision. He agreed that Ian might not be the best facilitator, but that his many responsibilities meant he could not dig too deeply into the many problems facing Adacel.

I must have made a more favourable impression on Ian Russell than he made on me. He called me back again with a view to evaluating the worth (if any) of the remnants of Adacel Communications Pty Ltd. The communications company had the exclusive marketing rights for a product that I had admired: OPNET, optimum network performance modelling tools. I looked at the customer base of the product and could see $50,000 per annum in renewable business that should not need any great effort. I advised Ian Russell of my thoughts and he responded by saying that Adacel would be prepared for me to work in its offices part-time to test this assertion. This was not a burden, so I did so. I gradually got sucked into the OPNET opportunity. There was good new business to be had.

Afterword

This formal narrative ends with me facing the challenges of running my own software distributorship from 2001. It was energising. It was another change in the role I had to play. I learned to operate, and demonstrate if required, three sophisticated software packages, the discrete event-driven network modelling software from OPNET Technologies, the call-centre insurance sales software from Vulcan Solutions, and the basic accounting system I used to operate Alltech Communications.

It was a very different environment to working for an established multinational company. One early task was to establish a network of contacts to whom what I was doing might be of interest. In Canberra, this was not a problem. The government was keen to support small- and medium-sized businesses. Immediately available were Australian Business Limited, providing services to small- and medium-sized businesses; Austrade, promoting Australian export activities; the Australian Computer Society — I was an associate through membership of the British Computer Society; the Armed Forces Communications and Electronics Association, where ex-defence senior officers seek white-collar jobs; the Simulation Industry Association of Australia; and the Australian Electrical and Electronic Manufacturers' Association. The ACT Government also sponsored IT briefing sessions at the National Press Club, through which I established some good relationships.

I needed to employ two exceptional software systems engineers to provide high-level technical support. My first call was to the professor of systems engineering at The Australian National University. I couldn't get the professor, but eventually I spoke to the acting dean of the systems engineering department, who advised me that postgraduate students were allowed to work one week in four, and earn $11,000 per annum without prejudicing ANU rules or any scholarships they might have been awarded. He asked me to put in writing Alltech's requirements for part-time systems engineers. My thinking was to employ two postgraduate students for one week per month as my technical support, so that I would have a technician with me for two weeks per month. When I put these thoughts into an email, the acting dean responded immediately by asking for a job and requesting an interview for himself. Joking aside, he told me that he would arrange for me to meet the two 'brightest students ANU had ever had'. These two had won every undergraduate prize available in their final year and were embarking upon their doctoral studies and research. I employed them both after fun interviews.

Government contracts are usually big and there is a high probability that you will get paid. But government does not have the manpower to understand every product that manufacturers want to sell to it, so it issues tenders in order to be able to appoint from a panel of experts — in system integration, for example. We worked hard to get on the list of small- and medium-sized businesses capable of supporting the recognised systems integrators. In 2001, the biggest government contract was going to be for the Defence Messaging and Development Environment. Defence terminals could not readily talk to one another, as the Department of Defence had three different security levels and was using two different software packages in the network. By the end of the year, the shortlist had been cut to two suppliers: Computer Sciences Corporation (CSC), and Motorola. Alltech was a subcontractor to CSC of the United States — a big player — but the Motorola submission included Alltech software produced simulations, and I felt confident that Alltech would be a winner no matter who was appointed the prime contractor.

I was amazed and disappointed when the Computer Sciences project manager told me that there would be no business for Alltech. The contract CSC had signed was with 'e-Defence', as the project was now named. CSC had signed an additional time and materials contract with the Department of Defence for work not included in the prime contract, and CSC would make a lot more money by charging the Department of Defence to write the simulation and modelling software from scratch, rather than buying it from Alltech — guaranteed to work and with support. When I discussed this with colleagues in Canberra, they were not at all surprised. The big players had the reputation of using local small- and medium-sized business to win contracts as prime contractors and to meet government local content requirements. They would then renege on the agreements that did not serve their desire for profit.

AFTERWORD

Greed was the motivator in the early 2000s. The network modelling software was produced by OPNET and as OPNET's distributor Alltech sold and supported the product in return for 50 per cent of the software price. Alltech was doing well; so well, in fact, that OPNET decided to replace Alltech with its own selling team in Australia. The businessman in me could understand the logic. The sums were easy. OPNET was a newly Nasdaq-listed company, and it needed the numbers. But they were not achievable by OPNET Australia, who failed catastrophically.

When working for oneself, any problems, however large or small, are yours to resolve. It was invigorating, but by 2005 I was ready to retire.

In discussing this decision with my wife, Audrey, she asked — sensibly as ever — what I thought retirement meant. We had kept our home in New Zealand when we moved to Australia, expecting to retire in New Zealand, and were favouring living on the Coromandel Peninsula on the North Island. My thinking had not progressed any further than living on a trout stream with access to the sea. Audrey, on the other hand, had given the subject some consideration. She presented to me a list of amenities that were her minimum requirements for retirement. It was a list that I immediately endorsed. Canberra was the city that met these criteria for us both.

Audrey's list included, as number 12, 'opportunities for personal development'. Audrey was working in the public service as a tour guide at Old Parliament House, and initially we were able to expand our interests through opportunities presented by government in the nation's capital. Then we found the University of the Third Age (U3A) through which persons over 50 set out to educate and entertain one another through a university-style set of courses. U3A is very strong in Canberra, where a highly-educated, older population seems determined to make the most of living. We both took courses that suited us.

I had already written the draft of this book when I joined the ACT Writers Centre to investigate writing for public consumption. The centre had a scheme where sample chapters of a manuscript were reviewed by Aruna Press. My original draft had included a description of my passion for rugby and athletic activities, which was sustained in each place we lived. The Aruna Press evaluation of my work history was that it was probably commercial, but the sporting sections were 'rubbish'. These sections were compiled into a small book I self-published as *Me and Rugby* in 2007. What to do with the meat of the story? Aruna recommended a literary agent who was also positive about the text, although she did suggest a change in tense from passive to active. Fair enough, but could I take positive action?

After a serious look at The Australian National University curriculum, one discipline seemed to be a natural fit. I approached the science communication department. At my initial interview, the department indicated that my application to do a Master of Science Communication would be accepted, as I had a science degree and business experience. I completed a MSc, and then a PhD with a science communication study titled 'The Representation of Science and Scientists on Postage Stamps' and published a book with the same title via ANU Press in 2015. At the end of 2016, I am a Visiting Fellow of the Australian National Centre for the Public Awareness of Science at ANU.

I have made few changes to the text I had written prior to joining academia. I hope you have enjoyed the outcome.

www.ingramcontent.com/pod-product-compliance
Lightning Source LLC
Chambersburg PA
CBHW041924220426
43670CB00032B/2956